# THE POINT OF IT ALL

Understanding The Designs and Variations in Antique Barbed Fencing

# THE POINT OF IT ALL

Understanding The Designs and Variations in Antique Barbed Fencing

**James R. Newman**

Astragal Press

An Imprint of Finney Company

Notice to Reader

The information and material in this book, to the best of our knowledge, were accurate and true at the time of writing. All recommendations are made without guarantee on the part of the author or the publisher. The author and publisher disclaim any liability in connection with the use of information contained in this book or the application of such information.

All rights reserved. No part of this publication may be reproduced or transmitted in any form or by any means, electronic or mechanical, including photocopy, recording, or any information storage and retrieval system without the written permission of the publisher.

Design and Layout: Sonya Boushek
Editing: Sarah Fitz Simmons
Indexing: Dianna Haught, Words by Haught
Publisher: Alan E. Krysan

Astragal Press
An Imprint of Finney Company

5995 149th Street West, Suite 105
Apple Valley, MN 55124

www.astragalpress.com

Printed in United States of America

# Contents

# Foreword

It was September 1965, Jim Newman and I were enrolled in our first semester as graduate students on the Davis campus of the University of California. He was beginning work on a Ph.D. in Zoology.

With a shortage of student housing at that time, we were fortunate being assigned to Ash Hall. It was a two-story former Army barracks used by the Signal Corps during World War II, and was the only on campus residence hall for male graduate students. It was there that Jim and I formed a relationship that has lasted to this day.

We had many of the same likes and dislikes, enjoyed the out-of-doors, and had close family ties. As undergraduates, we both had taken a number of philosophy courses, and perhaps because of that, spent what seemed like countless hours arguing the position of great philosophers on the origins of the universe, life, and death, and the existence of an afterlife.

Jim's zoological studies eventually led him to researching the habitat and lifecycle of the shrew, a mouse-like terrestrial mammal. During the second semester of our studies, he invited me to tag along to the location of his fieldwork, where he frequently went to check on, reposition, and bate live animal traps. It was about 50 miles from Davis at a large salt marsh bordering on San Pablo Bay that is part of the San Francisco Bay-Estuary fed by the Sacramento River and Delta.

Upon our arrival, it was all business, as Jim and I put on wading boots and he carefully tucked a notepad and assorted other gear into the large pockets of his jacket. As we left the car behind on the dirt road off Highway 37, I could sense the excitement Jim was feeling as he awaited what an inspection of the traps might reveal. We spent several hours surveying the marsh, noting the vegetation and visible wildlife, and carefully checking each of the traps. Nevertheless, it was on our way back to the car that I saw Jim's face "light up" like at no other time that day. I was walking behind as he bent over and picked up a piece of twisted and rusted barbed wire.

I knew that Jim was interested in the history of the American West, and a few times had heard him mention that barbed wire played an important role. However, not until then did I begin to appreciate his considerable knowledge of the subject and the significance of his collection. Moreover, little did I realize that day in the salt marsh would be the beginning of my own exploration into the subject's rich and complex history.

Working diligently on our graduate degrees left little time for either of us to research, much less go about collecting barbed wire. We did, however, talk about it from time to time and vowed to someday write a book on the subject. We even went so far as to sketch an outline of the Table of Contents we had imagined.

Jim was married prior to completing his degree and had started a family. His first employment opportunity was a university faculty position out of state, and our close ties were interrupted by distance and the demands of family life and new careers. The months turned into years and the years into decades. However, whenever we talked on the phone or occasionally visited each other, barbed wire was always part of the conversation.

I knew that for the past several years Jim had been "phasing" into retirement from a highly successful environmental consulting company he started in Florida following several years of teaching. However, it was somewhat of a surprise the evening he called to tell me he was sending a draft manuscript he had written on the subject of barbed wire.

He made a convincing argument that there still was plenty of research and writing to be done, and invited me to co-author. Naturally, I was flattered but knew that Jim's knowledge of the subject far exceeded mine, and that my participation would be more of a burden than a contribution to the progress he already had made. Following several subsequent phone calls and email communications, he relented with the proviso that I agree to write this forward. I hope that the foregoing introduction provides a frame of reference to the origin of a relationship (now having lasted nearly 50 years) and of Jim's journey leading up to this very accomplished work.

*The Point of It All* is an outstanding piece of research and writing about the too ignored role that barbed wire has played in the history of this country. Everyone who reads this book cannot help but be fascinated by the manner in which Jim's training and experience as a scientist is reflected in his writing about how the inventors of barbed wire, its designs, descriptions, classification, uses, components, patents, and associated tools helped shape who we are today.

The casual reader of this book will marvel at how much one can learn about what otherwise might have been an easily overlooked fence. The serious collector will be amazed upon discovering a wealth of references heretofore not known.

For the historian, *The Point of It All* is a "must read." For anyone wanting to know more about the American West, it is a treasure trove of information not found so authoritatively presented in any other publication. No one should claim to be a serious collector without having read it, and no library should be without it.

Fred Costello

May 15, 2015

# Preface

My great grandparents and my great great-grandparents were farmers in New York and Indiana and as a child, my family would visit our old family farms. I spent hours exploring our farms lands and more than once "ripped" my pants crossing a fence but never paid much attention to which type of wire cause the rip or scratch. Later as a wildlife biology student in California I also explored farm and ranch lands studying wildlife but this time I paid attention to avoiding "ripping" my pants and noticed that not all barbed fencing was the same and started collecting different pieces here and there.

As the different pieces of fencing in my "collection" increased I looked in the agricultural library at UC Davis for old agricultural journals and found that there could be scores if not hundreds of different kinds of barbed fencing could be found. This experience led me to getting "religion" and buying Jack Glover's "The Bobbed Wire Bible" in 1969. As a field biologist, my equipment included a pair of binoculars, camera, notebook and wire cutters. I kept notes of birds and mammals I observed as well as the locations where I collected "barbed wire." As the book points out the term should be expanded to "barbed fencing" since not all "barbed wire" is wire.

I was and still am intrigued by the questions of why so many different designs and what was the rationale for these different designs. The value of collecting barbed wire took on a new meaning while I was attending at scientific conference in Boulder Colorado in the late 1960s and visited store with Western memorabilia. On entering the store, my wife almost immediately pointed to a display of half dozen pieces of barbed wire mounted on board for sale for $200. She said to me ""Don't you have these?" I said "Yes, I do and more." She said "Bring them in from the garage and put them in our living room." My good friend, Fred Costello, and our wives would joke about our common if not strange interest in "barbed wire" and as young graduate students said we should write a book on "barbed wire" when we "settled down." We have "settled down" so I is time to write the book.

Collecting barbed fencing is fun, interesting, gets you outdoors, and it tells us something about the agricultural history of the farms of the East and ranches of the West. Barbed fencing was invented in the late 1870s and immediately led to an explosive creative period of inventing after the Civil War when farmers, ranchers, manufactures, and steel companies are changed how livestock was managed and put fences that would "rip" pants of future generations exploring old fields.

# Acknowledgments

First, I want to acknowledge my wife, Denis, for her patience and understanding with this "obsession," her insight into the purpose of the book, and above all, her love and encouragement to see it through. In 1968, she recognized the value to collecting antique barbed fencing. To my children, Christian, Rachel, and Beth Anne, for their encouragement of my collecting interests. To Sadie, Jack, and Charlotte, my grandkids, for distracting their grandmother in Columbia and Del Ray so I could work on the book. To my other grandkids, Raney, Aidan, and Maggie, in Gainesville for their support and enthusiasm for this endeavor and their help and advice on Collectors Day 2015 and 2016. I also want to thank the Purintons of Elm Tree Farm in Norway, New York, including Nathan for finding the wooden corner post on their farm with four different antique barbed strands and strips including Allis and Crandal patents; this illustrates that antique barbed fences are not just a Western phenomenon. Thanks also to Karen Hill and Marilyn Fitzpatrick for their editing help and overall suggestions. I would like to thank Dwight Bennett for his advice on publishing and also Bob Spencer, the editor of the Antique Barbed Wire Society for his peer review. Harold Hagemeier is acknowledged for his herculean effort in identifying the more than two thousand various patents and patent variations. It was a great resource used in this analysis. A special acknowledgment goes to my good friend and early collecting buddy, Fred Costello, of Davis, California, who was instrumental in suggesting that we write a book on barbed fencing. Finally, I would also like to thank all my friends for their interest and patience in listening to my many discourses on the subject of antique barbed fencing.

# 1) INTRODUCTION

» Barbed Wire Versus Barbed Fencing

» Components of Barbed Fencing

» Advantages and Disadvantages of Barbed Fencing

» Purpose of the Book

Driving past pastures and farm fields in the Northeast and Midwest and ranches and range lands in the Southwest and West, one sees barbed wire stretched between fence posts or sticking out of the trunks of old trees. A closer look reveals that this barbed wire or barbed fencing often differs in structure, form, and shape. Barbed wire can have single or multiple wires twisted to form a wire strand with barbs, or in some cases, a flattened metal strip with barbs called ribbon wire. If one is lucky, large barbed metal horizontal structures (e.g., bars and rods) may be encountered as fencing. Wooden fences with barbs existed, but most of these have likely decayed and fallen down.

## BARBED WIRE VERSUS BARBED FENCING[1]

Most discussions of antique barbed fencing use the term "barbed wire" to discuss antique barbed fencing. Other terms found include "bobwire," "barbwire," and "barb wire." The term barbed wire can be defined as a series of horizontal strong wires or metal strips

---

1    Fencing is a contraction of the word "defense" and means a physical barrier defining a boundary or a barrier to prevent intrusion or escape. In this case, a barrier with barbs.

with sharply pointed metal barbs attached at regular intervals to these wires or strips which in turn are attached to wooden or metal posts or trees for the purpose of controlling livestock. However, barbed wire itself is just one of several types of antique barbed fencing types invented in the late 1860s and early 1870s. Technically speaking, the term barbed wire is somewhat of a misnomer since it includes not only wire–like metal wire stands, but also a variety of non-wire-like metal barbed fencing types including barbed sheet metal strips or ribbon wire, metal rods, bars, and barbed wooden rails.

## COMPONENTS OF BARBED FENCING

Barbed fencing has three major components: (1) horizontal components, (2) attachments, and (3) vertical components.

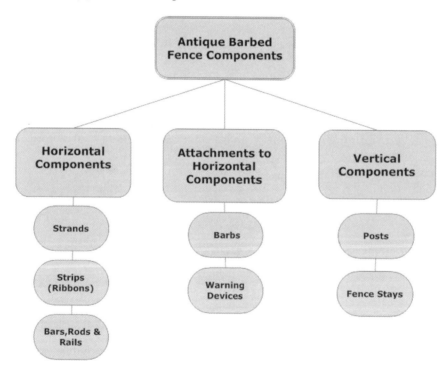

Figure 1. Components of Antique Barbed Fencing

The first two components, the horizontal components and attachments, are the subject of this book. The horizontal components include barbed wire strands, sheet metal strips, iron bars, rods, and rails (both metal and wooden). The attachments include barbs and warning devices. The vertical components include posts and fence stays. Vertical components (i.e., posts and stays)[2] are not covered in this edition with exception of fence designs where stays are part of a barbed fence for holding barbed wire strands in place (see Interlaced Multi-Wire Strand Designs). In this edition, the term barbed fencing covers all varieties of barbed fencing.

In general, antique and modern barbed fences have three to five strands of wire (or strips) stretched between posts that are twelve to twenty feet apart.[3] Sometimes sheet metal strips are found in place of wire strands. An 1884 guide to farming, *The American Farmer* (Flint 1884), recommended that two strands be placed "twenty-one inches from the ground and from each other to turn horses, cattle, cows and young." Three stands, the "lowest being placed twelve inches from the ground, and second twenty-three inches, and third forty-two inches from the ground will, of course, be better and make a more substantial fence. Four strands are most commonly used, while even five are frequently employed when some special object is desired, such as excluding dogs, pigs, poultry, and other small animals" (Flint 1884).

---

2    Designs of vertical components are not discussed here. Identification guides exist for these vertical components (e.g., Sowle, D. *Fence Stays: A Collectors Guide* 2007).

3    Virginia Cooperative Extension 2003.

## ADVANTAGES AND DISADVANTAGES OF BARBED FENCING

Barbed fencing was primarily invented to control livestock, especially cattle. It was used by homesteaders to define their property; by farmers to divide their land into lots and fields for grazing rotation and for confining weaning of cattle to certain pastures; by ranchers to improve the grade of livestock by confining animals to areas, especially during winter months so that water and hay could be provided; and by railroad companies to minimize the injury to livestock and resulting liability from passing trains. As the population grew, barbed fencing was used by landowners to define travel along roads rather than crossing fields (Hayter 1939; Hornbeck 2010). Although legal in all states in 1890,[4] two states had passed laws prohibiting the erection of barbed fencing next to certain land used: next to school grounds (New Hampshire) and within six feet of highways with sidewalks.

Reading the agricultural literature shows that the limitations of barbed fencing for certain species of livestock were recognized early. After the first few years of its use, many types of barbs were considered very injurious to cattle and other livestock. These have been called "vicious" barbs[5]. In reaction to these injurious barbs, less injurious barbs were designed (i.e., "obvious" barbs) along with warning devices for livestock of various kinds. Some states even tried to pass legislation banning the use of barbed fencing (McCallum and McCallum 1985).

There are references to the value of fencing to control difficult cattle such as breachy cows. For example, in the "Illinois Farmers' Institute of 1900" annual report (Stoddard 1890), there is a commentary on difficult cows and fencing: "It's an old adage that poor fences make 'breachy cows', so fix your fence first and insist the cow stay in or out as the case may be. Some cows seem to be descendents of the cow that jumped over the moon and still

---

4    *American Agriculturist* 49 (1890): 87.

5    McCallum and McCallum 1985.

'keep her memory green.' If yours is such a cow, speed her away to a slaughter house and her wings over your home and your neighbors will rise up and call you blessed."

Over time it became apparent which livestock should or should not be fenced with barbed fencing. The Virginia Cooperative Extension (2003) provided present day recommendations for the use of barbed fencing for different species of livestock. The following is a summary of these recommendations on the appropriate uses of barbed wire for different types of livestock:

» For cattle, barbed wire strand fences have traditionally been used. Four- or five-strand barbed wire fences are adequate for cattle.

» For sheep and goats, barbed fences have been typically used. These fences are not recommended for sheep since barbs pull the fleece. Barbed wire strand fences do not effectively confine goats when moderate grazing pressure occurs in a fenced-in area.

» For swine, barbed wire fencing is not effective. Woven-wire fences with one or more strands of barbed wire placed on the bottom are recommended.

» For horses, barbed fencing is not desirable. Visibility is the most important characteristic of horse fencing. Poorly visible fences such as barbed wire fences should not be used with horses; the animals may incur severe injuries (e.g., deep lacerations and broken bones) if they become entangled in fence wires.

In 1880, the *American Agriculturist*[6] discussed the advantages of wire fences over other fence types, especially wooden fences, and described the fact that wire fences took up less arable space in the field. For example, in wheat fields there is less drifting of snow, allowing for more growing area and an earlier planting for wheat next to the fence lines. In 1882, Washburn and Moen Co. published a booklet entitled "*The Fence Problem in the United States as Related to General Husbandry and Sheep Raising. Fact and Statistics from Authoritative Sources with a View of Fence Laws and Customs,*" in which they listed a number of reasons for using Glidden barbed wire fencing (which they manufactured along with

---

6    Volume 39, page 92.

other patent designs). These reasons included that it was strong, easy to handle and transport, easy to erect, and that is was imperishable, cheap, and efficient in use. Casey (1990) cited a publication, "The DeKalb County Manufacturer of 1882," which listed the following advantages barbed fences had over other forms of fencing:

» cheap and inexpensive to transport

» easy to erect and maintain

» nearly indestructible

» resists fire, wind, flood, animals, and trespassers

» does not cause snow drifts or harbor weeds and vermin

» not stolen for fuel

» does not decay

» light to handle

» allows weeds and grasses to be burned without harming the fence

» does not require fire insurance or monitoring

One of the biggest advantages of wire or barb fencing over other types of fencing is greater productivity that a field will have. Washburn and Moen (1879) provided quotes of the lost acreages or uncultivated land using the conventional wood and stone fencing of the time. For example, they cited that a farm of 160 acres had twenty acres with fencing that could otherwise be cultivated. A second example they cited was of a farm in Sutton, Massachusetts, that had two acres out of twenty-four covered with stone fences. Finally, they provided an estimate that four feet of land on both sides of the traditional fence was uncultivated and was "worse than useless."

Why use fencing at all? The reasons may seem obvious, but a 1916 paper presented by H. E. Horton[7] at the Ninth Annual Meeting of the American Society of Agricultural Engineers in Chicago provided three emotional reasons for someone to use fencing:

1. The prime reason is imitation: his neighbor has fences.

2. Another reason is selfishness, for the real ownership of land is not felt unless it is guarded against intrusion.

3. Another reason is to make money.

The author then went on to describe several benefits of fencing:

Thinking of fields, and in a superficial way, the fence will of itself neither directly raise nor lower the yield of potatoes, grains, etc. Indirectly, and through livestock keeping, fence means the major part of maintaining permanent fertility for the soil and increased income from the sale of livestock.

There is always material produced on the farm which has no, or doubtful, market value—weeds, stubble, straw, corn stalks. Through the medium of livestock these materials may be converted into meat on the hoof, which has a value the world over.

A flock of sheep, a bunch of swine, a herd of cattle, furnish manure and meat. Shut in stalls, these domestic animals do not make the most economical gains, for these come only when stall feeding is supplemented with feeding in the field. Fence makes possible this profitable combination.

---

7    He was Agricultural Commissioner for the American Steel and Wire Co. of Chicago.

The author concluded with a comment on the influence of barbed fencing on farming history and alluded to the early problems of barbed fencing that resulted in changes to barbed fencing designs: "The invention and rapid production of <u>barbed wire marked an epoch in farming history of this country</u>. In the beginning, it was believed by many that barbed wire solved all fence problems. As time passed barbed wire was execrated more and more, but still its production and distribution continued in quantity."

## PURPOSE OF THE BOOK

This book examines the invention of barbed fencing and provides an understanding to complexities of the designs and patterns of antique barbed fencing. Because of its place in American history, antique barbed fencing has become of interest to collectors and historians. There is a national collecting society, the Antique Barbed Wire Society headquarters in La Crosse, Kansas,[8] museums (e.g., Kansas Barbed Wire Museum and Devils' Rope Museum)[9] dedicated to barbed fencing, and state barbed wire associations (e.g., California, Colorado, New Mexico, Nebraska, and Ohio). There are annual meetings and shows associated with different state organizations. Some thirty state and local barbed fencing organizations have been formed over the years. A national magazine, *The Barbed Wire Collector*, is published by the Antique Barbed Wire Society. Antique barbed fencing is sold on eBay, in antique stores, and at auctions.

---

8  http://www.antiquebarbedwiresociety.com/directors.html

9  http://www.barbwiremuseum.com/ and http://www.rushcounty.org/barbedwiremuseum/

For the casual reader interested in antique barbed fencing or for the serious collector or farming historian, understanding the complexities of the some 2,000 patent designs and variations of antique barbed fencing can be confusing. The point of the book is to provide an understanding of the different patent designs and variations found in antique barbed fencing, and the factors that influenced these designs and variations over time. This book provides a classification system based on the designs of antique barbed fencing that can be used by collectors and fence historians for grouping and classifying barbed wire into similar designs. This book is intended for antique barbed fencing collectors, farming historians, and those of us who have ripped our pants crossing barbed wire fences.

This analysis is based on an examination of the differences and similarities of the different barbed fencing designs found in the patent designs and variations, books and other publications on barbed fencing (see references), as well as internet searches on barbed fencing. The analysis is also based on a review of more than 350 patents records from the United States Office of Patent and Trademark Office (USPTO) using Google Patent Search and augmented by Campbell and Allison's 1986 book on barbed fencing patents, as well as information from barbed wire organizations and museums. Key publications used to characterize antique barbed fencing and its designs include the books by Robert Clifton (1970), Henry and Frances McCallum (1985), Robert Campbell and Vernon Allison (1986), Jack Glover (1969), and Harold Hagemeier's (2010, 2012) comprehensive identification book. It should be noted that occasionally some differences between authors occurs in their identification of patents. Also, patent variation was found; some of the numbers of patents and patent designs may be slightly different depending on which author is quoted. Finally, this characterization of designs has been aided by examination of the design variations from my own collection of barbed fencing. USPTO patent classifications are provided in the discussion of different patents to better understand how the USPTO viewed barbed fencing compared to other forms of fencing. Common names are used to characterize some patent designs and followed Hagemeir's common names when available or Clifton's common names if Hagemeir's were not available.

Since the 1900s, barbed fencing has been adapted for other uses such as in war for impeding the movement of troops, in prisons to control inmates, and for protecting property from unwanted intruders. These uses are not the focus of this book; only barbed fencing that was invented and manufactured for the use in controlling livestock is considered in this analysis. This analysis also does not discuss modern barbed fencing patents and their variations, although their designs have a similar basis as antique barbed fencing.

This book is divided into a number of chapters which include an overview of antique barbed fencing, including its origins; a discussion on plain wire fences, the forerunner of antique barbed fencing; and the number of patent designs and variations that have been identified over the years. These chapters are followed by discussions on the designs and patterns observed in components of antique barbed wire fencing (i.e., barbs, strands, strips, bars, rods, and rails). The changes in designs over time and the reasons for the myriad of designs and patterns seen in antique barbed fencing are discussed. An antique barbed wire classification system based on these designs is developed and presented.

# 2) ANTIQUE BARBED FENCING

» Early Fencing in the United States

» Origins of Barbed Fencing

» Transition from Plain Wire Fencing to Barbed Fencing

» Regional Patterns in Barbed Fencing

## EARLY FENCING IN THE UNITED STATES

The 19th century, known as the Industrial Revolution period, was also an agricultural revolution period; fencing contributed greatly to the industrialization of agriculture. The four major fence types found in the United States in the 19th century, before the invention of barbed fencing in the late 1870s, were: (1) wood fences, including Virginia rail or "worm" fences, pole fences, board fences, and picket fences; (2) earthen fences, i.e. stone walls and sod fences; (3) hedges (referred to as "living fence" by Washburn and Moen in 1879); and (4) metal or plain wire fences.[10] These fence types were used to control the movement of livestock on farms and pastures and define boundaries for property and buildings (Martin 1892; Hornbeck 2009). Martin's (1892) book *Fences, Gates and Bridges, A Practical Manual*, provided a detailed discussion on the early fences in the United States up to the 1890's. He provides detailed discussions on their uses, construction and limitations for more than a half a dozen fence type including wooden rail fences, stone and sod fences, hedges, picket

---

[10] "Wire" fences manufactured from mild steel were common in the Eastern US from 1850s and were the forerunner of barbed fencing (See later discussion on Plain Wire Fencing)

fences (with and with out wire), fences with boards and barbed wire, and barbed wire fences. According to McCallum and McCallum (1985), the growing need for fences in the United States was reflected in the number of patents for fencing issued. In the first seventy-five years of the 19th century there were approximately 1,200 patents issued for farm and field fences, including some 368 patents immediately after the Civil War (1866 to 1868). Available fence resources (e.g., timber and stone), economics, industrial development, regional agricultural expansion, and innovation in designs contributed to fence development. In the early and mid 19th century, fences in New England were mainly stone and wood. In the Middle Atlantic states with less stone, wooden fences were the primary fence type. In the South, with even fewer stones, wooden fences were used almost exclusively. In the Midwest, wooden fences were the primary fence type along with hedge fences. In the prairie states (e.g., North and South Dakota) and the Southwest, there was very little fencing compared to other regions (Hornbeck 2007, 2010).

Similar quantitative data for the Northeast and South were not available but the trends reflected in the attitudes of Eastern farmers to fencing can be established from the historical literature. The barbless fence types used up to the 1870s had their limitations in the effectiveness in controlling livestock and were expensive to set up and maintain. An 1882 meeting of the Massachusetts Department of Agriculture (1882) listed the following limitations for wire fencing: it sagged, snapped in the cold, and presented no terror for cattle. The conditions were right for inventing barbed fencing. There was a demand for better control of livestock by farmers to protect their crops from roaming livestock, by ranchers wanting to protect their cattle from injury by railroads crossing their ranches, and by cattlemen wanting to expand cattle production in the West. In addition, the US steel industry, in particular the wire manufacturing sector, in the Northeast was well established several decades before the invention of barbed wire fencing and aided in the manufacturing of barbed fencing. An example of existing metal fencing industry is found in the early hardware and fencing catalogue, e.g. Fiske Iron Works. (1875). Illustrated catalogue and Price List. New York: J. W. Fiske. In their 1875 catalogue there are advertisements and descriptions for iron and wire railings, galvanized wire fences and ornamental wire work. The catalogue states that they manufacture iron and wire products for public and private buildings, parks, cemetarires, balconies, farms, lawns, "heneries", and "sheepfolds[11]". The wire manufacturers were looking for new business opportunities (McCallum and McCallum 1985; Hornbeck 2007, 2010). The Washburn & Moen Company (1876) of Worcester, Massachusetts, was an early manufacturer of plain wire fence. They claimed in their 1876 pamphlet that they were the first to introduce plain wire for fencing into the West "twenty-five years ago." They contrasted barbed wire versus plain wire and pointed out that "cattle, from familiarity with it (plain wire fences), learn to press against it or crowd through and break it."

## ORIGINS OF BARBED FENCING

No one person invented barbed fencing. It was an idea that started in different regions of the country by farmers, ranchers, fence manufacturers, and others who recognized the limitations in existing fences (e.g., ineffective in controlling livestock), and in particular, the limitations of plain wire in common use in the 1860s and 1870s. McCallum and McCallum (1985) discussed a number of examples of Iowa and Illinois farmers, merchants, and blacksmiths who claimed they experimented with barb fencing in the 1850s and 1870s before the formal patent era starting in the mid-1870s. Supreme Court records (i.e., "The Barbed Wire Patent Case" 143 US 275 of 1892 involving Glidden's 1874 patent

---

*11*     Old terms for enclosures for sheep ("sheepfold") and chickens coop ("henneries")

[#157,124]) established that this early idea was prevalent. The summary opinion described that in the late 1850s the "existence, public exhibition and use of number fences" known as the "Morley Fence" occurred in Delaware County, Iowa. The unpatented design by Alvin Morley, a farmer, was a wire fence which had short pieces of wires twisted around the wire. The summary opinion described testimony from the plaintiffs that the idea of barbed wire occurred before Glidden's patent. However, this testimony was only oral testimony without proper documentation to establish the design specifications; therefore, it did not sway the Court's opinion in favor of Glidden. From the Supreme Court record it appears that several local farmers in northern Illinois and eastern Iowa were experimenting with unpatented barbed fences identified in the Court records[12] as "Morley's Fence," "Hutchinson's Fence," and "Beer's Fence."

Between 1867 and 1873 and prior to the DeKalb County Fair in 1874, there were six barbed wire patents from five inventors - (1) William D. Hunt, (2) Michael Kelly, (3) Lyman P. Judson, (4) Henry M. Rose, and (5) Lucian B. Smith - that comprised the initial barbed fencing designs. They addressed the common problem of cattle breaking wire fences by designing fences using barb-like attachments. Their patents included the basic design features of future barbed fencing designs (i.e., the use of longitudinal wire strands, sheet metal strips, and wire points or barbs) (see Chapter 3 discussion of Initial Antique Barb Fencing Designs).

According to McCallum and McCallum (1985), some dozen years before the recognized invention of barbed wire fencing in the mid 1870s there were five inventors, three from France and two from the United States, who came close to inventing barbed wire and patenting their designs. These patents occurred within a few years of each other

---

12    Washburn & Moen Mgt. Co. vs. Beat' Em All. Barbed-Wire Co. ("Barbed Wire Patent Case") 143 US 265 (1892).

(1860–1867). The first French patent was by L. E. Grassin-Baledans in 1860 for twisted sheet metal with points designed to protect trees from livestock. He was the first to propose the use of twisted wire with metal projections as means to protect trees from grazing cattle (Krell 2002). The two other French designs were by L. F. Jannin and G. Gavillard. Jannin's 1865 French patent was for a fence with two twisted wires that secured sheet metal diamond or three-point star-shaped barbs (Tanner 1889).[1] Gavillard's 1867 patent was for a "T" shaped metal spine held between three wires. All three French designs had the theme of using metal thorn-like projections, which were likely mimicking the thorny hedges used as fences at the time. These French designs were not copied or used in the United States, although Gavillard's 1867 design was very similar to Kelly's 1868 US patent for a thorny fence (McCallum and McCallum 1985).

The two US inventors with the earliest barb fencing patents were Lucien B. Smith of Kent, Ohio, in 1867, and William Hunt of Scott, New York, in 1867. They were the first to attach a device to plain fence wire as a more effective way to control livestock, a problem recognized by farmers and ranchers for more than a dozen years. Smith's June 1867 patent (#66,182) was for a wire fence consisting of cast iron posts with two or more "stout wires between the posts" and rotating wooden or cast iron spools with four short wire spurs or nails hung on the wire a few feet apart.

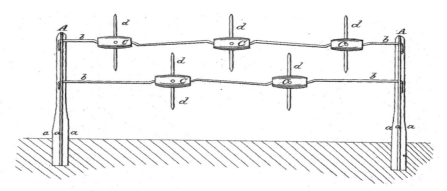

Figure 2. Smith, L. B. 1867 (#66,182) "Wood Spool Four Point"

The purpose of Smith's patent was an improvement of a wire fence to be used in the prairies of the western states "where timber is scarce and fires frequent." Although it was barbed and designed for livestock use, the design was not practical and did not go into commercial production (McCallum and McCallum 1985). Technically speaking, it could be considered the first barbed wire patent but there is some controversy as to Smith's filing date compared to W. D. Hunt's patent (McCallum and McCallum 1985) and who actually had the first US patents for barbed fencing. In July 1867, W. D. Hunt was issued a patent (#67,117) for a wire fence with sharpened "spur wheels" made of sheet metal designed to keep animals from pushing against the fence (Figure 3).

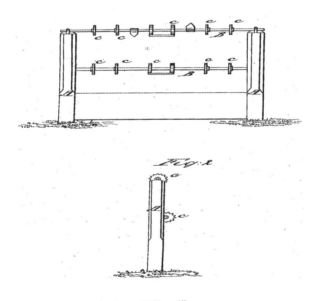

Figure 3. Hunt, W. D. 1867 (#67,117) "Spur Wheel"

Hunt is given credit for the first actual barbed wire fence design (McCallum and McCallum 1985), which was subject to litigation over the next decade by other patentees such as Joseph Glidden. It also was not commercially successful (McCallum and McCallum 1985), but as Hayter (1939) stated, Hunt's design was one of the early ones that served as the basis for the successful barbed wire designs that followed.

Although mentioned in recent literature (e.g. McCallum and McCallum 1985) as an early "barbed wire" patent design by A. Dabb of Elizabethport, New Jersey, in 1867 (#63,482) for a "wrought-iron bar or strip" or "cast-iron pickets" to be attached to the top of wooden picket fences. For this analysis this design is not considered antique barbed fencing since it was not designed for controlling livestock but was designed for ornamental purpose and more specifically for security purposes (e.g., keeping "juveniles" from climbing over a picket fence). In the 1860s there was considerable manufacturing of ornamental fences for houses and commercial buildings (See Fiske 1870).

It wasn't until some six years later in 1873 at a county fair in DeKalb, Illinois, that the idea of using wire with more practical barbs to control livestock was seen as a better way of fencing livestock. Although other inventors including a merchant (L.B. Smith) from Ohio and a blacksmith (M. Kelly) from New York already had barbed fence patents, H. M. Rose from Waterman, Illinois, is credited with generating the idea of barbed wire to other inventors by displaying his design at a county fair in Illinois. Rose demonstrated his fence patent (#138,763) at the DeKalb County Fair in the summer of 1873. He considered his design an "Improvement in Wire fences." It was a long strip of one-inch square wood with metallic points inserted six to eight inches apart. This strip of wood was attached to plain wire stretched between two posts sixteen feet apart. According to Rose, the metallic point could also be inserted on an ordinary board fence (Figure 4).

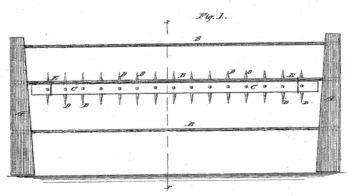

Figure 4. Rose, H. M. 1873 (#138,763) "Barbed Wooden Rail"

Rose's fence design is considered the triggering event for the invention of barbed fencing (McCallum and McCallum 1985). Three other DeKalb County residents, Isaac L. Ellwood, Jacob Haish, and Joseph F. Glidden, and possibly a fourth, Charles Kennedy also of DeKalb County, supposedly attended the fair and independently came away with different ideas for a wire fence design using barbs. Within a year, each had obtained patents for their barbed wire fence designs. According to McCallum and McCallum (1985) the need for better wire fences, the economic environment of the time, an inexpensive way of making steel from iron (i.e., the Bessimer Process), and regional agricultural conditions played a role in the success of the DeKalb patents. Most of the early inventors lived in Illinois next to the prairies and plains of the West where the cattle industry was expanding. They had access to manufacturers to make the wire and to promote it to cattlemen and ranchers.

Fifty percent of the early inventors came from the DeKalb County area of Illinois (Clifton 1970; Campbell and Allison 1986). After Smith, who was from Ohio, and Hunt and Kelly, both from New York, most of the early inventors (1874 to 1876) of barbed fencing came from Illinois (forty out of fifty-four inventors, more specifically most came from the DeKalb County area of Illinois where the idea of such a fence improvement was publically demonstrated). For the next three years (1874–1876), fifty-nine percent (thirty of fifty-one) of the patents came from the vicinity of DeKalb County or within a fifty-mile radius of DeKalb, Illinois. Four of the five patentees in 1874 were from DeKalb County, Illinois. In 1875, ten of the eighteen patentees were from a fifty-mile radius of DeKalb, Illinois. The other patentees were from other places in Illinois (two), Iowa (three), and Connecticut (three). In 1876, twenty-one of thirty-seven patentees were from a fifty-mile radius of DeKalb, Illinois; the other inventors were from other parts of Illinois, Iowa, Nebraska, Wisconsin, New York, and Washington, DC.

Barbed fencing was not without controversy. Soon after it became commercially available, some states (e.g., Connecticut, Vermont, New Hampshire, Colorado, and Texas) attempted to pass legislation to ban the use of barbed wire because of its injurious nature not only to livestock but also humans (Bennett 2012). *The American Agriculturist* of 1880[13] had editorial comments in the January issue calling for comments on the pros and cons of barb wire. At that time the editor was "ready to condemn nearly all … barbed wire fences" because the editor knew of "… many instances of severe injury to valuable animals, and from the strong objections against their use expressed by intelligent men of good judgement." But in the February issue, his position was "somewhat modified by recent letters from our readers…" reporting of the observations from readers of animals learning to stay away from barbed fences after contact and discussions on ways to get the attention of animals before they contacted the fence. In the 1880s, range wars occurred in the West, especially in Texas over the restricted grazing of land with barbed fencing (McFadden and McFadden 1985).

---

13      *American Agriculturist* 39 (1880): 10, 51-52.

In 1910, R. Horton, an agronomist for the American Steel and Wire Co. of Chicago, Illinois, presented a paper at a meeting of the American Society of Agricultural Engineers entiltled "Fencing the Farm" and stated that "no other fence (barbed wire) ever proved so useful…and has retained its hold and increasing use and the end is not in sight." A hundred years later this view would be changed with the invention of electric fences.

## TRANSITION FROM PLAIN WIRE FENCING TO BARBED FENCING

Plain wire fencing use was established in the East and the Midwest. Between the years 1850 and 1870 over 350,000 miles of plain wire fencing was in use in Massachusetts (Massachusetts Board of Agriculture 1882). Its use overlapped the invention of barbed wire. It was a minor fence stock in the Midwest and West before the 1880s but was an important fencing alternative in the East. It had its limitations. It sagged in the heat and snapped in the cold (see earlier discussion on fence stocks). Plain wire fencing was the forerunner of antique barbed fencing. Of the four fence types discussed above, plain wire fences were the most versatile. This fence type took up the least amount of space in a field compared to the other forms of fencing and was more easily erected and taken apart. It appears that plain wire fences were common in the East given their mention in early 19th century agricultural literature from the region. This fact may explain why a number of early inventors came from the Northeast (e.g., M. Kelly, a blacksmith, from New York City). The use of plain or barbless wire fences to control cattle was proposed in as early as 1816 and 1821 by farm societies in Philadelphia and Baltimore (Massachusetts Board of Agriculture 1882).

In 1847, the New York Agricultural Society awarded their silver medal for wire fence as cheaper and more effective for farm use than wood. According to records,[14] the earliest[15] plain wire fence patent was issued to C. Hall of Meridan, Connecticut, in 1829 for making a fence of wire or cords or twine and for making seines or nets of wire (Figure 5).

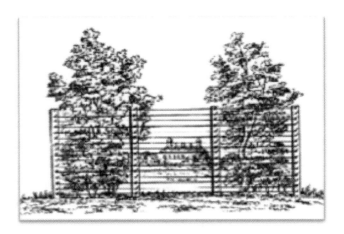

Figure 5. Hall, C. 1829 (#5702 ½) "Wire Fence"

A few years later in 1833, Samuel F. Dexter of Auburn, New York, was issued a patent for a wire fence. A fire in December 1836 destroyed most existing patent records and no patent description or drawing is available.[16]

---

14      http://www.datamp.org/patents/search/advance.php?id=46799&set=2

15      Early patent records were destroyed in a fire in 1836.

16      Washburn and Moen in their 1879 brochure listed six early patents, including Dexter's patent for a wire fence.

The earliest fence wire patent where a patent description is available is for Zephaniah Knapp of Pittston, Pennsylvania. He was issued a patent (#5,884) in 1848 for a method of fastening horizontal wire using wooden or "iron wedges" to fence posts, thus making it easier to straighten out and repair such fences (Figure 6). This patent was classified as an "Improved Method of Fastening Fencing Wire to Fence Posts."

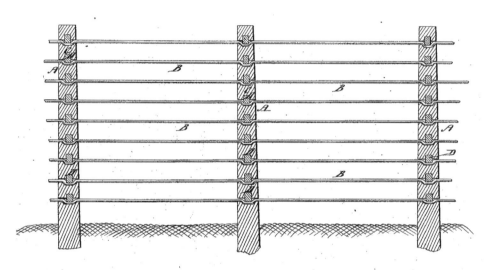

Figure 6. Knapp, Z. 1848 (#5,884) "Wire Rod Fence"

According to the Washburn and Moen Co. (1879), the first patent for a fence made of wood and metal was in 1801 by Kim[17] for a post-hole-making device. They stated that the number of patents increased rapidly, especially in the late 1860s; during that time there were over 386 patents issued for modification and improvement in common materials for field and farm fences. The Massachusetts Board of Agriculture (1882) estimated that between 1850 and 1870, 350,000 miles of plain wire fence were manufactured for use in fencing in Massachusetts.

---

17    Unable to find other records or pictures.

22

Table 1. Plain Wire Fence Patents (Non-Ornamental) 1848 to 1870

These patents often attempted to address the limitations found in plain wire fences (e.g., Hunt [1856] and Bundy [1866]).

| Year | Patentee | Patent Number | Classification of Patent | Comments |
|------|----------|---------------|--------------------------|----------|
| 1848 | Z. Knapp | 5,884 | Improved Method for Fastening Wire to Fence Posts | Attaching wires to posts |
| 1853 | W. H. Meriwether | 10,211 | Wire Fence (Improvement in Construction of Wire Fences) | Wire fence |
| 1854 | J. Nesmith | 19,743 | Improvement in Machines for Making Wire Netting | Machine |
| | M. F. Coons | 10,781 | Improvement in Construction of Wire Fence | Method to minimize temperature, wind damage, ice, and sleet |
| | W. G. Lavers | 11,376 | Device for Securing Ends of Wires in Fence Post | Holding wires against pressure |
| 1856 | J. Burk | 14,751 | Device to Allow for Contraction and Expansion of Wire Fences | Lever system to stretch and tighten |
| 1857 | J. G. Hunt | 16,236; RE 474 | Improved Portable Field-Fence | Wood fence designed to turn cattle, can allow smaller animals (e.g., sheep) and swing by removing a slat |
| 1858 | D. M. Heikes | 21,073 | Field Fence | Wood and wire |
| | O. Williams | 21,459 | Method for Allowing Expansion and Contraction of Wire Fences | Wire fence |
| 1859 | P. S. Clinger | 25,387 | Improvement Device for Stretching and Retaining Wires | Wire stretcher for plain wire wooden fence posts |

| 1863 | E. Gale | 39,563 | Improvement in Wire Fences | Attempts to address the problem of cattle pressing against the fence, allowing expansion |
|---|---|---|---|---|
| 1864 | I. Knapp | 43,032 | Improvement in Wire Fences | New kind of fence post |
| | W. Robinson & J. Behel | 44,221 | Improved Device for Stretching the Wires of Fences | Wire stretcher |
| 1865 | J. W. Norcross | 45,852 | Improved Wire Fence | Wire tightener |
| 1866 | P. S. Crawford | 54,119 | Improvement in Device for Tightening Fences | Wire stretcher |
| | J. Bundy | 59,176 | Improvement in Fence | Attempts to address the problem of cattle pressing against the fence, protecting the wires |
| | J. W. Larmore | 56,766 | Improvement in Wire Fences | Add wood to top of wire fence to protect horses when jumping |
| | A. Morley | 56,249 | Improvement in Stock Yards | Triangular wood structure on wheels attached to wire fence to move cattle in stock yard |
| | A. Betts | 56,884 | Improvement in Tools for Holding | Device for holding staples when attaching fencing wire |
| 1867 | S. S. Griffling | 62,840 | Improvement in Fences | Wood wire fence |
| 1868 | S. B. Hewett | 75,759 | Improvement in Wire Fence Key | Wire tightener |
| | G. Fletcher, Sr. | 84,180 | Improvement in the Mode of Making Combined Wood and Wire Fence | Using poles and sticks |
| | H. K. Flinchbaugh | 75,145 | Improvement in Iron Posts for Wire Fence | Patent design picture is like an advertisement |
| | G. W. Ensminger | 84,810 | Improvement in Wire Fence | Portable wire fence |
| | W. B. Hayden | 81,367 | Improvement in Wire Stretcher for Fence | Wire stretcher |

| 1869 | D. W. Eaton | 93,967 | Improvement in Device for Tightening Wire Fence | Wire tightener |
|------|-------------|--------|--------------------------------------------------|----------------|
| 1870 | F. Fanning | 101,601 | Improvement in Tightener for Wire Fence | Wire tightener |
| | L. E. Lockling | 103,903 | Improvement in Fences | Wood wire fence |
| | T. Crosby | 108,766 | Improvement in Line and Wire Tighteners | Wire tightener |
| | B. Wilson & F. P. Grimes | 109,858 | Improvement in Wire Fences | Wire fence with swinging boards to make fence visible to cattle |
| | P. L. Sherman | 107,297 | Improvement in Fences | Attachment for posts and trees for wire |

The plain fence wire design that is considered as a prototype for later barbed wire fences is the design by H. Meriwether (#10,211) of New Braunfels, Texas, issued in 1853 (McCallum and McCallum 1985). It was a barbless smooth undulating wire fence that also used wood slats. This design provided features used in later barbed wire fences and consisted of wooden or cast iron posts with four non-barbed strands of undulating wire with a wooden rail below the top wire (Figure 7).

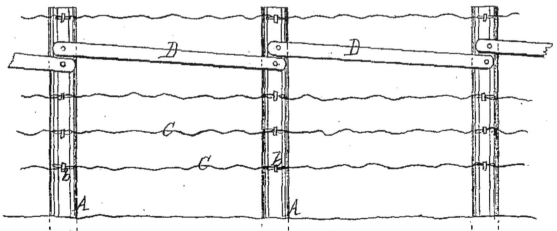

Figure 7. Meriwether, W. H. 1853 (#10,211) "Wire Fence"

The purpose of Meriwether's design was to improve wire fences by making them "stiffer and more visible to cattle." Meriwether claimed that the undulating (barbless) wires provided a springiness to bend and would not break from the pressure of cattle moving against the fence. He stated that the wooden rail provided visibility to cattle. Although earlier wire fence patents had been issued (e.g., Cole in 1829, Dexter in 1833, and Knapp in 1848), Meriwether's design was the first to specifically address cattle pressing against wire fences. However, McCallum and McCallum (1985) stated that this design was not practical and not commonly accepted.

Inventors tried to address these limitations in other ways than with barbs. A search of wire fence patent records from the 1840s to the mid-1870s shows that there were a number of inventors trying to improve one of the major limitations of plain wire fences. In 1857, J. G. Hunt of Scott, New York, was issued a patent (patent #16,236 and re-issue #474) for a portable field-fence. This wire fence was designed to turn cattle and allow smaller animals like sheep to pass through while restraining the larger animals with the use of "spur wheels." In 1858, O. Williams of St. Louis County, Missouri, was issued a patent (#21,459) for a wire fence with intermediate non-anchored posts and wires on friction rollers that removed the friction from the wires when pressed by cattle. In 1863, E. Gale of Pavilion, Illinois, was issued a patent (#39,563) for looping wire around a number of posts not secured in the ground and allowing for expansion when pressed against. In 1866, J. Bundy (#59,176) of West Liberty, Iowa, attempted to address this problem of protecting the wires by combining wood rails and wires (Figure 8).

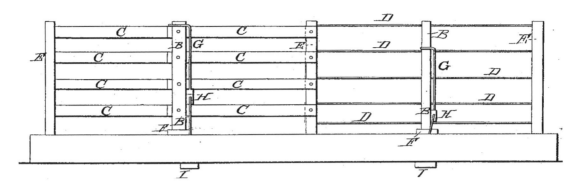

Figure 8. Bundy, J. 1866 (#59,176) "Wood and Metal Rail Fence"

In 1870, B. Wilson and F. P. Grimes of Dayton, Ohio, (#109,858) designed a wire fence with swinging boards[18] to make fence visible to cattle. Their designs were classified by USPTO as "Improvement in Wire Fences."

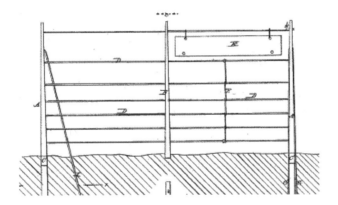

The conversion of plain wire fences into barbed fences led to the inventions of hundreds of barbed fencing designs. An example of the transition from plain wire fences to barbed wire fences was found in the patent (#182,928) of P. Hill from Alta, Illinois, in 1876; he was issued a patent for short strands of wire with barbs that could be linked and attached to ordinary plain fence wire to create a barbed fence (Figure 9).

---

18    Early example of warning plate used later in barbed wire.

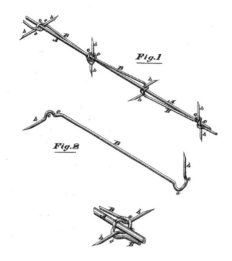

Figure 9. Hill, P. P. 1876 (#182,928) "Parallel Strand Hooked Link"

He discussed the merits of his invention as being able to easily attach and detach the barbed links from plain wire fences. Another example in 1878 was P. Miles of Worcester, Massachusetts, who was issued a patent for using common fence staples as barbs (Figure 10).

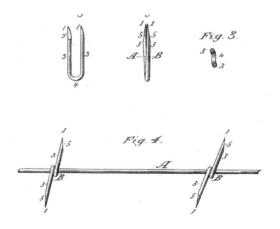

Figure 10. Miles, P. 1878 (#208,688) "Applied Staple Barb"

Miles stated in his patent description that one of the purposes of his design was to render "old plain wire fencing" with as "much utility and value as the new barbed fencing generally known as the 'Glidden barbed fence-wire'." He acknowledged "… many different kinds of barbs have been devised for the purpose of being applied to plain wire fencing." His invention was an improvement on a staple and did not require a separate stock of barbs. What is interesting in reading his patent is that he mentioned the success of other existing barbed wire fence designs, such as those of Glidden. He also described that there was a large amount of old plain wire fencing that could be converted into barbed fencing by using his patent design. Besides using his redesigned plain fence staples as barb, he said his design was a better fence staple. He called his design a "double pointed tack." Living in Worcester, Massachusetts, he would have been familiar with Glidden barbed wire manufactured by the Washburn and Moen Co. in Worcester.

St. John's design was for a staple used as a barb that could be attached to plain wire fences (Figure 11).

Figure 11. St. John, S. H. 1878 (#199,330) "Locked Staple Barb"

These are other examples of inventors adapting plain wire fences using nails and staples as barbs. Underwood's 1878 "Single and Double Tack" patent (#206,754) used ordinary carpet tacks for barbs (Figure 12).

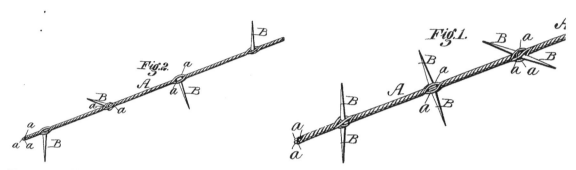

Figure 12. Underwood, H. M. 1878 (#206,754) "Single and Double Tack"

Another early inventor who wanted to capitalize on existing plain wire fences was M. Knickerbocker of New Lenox, Illinois. He was issued a patent (#185,333) in 1876 for a three-point sheet-metal-barb design that could be attached to existing fencing with the barbs vertical to the ground so only animals pushing through the wire were affected[19] (Figure 13).

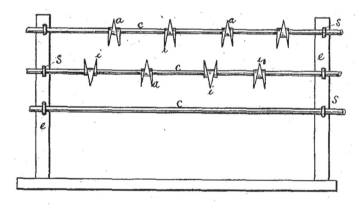

Figure 13. Knickerbocker, M. 1876 (#185,333) "Three-Point Single Strand"

---

19    Example of the early recognition of the need to minimize injury to livestock.

As mentioned, for the first couple of years after the invention of barbed wire in 1874, inventors rushed to design barbs and barb-attaching tools to convert plain wire fences into barbed wire fences. Table 2 shows a representative list of these patentees and their designs. The majority of these types of patents occurred in the first few years after the 1874 patents of Glidden, Ellwood, and Haish. These patents included not only barb patents but also tools for attaching these barbs to plain wire fences. Twelve patent designs were issued in 1875 and nineteen designs were issued in 1876. Haish was issued patents for adapting plain wire fences and a patent for a barb design for a wooden fence. The number of patents for adapting existing fences declined after 1876, likely because of the success of new barb fencing designs. As late as 1897, inventors like Perry (#588,774) were still trying to invent a way of attaching barbs to plain wire fences (Table 2).

Table 2. List of Inventors, Patents, and Design Descriptions For Adapting Plain Wire Fencing to Barbed Wire Fencing - 1874 to 1897

| Inventor | Year | Patent # | Design Description |
|---|---|---|---|
| Kennedy | 1874 | 153,965 | Seven sheet-metal-barb designs for attaching to wire |
| Wilson | 1875 | 158,451 | Four-point wire barb attached by staple to fence rods |
| Mack | | 162,835 | Two-point spiral twist end wires |
| Kennedy | | 164,181 | Four-point barbs to slip on wire |
| Haish | | 164,552 | Two-point sheet metal barb |
| Stover | | 164,947 | Two-point sheet metal |
| Duffy & Schroeder | | 165,220 | Two-point grooved sheet metal barb, crimped |
| Dobbs & Booth | | 166,511 | Tool for attaching two-point wire barb |
| Haish | | 167,240 | Two-point wire in the form of a "S" for double- and single-strand wire fences |
| Devore | | 168,886 | Two-point crimped barb |
| Stover | | 169,947 | Two-point cast iron barb applied to two wire strand |
| Dulin | | 170,354 | Tool to use with hammer, etc., two-point wire barb |
| Dobbs & Booth | | 171,104 | Two styles wire barbs and hand tool |
| Dobbs & Booth | | 171,105 | Two-point wire barb |
| Hill & Jayne | 1876 | 172,437 | Tool for attaching four-point wire barb |
| Knickerbocker | | 172,452 | Tool for attaching two-point wire barb |
| Pooler & Jones | | 174,435 | Tool for attaching three-point barb |
| Jayne & Hill | | 176,120 | Four-point wire barb |
| Jayne & Hill | | 176,12 1 | Improved tool for attaching four-point wire barb (see #172,437) |
| Emerson | | 176,523 | Two-point wire barb for attaching to fences |
| Prindle | | 178,954 | Tool for attaching two-point wire barb by twisting |
| Harsha | | 179,555 | Three-point sheet metal and nail barb |
| Swan | | 179,625 | Tool for attaching two-point wire barb |
| Allen | | 180,185 | Four-point wire barb for attaching to wire fence with pincers |
| Kennedy | | 180,351 | Tool for attaching three-point wire barb |
| Wilson & Bartlett | | 180,405 | Tool for attaching two-point wire barb |
| Miller | | 181,533 | Two-point wire barb ("pliable" wire), no tools or skill needed for attaching |
| Pooler & Jones | | 181,537 | Three-point wrought iron or sheet metal barb |

| Inventor | Year | Patent # | Design Description |
|---|---|---|---|
| Hill | | 182,928 | Clip-on sections of barbed wire |
| Harsha | | 182,819 | Two-point with special designed opening for attaching to fence |
| Dobbs | | 183,379 | Tool for attaching two-point wire barb |
| Knickerbocker | | 185,333 | Three-point sheet metal barb for attaching to fence |
| Nelson | | 185,346 | Two-point wire clip-on barb |
| Scutt | 1877 | 193,557 | Four-point sheet metal barb for attaching to single-wire strand or double-wire fences |
| St. John | | 199,330 | Four-point barb created for two intertwined staples on single-wire strand |
| McNeill | 1878 | 199,162 | Four-point sheet metal barb for attaching to single- or two-strand wires |
| St. John | | 199,330 | Four-point wire (staple) barb for attaching to single- or two-strand wires |
| Edwards | | 199,995 | Tool for attaching two-point wire barbs, called pincer |
| Brunner & Reynolds | | 200,125 | Two-, three-, and four-point wire barb (staple and sheet metal washer) for attaching to single- or two-wire strands |
| Wing | | 200,783 | Four-point wire barb attached with pincers |
| Nadelhoffer | | 201,889 | Two-point staple shaped wire for attaching to double-strand wire fence |
| Eberhart | | 207,405 | Tool for attaching four-point wire barb |
| Sellers | | 207,449 | Tool for attaching two-point wire barb |
| Knickerbocker | | 208,403 | Tool for attaching two-point staple wire barb |
| Miles | | 208,688 | Two-point wire staple barb, hand mounted |
| Wilkes | 1879 | 216,637 | Four-point barb from two interlocked staples attached to single-strand wire |
| Baker | 1883 | 273,219 | Two-point sheet metal or wire flat barb to be attached by suitable machinery |
| Randel & Brockner | | 286,636 | Tool for affixing staple wires to fence wire |
| Perry | 1897 | 588,774 | Method for welding two-point wire barbs to barbless wire fences |

One design that had the purpose of adapting barbless wire fences involved designing a barb that could be attached to a two-wire-strand barbless fence. In 1878, Nadelhoffer (#201,889) designed a two-point wire barb that could be inserted between a two-strand plain wire fence (Figure 14).

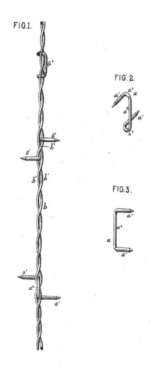

Figure 14. Nadelhoffer, J. W. 1878 (#201,889) Crossover "Z" Barb

Besides Haish (1874, #147,631), other inventors tried to adapt existing wooden fences, as was being done for existing plain wire fence, by developing barbs to be inserted on or into a wooden rail. In some cases these designs using wooden rails were seen as making barbed fencing more visible by utilizing existing wooden rail fences with barbs. Along with Rose's 1873 design (#138,763) which initiated the idea of barbed wire fencing, the following is a list of other early barbed fence patents utilizing wooden fencing:

- » Haish (1874) #147,631 – Four-point sheet metal barbs for attaching to wooden rails

- » Stout (1875) #163,116 – Three-point mild steel barbs inserted into wooden board suspended between two single-strand mild steel wires

- » Richards (1877) #191,468 – Tool and barb (single sheet metal point) to convert wooden fences into barbed fences

- » Topliff (1877) #191,818 – Serrated metal edge placed in a grooved wooden rail

- » Housum (1878) #204,734 – Tool for attaching one-point wire barbs in wooden rails (he had two barb designs)

- » Walsh & Dutol (1880) #223,780 – Grooved wooden rail with reinforcing rod held together with alternating barbs

- » Orwig (1880) #225,717 – Wooden rail with wire barb inserts (purposely designed to eliminate use of metals and be more visible)

- » Chapman (1881) #246,866 – Three-point brad barbs staggered along edge of wooden rail

It should be noted that sheet metal strip fencing and wooden strip fencing with barbs were included under the USPTO Classification "Improvement in Wire Fences" in the early 1870s.

Plain wire fence patents continued to be applied into the 1890s in spite of the acceptance and expansion of barbed fencing. For example, S. H. Gregg of Crawfordsville, Indiana, patented a barbless single-wire strand in 1890 (#441,005). His design was an "Improvement in Wire Fences." The design remedied the "questionable features" of barbed fences (i.e., "…liability to lacerate, maim, and destroy the lives of animals, rent clothing and wound persons coming in contact with them") and the disadvantages of barbless wire fences (i.e., "…the difficulty of seeing same and troubles resulting from the expansion and contraction under heat and cold"). His design was a single-strand fence with undulating oval wires (Figure 15).

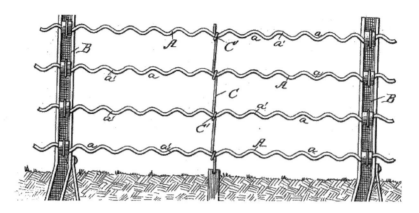

Figure 15. Gregg, S. H. 1890 (#441,005) "Single Strand Snake Wire"

## REGIONAL PATTERNS IN BARBED FENCING

Antique barbed fencing is found throughout the United States and is not just a Western United States phenomenon or invention. In an 1882 publication by Washburn and Moen Co. they claim that barb fencing is used in "all parts of the Globe" including "large estates in the Amazon", Australia, India and South Africa (Washburn and Moen 1882). Although barbed fencing was used extensively in the West, it was invented in the Midwest (e.g., J. Glidden, I. L .Ellwood, and J. Haish) and in the East (e.g., M. Kelly, L. B. Smith, and W. D. Hunt). Once invented, it was used in farming and ranching throughout the United States. Barbed fencing was especially important in the East in allowing the use of otherwise unusable hilly forestland once cleared to be used for pasturing. One Vermont farmer was quoted as saying, "I am getting a return on twenty-four hundred dollars from land that has been worthless to me, and would not pay for solid fencing" (Massachusetts Board of Agriculture 1882). The Board stated that in New England "it (barbed fencing) will make an effective barrier with one, two, three, four, or five strands, varying with the farmer's needs. In the first form, of a single strand attached to trees through woodlands, it is to-day furnishing thousands of miles of effective barrier to large stock on hill pastures in New England, where a more efficient and costly fence is not believed to be warranted."

For the South, the Massachusetts Board of Agriculture in 1882 attributed a comment regarding the use of barbed fencing to Edward Atkinson, a well-known economist of the time: "In the South …under its new system of divided farm lands, such writers as Edward Atkinson are pointing to the utility of barb wire as cheap and available in protecting the crops of the new and small farmers, helping the raising of cotton and the breeding of sheep; and sheep-breeders, everywhere, are beginning to study how the barb may antidote the sheep-killing dog and bring back sheep-raising to regions whence the mutton-loving canines long ago banished or impoverished it."

The Board went on to say that "barb wire is rapidly doing away with the system of free ranges in the great open regions of the South-west and the interior, and on the Pacific slope, where, not long ago, fencing was not dreamed of as possible."

Once barbed fencing was invented, the wire industry in the East and Midwest quickly moved to manufacture and distribute this inexpensive wire fencing with barbs. In 1881, nearly all of the barbed wire manufacturing occurred in the Upper Midwest and Northeast (Figure 16).

Figure 16. Centers of Barbed Wire Production in 1881 (Adapted from Netz 2004 and The American Steel and Wire Records housed at Harvard Library in Boston).

It should also be noted that barbed fencing, manufacturing, and patenting occurred across the border in Canada. Three cities in Canada were identified by Netz (2004) as production centers: (1) Montreal, (2) Toronto, and (3) Woodstock, Ontario. Canadian barbed fencing advertisements have been found (e.g., Dominion Barb-Wire Company of Montreal and Toronto, Canada), as has a history of Canadian business from 1867 to 1914 (Naylor 2006) that shows the importance in manufacturing and use of barb fencing in Canada. These sources referencing testimony regarding the monopolization of barbed fencing in Canada indicate that barbed fencing was both manufactured and imported to Canada. Dominion Barb-Wire Company had a licensing agreement with Washburn & Moen Co. to manufacture and sell barbed fencing. The distribution of barbed fencing was national and reflected its use in the West (Figure 17).

Figure 17. Centers for Delivery of Barbed Wire in 1888 (Adapted from Netz 2004 and The American Steel and Wire Records housed at Harvard Library in Boston).

For the next twenty plus years there was an explosion in the designs, patents, and manufacturing of barbed fencing in the United States for the purpose of fencing livestock. By 1910, not only had the overall fence stocks increased by twenty-five percent since 1870, but there was a dramatic shift in the proportion of the type of fence stocks (Figure 18).

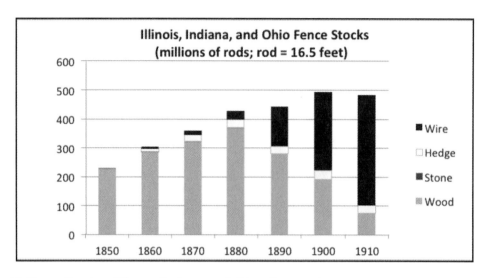

Figure 18. Fence Stock in Illinois, Indiana, and Ohio from 1850 to 1910
(Adapted from Hornbeck 2010)

In 1870, wood fences accounted for eighty-nine percent of the fence stocks in the Midwest. By 1910, wood fences accounted for only fifteen percent of the total fence stocks. Wire fences accounted for seventy-nine percent of the total fence stock in the Midwest. It is interesting to note the continued use of hedges for fencing (one percent of total stocks in 1910).

In New England, there was commentary in the 1882 Annual Report of the Massachusetts Board of Agriculture about the use of barbed wire to make old stone walls effective: "Another thing it (barbed wire) is one of the best things to use on an old stone. If you have an old wall that needs building over, and you have not the time to do it, just set up a few stakes, and put up one or two strands of wire, and you have got one of the best fences that can be made. One of the things that I like about it very much is that it won't winter-kill, and it don't burn up."

Similar trends in the increased use of barbed wire fencing were seen in other regions. In the prairies of North Dakota, South Dakota, Iowa, Nebraska, and Kansas - areas without large quantities of trees and stone - little fencing occurred from the 1850s to the 1870s compared to the Midwest where fence stocks were primarily wood fencing and hedge fencing. However, the passing of the Homestead Act in 1862 brought farmers and ranchers to these areas. The Homestead Act allowed citizens and immigrants intending to become citizens to get title to 160 acres of land for a small fee if they agreed to live on the tract for five years and make a few improvements. The demand for adequate fencing rose. This resulted in the expansion of cattle production in this region.[20] The fencing was dominated by wire or barbed wire fencing (Figure 19).

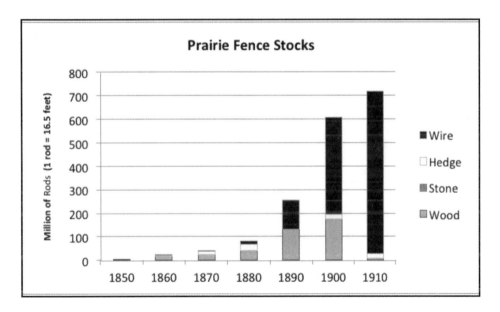

Figure 19. Fence Stock in the Prairies from 1850 to 1910 (Adapted from Hornbeck 2010)

---

20    *The Farming Frontier*, Digital History ID 3151. Available from http://www.digitalhistory.uh.edu/disp_textbook_print.cfm?smtid=2&psid=3147

By 1910, ninety-five percent of the fence stock, or more than 700 million rods (about two million miles), was wire fence, primarily barbed wire. Barbed and barbless woven wire was introduced during this period, especially in the 1890s and 1900s (see Chapter 5).

The pattern of switching from pre-barbed wire fencing of wood, stone, and hedges was also seen in the new construction of new fences during this period. In Illinois, Indiana, and Ohio, new barbed wire fence accounted for ninety-six percent of the new construction in the 1880s and one hundred percent in the 1890s and 1900s (Figure 20).

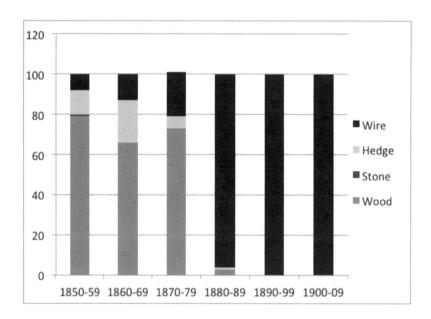

Figure 20. Comparison of New Fence Construction (Percentage of Total Fence Stocks) in Illinois, Indiana, and Ohio (Adapted from Hornbeck 2010)

A similar trend in new fence construction (i.e., wire fences) was seen in the prairies although starting 10 years later. New wire fence construction comprised eighty-two percent of the new fence stocks constructed from 1890 to 1899, and 100% constructed from 1900 to 1909 (Hayter 1939) (Figure 21).

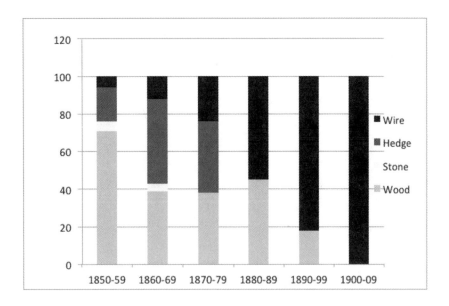

Figure 21. Comparison of New Fence Construction (Percentage of Total Fence Stocks) in the Prairie Region (Adapted from Hornbeck 2010)

Detailed statistics for changes in fence stocks for the Northeast and Southeast are not available, but the same trends occurred with the greater use of barbed wire over other fence stocks. This pattern is reflected in the discussions of agricultural literature of the time (e.g., Massachusetts Department of Agriculture 1882) and in the finding of antique barbed wire attached to the top of old stone walls in Vermont.

As discussed earlier, the amount of antique barbed fencing used in different parts of the country depended upon the available fencing resources in a region and experience with fencing. The East, with a longer history of using plain wire fencing and other fencing types (e.g., stone walls and wood fencing), barbed fencing was added and combined with these existing fencing types. In the Midwest, the same trend occurred in states such as Ohio, Indiana, and Illinois with existing fencing resources (e.g., timber and hedges). Existing fencing was supplemented and supplanted with wire fencing, including barbed wire and woven fence wire. In the North-Central states, with fewer basic fence resources (e.g., timber), barbed fencing quickly became the dominant fence type. Besides regional differences in barbed fencing, subregional patterns are found and relate to the available fencing. This is seen in the 1916 patterns of fencing in the North-Central States (Figure 22).

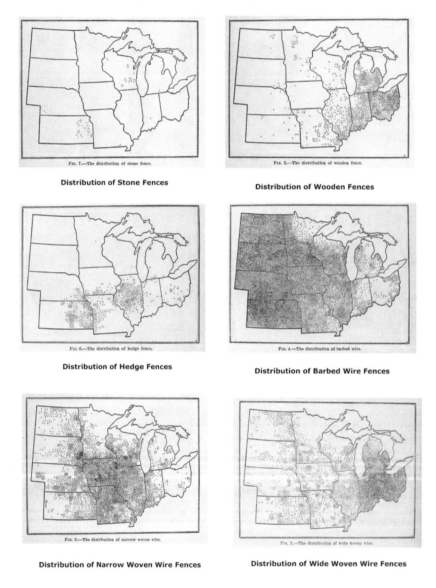

Figure 22. Distribution of Fencing in the North-Central States in 1916 (Humphries 1916)

Few stone, hedge, and wooden fences appeared in the Midwest in 1916, primarily because these fence materials, (stone, hedges, and timber) were scarce compared to the eastern parts of the U. S.. The rapid expansion of cattle production in the Midwest required fencing, and barbed wire and narrow woven wire were the dominant fence types.

Collectors of antique barbed wire should not assume that "old" or antique barbed fencing can only be found in the West. The previous discussion indicates that all parts of the country adapted and adopted barbed fencing. Comprehensive regional inventories for occurrence of different designs have not been identified in the literature. McCallum and McCallum (1985) did provide some indication where a few patent designs they considered were found, but their information is not comprehensive. For example, they indicated that Crandal's 1879 "Zigzag" design (#221,158) had been found in California, Texas, and Oklahoma. I have barbed fencing specimens from a farm in upstate New York that includes Crandal's 1879 "Zigzag" (#221,158) and Allis's 1881 "Buckthorn" (#244,726) wires. Both were found on the same corner post in an old farm field in upstate New York that now is a woodland. Rolls of Allis's 1881 "Buckthorn" (#244,726) wire sit in the Adirondack Museum in Blue Mountain Lake, New York, and the Mill House Museum in *Occoquan*, Virginia. A history[21] of small sheep and dairy farms on an island (South Hero, Vermont) in Lake Champlain records the use before 1900 of T. V. Allis's 1881 "Buckthorn" (#224,726) and N. G. Ross's 1879 four-point barb (#216,294). The "Buckthorn" fencing was a type of fencing apparently utilized by sheep farmers. Finding "Buckthorn" fencing in southern and northern Vermont, New York, and Virginia, suggests that this patent design was in common use in the East at the turn of the 19th century. Barbed wire organizations and museums should consider inventorying the regional occurrences of antique barbed fencing designs to understand the use and distribution of specific designs.

---

21    http://www.uvm.edu/~clpp/conservationleadership/site/?Page=fencing.html

Although antique barbed fencing is associated with the United States, it is also found in other countries, such as Canada in the 1880s (see earlier discussion). Barbed fencing is mentioned as being used in England and Germany, however, antique barbed fencing use in Australia may be the second place where it was extensively used compared to the United States. The Museum Victoria[22] is a state museum with several specialty museums in Melbourne, Australia; it has a collection of more than 1,400 pieces of antique barbed fencing including almost 900 different types of barbed wire, numerous samples of plain and kinked wire, ribbon wire, warning devices, and other wire accessories. The collection includes the familiar patents found in the United States, including Glidden, Crandal, Brinkerhoff, Scutt, Kelly, and other inventors. The collection is called the "Jack Chisholm Fencing Collection." According to the museum, most of these pieces were collected in Australia, but only eight to ten examples were actually made in Australia. According to the museum, barbed fencing was introduced to Australia in the 1880s. There were local manufacturers, but many types were imported from the United States. On the lighter side, there is a bar in Spalding, South Australia, called "The Barbed Wire Pub"[23] which features a barbed fencing museum of some 500 pieces and accessories that have been collected in the area. Kerr (1987) reported a collection of twenty-one different types of barbed fencing displayed at the Tamworrth Historical Society Museum in New South Wales.

---

22    http://museumvictoria.com.au/collections/items/404363/barbed-wire-sample-glidden-two-twisted-strand-two-point-illinois-1874

23    http://www.barbedwirepubspalding.com.au/

He discussed an "early interesting sample" of Allis's 1881 (#244,726) "Buckthorn" design collected in the Tamworth area, Bective Station. The author stated that for cattle, the most common fences were post and barbed wire, though post and two-rail fences were still preferred if timber was available.

No exhaustive review of the international distribution of barbed fencing has been found, but a news item in the 1904 *Hardware Dealers' Magazine* indicates that barbed fencing had truly international recognition and use. The news item described the action of the government of Iceland, which appropriated $26,800 for granting loans for the purchase of "galvanized barbed wire for the fencing of farms." The news item went on to say that this action "would seem to be an opening for American manufacturers." The 1906 edition of the *Hardware Dealers' Magazine* discussed the exporting of barbed wire to Brazil, saying that "three point wire barbs are the most popular."

# 3) MATERIALS USED IN ANTIQUE BARBED FENCING

» Metallic Materials

» Non-Metallic Materials

To understand antique barbed fencing designs, one needs to consider the materials used in the design and manufacturing of barbed fencing. These materials influence the structure, shape, form, and function of the designs. Barbed fencing evolved from the early fencing types, including plain wire fences, wood fences, and hedges. It is not surprising that early inventors developed designs that used many of the same materials. Below is an overview of the materials used in the design and manufacturing of antique barbed fencing. There are two basic groups of materials found in antique barbed fencing: (1) metallic materials and (2) non-metallic materials (Figure 23).

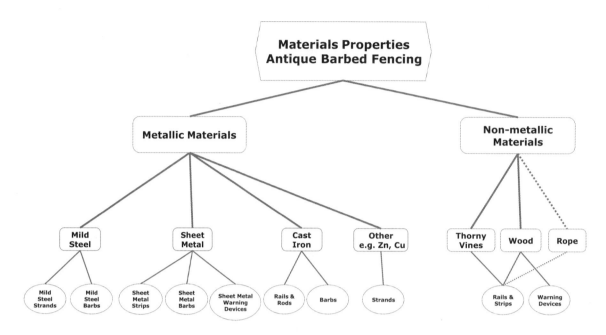

Various combinations of metallic and non-metallic materials are found in the designs of the horizontal components and    attachments

Figure 23. Material Properties of Antique Barbed Fencing

## METALLIC MATERIALS (MILD STEEL, SHEET METAL, AND CAST IRON)

The primary metallic materials used in antique barbed fencing are iron and its alloys (e.g., mild steel). Iron (Fe) is one of the basic elements. It occurs naturally and is mined. It has been used for thousands of years in tool making and building construction, especially when alloyed with other elements. When iron is heated, it liquefies and can be molded into objects like barbs. This type of iron is called cast iron. Cast iron is more brittle than mild steel. It has a carbon content from about two percent to four percent.

Steel is an alloy of iron and carbon with a lower carbon content than cast iron. There are two kinds of steel: (1) plain carbon steel or mild steel and (2) alloy steels produced from Bessemer and open-hearth steel manufacturing.[24] Mild steel has a carbon content of around 0.2% - 0.3%. The iron ore used in producing mild steel can have other elements in it, including copper. The copper content of iron ore used to produce mild steel was found to have a direct bearing on the durability of barbed fencing in the early 1900s. Studies by Storey (1917) showed that early mild steel barbed fencing with higher copper contents of 0.1% to 0.2% had a greater durability and less rusting than the later barbed fencing produced with lower copper steel. Plain carbon steel is divided into three types: (1) low-carbon steel, known as mild steel (used in antique barbed fencing); (2) medium-carbon steel; and (3) high-carbon steel. Two types of mild steel metals were produced: (1) rolled wire and (2) stamped out sheet metal referred to as sheet metal strips or ribbon wire. Rolled wire, sheet metal, and cast iron were used in manufacturing the horizontal structures and attachments for barbed fencing.

Cushman (1905) provided a detailed description of the manufacturing of wire at the turn of the 19th century. Wire manufacturers obtained their steel in the form of metal bars or billets from steel mills. Wire manufacturers then took the billets and heated and rolled them into 12 gauge or other gauge wires.

---

24    Bessemer process is a less expensive process of making steel from iron and was invented in the mid-1850s, twenty-plus years before the invention of barbed fencing.

Other metals found in antique barbed fencing patent designs include zinc and tin. They have primarily been used as coatings to prevent rusting. Zinc is the most common metal used to coat or galvanize wire, strips, and barbs to prevent rusting and was commonly used in early barbed fencing manufacturing. Galvanizing to protect metal from rusting was already established in the steel industry by the mid-1870s. W. A Root in his 1881 patent (# 237,130) described an improved manufacturing process for coating barbed wire and barbs using galvanization and other coatings. Hagemeier (2010) identified a copper-coated variation[25] of Ross's "Four Point Double Strand" (#216,294). Ross's patent description did not mention coatings. In 1885, M. Kelly described his two-point loop barb design (#322,108) and mentioned that the wires could be coated with tin. Other attempts besides galvanizing were used to retard rusting, including coatings of paint, varnish, annealing, copper, tin, cadmium, and zinc (McCallum and McCallum 1985). Horton (1916) provided a detailed description of the galvanizing process in the early 1900s.

One design that appeared as barbed fencing for use with livestock but was not was a design by T. H. Dodge of Worcester, Massachusetts. He patented a design in 1883 (#282,449) for a metal strand composed of a combination of a two-point mild steel barb twisted on a galvanized mild steel wire; both were then twisted with a copper wire forming a double-wire strand. This design was not used as livestock fencing, but rather as a lightning rod or conductor to protect building from burglars.

---

25      Hagemeier's 2010 identification (# 1093B).

Prior to this patent, Dodge had patented traditional barbed fencing using all iron materials. Modern barbed wire uses high tensile steel to provide greater flexibility and strength of barbed wire. Modern wires have been made of aluminum.[26]

Most barbs were primarily metal, although sometimes they were combined with wood (Figure 24).

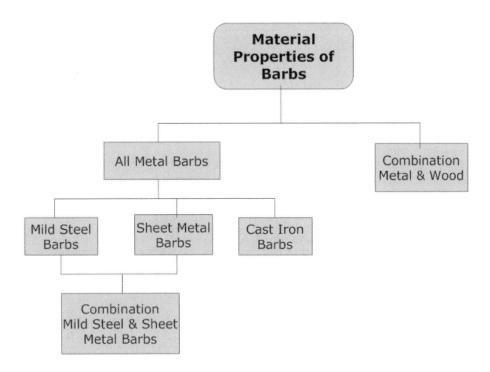

Figure 24. Materials Used in Barb Design

---

26    Hagemeier (2012) identified a barbed wire (#1845B) consisting of two parallel wire strands with a two-point aluminum "S" barb as a variation of Haish's 1874 patent (#167,240).

Table 3 provides a comparison of the types of materials found in antique barbed fencing designs. The vast majority of inventors used mild steel followed by sheet metal for their horizontal components and attachments.

Table 3. Comparison of the Number of Antique Barbed Fencing Patents and Patent Variations Associated with Different Metallic and Non-Metallic Materials (Adapted from Clifton 1970; Hagemeier 2010, 2012)

| Mild Steel | Metallic Materials* | | | | Non-Metallic Materials |
|---|---|---|---|---|---|
| | Sheet Metal | Cast Iron | Iron | Wood | |
| **Horizontal Components** | | | | | |
| Wire Strands | 600+ | | | | |
| Sheet Metal Strips | | 250+ | | | |
| Metal Rods/Bars | | | | <12 | |
| Wooden Rails | 4** | 2** | 2** | | |
| **Attachments** | | | | | |
| Barbs | 400+ | 190+ | <20 | | |
| Warning Devices | | 11 | | | 7 |
| * Cu, Al, and other metals reported in barb and strand variations but no patents found before 1914 | | | | | |
| ** Material of barbs or supporting materials | | | | | |

An all-inclusive metallic and non-metallic barbed fencing patent design is J. Fisher's design (#203,536) in 1878. Fisher, from Davenport, Iowa, patented a complete barbed fence system with metallic barbed wires, fence posts, and gates made of cast iron and mild steel wires with barbs (Figure 25). The design also had wooden boards. The object of his design was a more visible fence to animals and use of blunted prongs. It was classified as an "Improvement in Fences."

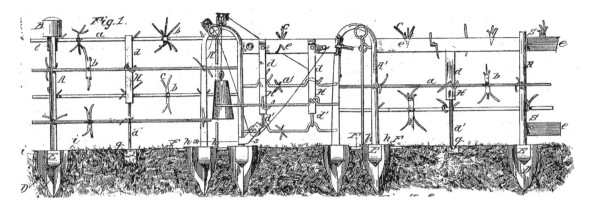

Figure 25. Fisher, J. B. 1878 (#203,536) "Metal and Wooden Fence System"

### Mild Steel Wire Fencing

Mild steel wire strands used for barbed fencing were made of rolled and drawn mild steel, or low carbon steel. A rolled wire was relatively inexpensive, malleable, and ductile. The gauge of the wires have varied from sixteen gauge (0.0625 inch) to eleven gauge (0.1205 inch). Twelve and one-half gauge is the most common gauge wire found in barbed wire. Orders for barbed wire could be placed for different gauge wires (Hagemeier 2010).

Mild steel materials were used primarily in wire strands and barbs and were the major material used in antique barbed fencing. They were occasionally used in combination with sheet metal strips as barbs and in combination with wooden rails as reinforcing material. The earliest use of a mild steel wire as barb was found in H. Rose's 1873 patent (#138,763) for a wooden strip with wire projections (see Figure 4 on page 18). He called them "metallic points."

55

The earliest granted design using mild steel for both a horizontal component and attachment was J. Haish's "S" barb patent (#146,671) in Jan 1874 for a mild steel wire strand and mild steel barb. (See later discussion first applied for and issued designs following Rose's use at the DeKalb Co. Fair in 1873).

Sixty-nine percent of barb patents and variations involved the use of mild steel wire barbs with mostly round shape. Twenty-seven percent involved sheet metal barbs. Only three percent of the barbs were made of cast iron and one percent were made of a combination of wood and metal (Figure 26). Copper and aluminum barbs have been identified as variations by Hagemeier (2010); however, no specific patents using these metals have been found.

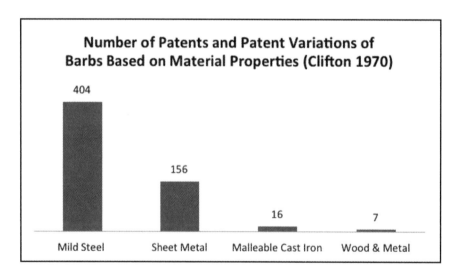

Figure 26. Number of Patents and Patent Variations of Barbs Based on Material Properties (Clifton 1970)

**Sheet Metal Fencing**

Sheet metal is the second most common attachment and horizontal component material used in barbed fencing. Sheet metal is a mild steel that is rolled or pressed into flat pieces of metal. It is also referred to as "hoop iron." In barbed fencing, it is found primarily as sheet metal strips or ribbon wire but also as barbs and warning devices on single- and multiwire-wire strands and wooden rails. It was invented at the same time mild steel strands and barbs were invented. The earliest sheet metal barb patent was W. D. Hunt's 1867 (#67,117) "Spur Wheel" design. The earliest sheet metal barb attached to a sheet metal strip was Judson's 1871 (#118,135) "Both Edges Single Cut Ribbon."

Sheet metal barbs were formed by being stamped out of a sheet metal strip. In 1875, T. Doolitttle and J. Ellis of Bridgeport, Connecticut, patented the first invention (#165,561) for manufacturing sheet metal barbs with a better set of designed punch and dies that resulted in sharper pointed barbs. J. Oliver of Allegany County, Pennsylvania, was issued a patent (#182,323) in 1876 for "Wire-Fence-Barb Blanks and Dies." The patent used "… waste hoop ends of cottons-bale hoops manufacture or other like waste hoop material…" to make sheet metal barbs. In his patent description, he made "no claim" on the barb but only on the way such barbs could be manufactured.

T. V. Allis was a prolific inventor of sheet metal patent designs from 1878 to 1895 (see Chapter 4). There are also a large number of variations in sheet metal strips based on their appearance and mode of attachment (Figure 27).

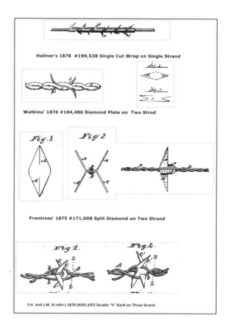

Figure 27. Examples of Sheet Metal Barbs, Single- and Multi-Wire Strands

Some barb designs involved combining iron wire and sheet metal as barbs (e.g., Hunt's 1877 [#193,370] "Plate Locked Link") (Figure 28).

Figure 28. Hunt 1887 (#193,370) "Plate Locked Link"

Hunt's design involved creating a four-point design by attaching a sheet metal diamond-shaped plate and single-point wire barb held in place by hooking a double-strand wire through a diamond plate and bending the ends of the wires perpendicular to the diamond points.

## Cast Iron and Bar Iron Fencing

Two types of iron are found in antique barbed fencing: (1) cast iron and (2) bar iron. Cast iron is an iron product that is heated until it liquefies and is poured into a mold to solidify. It is sometimes referred to as malleable iron. Cast iron contains from three to four and one-half percent carbon. This high proportion of carbon makes cast iron hard and brittle; it is liable to crack or shatter under a heavy blow and it cannot be forged (i.e., heated and shaped by hammer blows) at any temperature. Cast iron patents are primarily barb designs and make up a very small number of the total barb patent designs and patent variations (approximately three percent of the total) (e.g., Reynolds's "Cast Barb" 1877 [#187,049]). These barbs have distinct appearances (see later discussion on barb appearance) and are primarily associated with two-wire strand fences (Clifton 1970). Clifton identified six designs, including Bur, Cylinder, Disc, Pin, Star, and Wheel designs. One design by O. Phillips (#280,857) in 1883 called "cocklebur" was designed to mimic the cocklebur found in pasture that the inventor assumed cattle would be aware of and avoid (Figure 29). It was one of the obvious designs invented to reduce injury associated with wire barb designs (see Chapter 4 discussion on Change in Patent Designs).

Figure 29. Phillips, O. O. 1883 (#280,857) "Cocklebur"

Another example of cast iron barbs was Utter's 1887 "Cylinder" (Figure 30). It attached to a double-wire strand fence. He claimed the advantage for his design was that the movable barb caused less injury to livestock than stationary barbs did.

Figure 30. Utter, H. 1887 (#369,825) "Spiked Cylinder Barb"

Bar iron, or wrought iron, is another type of iron that is heated and then worked with tools to produce its shape and form.[27] It contains very little carbon (less than 0.035%). This material was used primarily to make horizontal components (i.e., bars, rods, and rails) in barbed fencing. According to patent descriptions, barbed iron rods could be produced by ordinary "rolling," "molding," "casting," or "dieing"[28] (see Perry's 1886 patent description [#333,887]).

---

27    http://www.reliance-foundry.com/blog/difference-cast-iron-wrought (Accessed December 2012)

28    Refers to the process of using a die for casting or molding.

Although not clear from patent descriptions, iron bars, rods, and rails were made of what we consider today wrought iron, a very low carbon iron. These iron bars were shaped by passing them through the rolls of a rolling mill. Barbs for iron bars were an integral part of the iron bar (see patent description of Sims 1876 [#178,195]). Bar iron with integral barbs was found in about half a dozen patent designs as bars or rods that could be set up and taken down in the field. These designs were generally for small enclosures (Clifton 1970; Hagemeier 2010, 2012) (see Chapter 5 discussion on bars, rods, and rails for examples).

## NON-METALLIC MATERIALS

Non-metallic materials in combination with metal materials were used for the manufacturing of rails, barbs, and warning devices. Fence posts (not covered in this analysis) were primarily wood,[29] although metal fence posts and rock posts were used as fence posts. They have been found in Kansas as limestone posts.[30] In Nebraska,[31] cement posts were erected by the railroads in the late 1880s. The use of non-metallic materials (i.e., wood) lent itself as the preferred barbed fencing post alternative to metal posts because of cost, prevalence of wood as a fence post resource, and existence of wooden fences already in use in the United States, especially in the East and Midwest in the 19th century.

The non-metallic materials for the horizontal component were primarily wood rails, although there was one patent design that included the use of thorny shrubs (see Chapter 5, W. B. Vanvleet 1879 [#218,342]) and one patent that incorporated rope (see Kelly 1868 [#74,379]).

---

29    The Massachusetts Department of Agriculture Report of 1882 stated that willow and chestnut posts were commonly used.

30    http://www.rushcounty.org/PostRockMuseum/

31    Blue, K. "Nebraska Cement Post." *The Barbed Wire Collector* 31, no. 5 (2014): 9.

Non-metallic materials in combination with metallic materials were patented as "Improvements in Fences." Since wood rails and wood used in barbs and warning plates could split, decay, or burn by prairie fires, the combination of wood and metal in barbed wire fencing was not as effective as all-metal barbed fencing wire and few patents were issued (Hagemeier 2010).

The longevity of wood material used in fencing was investigated in 1916 (Horton 1916). The best wood for wooden fences in north-central states were considered oak (live, white, and bur oak), chestnut, and walnut. In his study, Horton reported on the average life of different woods used in fence posts and showed that woods such as Osage Orange, Locust, and Red Cedar had an average useful life of more than twenty years while other woods such as Elm, Ash, Red Oak, and Willow had an average useful life of less than ten years. He also provided the average life of concrete as forty-eight years, stone as thirty-six years, and steel as thirty years. Horton (1916) provided more specific data on the durability of trees as wooden posts (Table 4). It is assumed that these numbers are for untreated wooden posts.

Table 4. Percentage of Failure of Trees Used as Fence Post in the Ground after Twenty Years (Adapted from Horton 1916)

| SPECIES OF TREE | PERCENTAGE OF FAILURE |
|---|---|
| Sycamore | 100 |
| Black Gum | 100 |
| Yellow Poplar | 100 |
| Willow | 100 |
| Birch | 100 |
| Sweet Gum | 80 |
| Pin Oak | 80 |
| Maple | 80 |
| Pine | 80 |
| Locust | 52 |
| Beech | 40 |
| Chestnut | 40 |

Some species, such as Sycamore and Black Gum, had to be replaced regularly. Horton (1916) provided advice on selecting and curing fence posts.

Woody materials are found in barbed fencing designs in combination with mild steel and sheet metal for horizontal components (i.e., wooden rails), attachments (i.e., barbs), and warning devices. Examples of combination wooden rails and metal include Walsh and Dutot (1880, #223,780), who invented a wooden rail fence with metal reinforcing rods (Figure 31).

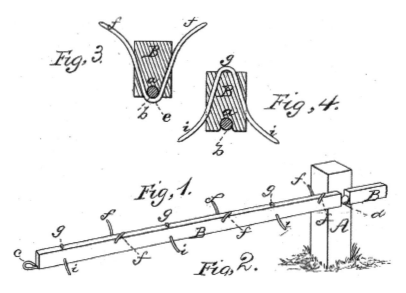

Figure 31. Walsh, J. and Dutot, J. 1880 (#223,780) "Wood Rail and Rod"

The post for the rails could be fifteen to twenty feet apart. It was classified as an "Improvement in Barb Fences." He stated that the advantage of his design was that it was "… more visible than under any ordinary circumstances to cattle, and that stock having once experienced their sting will carefully avoid them-a result that is not obtained in a barbed fence-wire."

In 1880, Orwig (#225,717) invented a wooden rail fence with short pieces of wooden rails (four feet) with two-point wire barbs penetrating the wooden rail sections and connected to one another by looped wire (Figure 32).

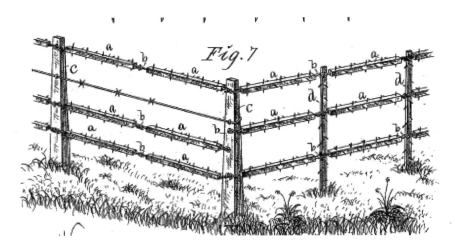

Figure 32. Orwig, T. G. 1880 (#225,717) "Square Rail with Point Barbed Inserts"

Wood is found in barb designs. The wood metal barb combination is referred to as a "Block and Nail" design by Clifton (1970). This combination was also one of the earliest patented barbed fence designs. In 1867, L. B. Smith (#66,182) patented a design comprising a single-wire strand with two-point cast iron barbs held in place by a wooden spool or cast iron spool. This design was never pursued as a popular barb design, although in the 1880s two inventors, A. Hulbert ("Block and Spike," 1884 [#296,835]) and H. Scutt ("Visible Barb Blocks," 1880 [#224,482]) patented two fence designs with a combination of wood and metal barbs. In 1893, Funcheon (#493,210) used a spool that could be made of wood or metal and four- point sheet metal barbs. The designs of the 1880s and 1890s had the purpose of making the barbed wire more visible to cattle and reducing unnecessary injury (see later discussion on antique barbed fencing designing period). These designs were not successful likely because of the lack of durability of wood on the wire. The following are examples of wood metal barb designs (Figure 33).

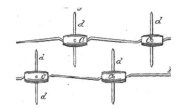

**Smith 1867 (#66,182) Block and Nail**

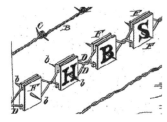

**Scutt 1880 (#224,482) Visible Barbed Block**

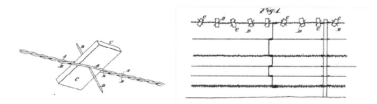

**Hulbert 1884 (#296,835) Block and Spike**

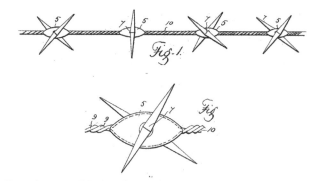

**Funcheon 493,210) Oval Spool & Four Point**

Figure 33. Examples of Combination Wood and Metal Barbs

A few combination wooden and metal warning devices were invented (e.g., Boone 1885 [#321,787] and Chappell 1889 [#401,133] were made of wood and attached to strands with wires) (Figures 34 and 35).

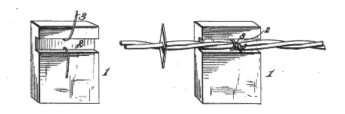

Figure 34. Boone, R. 1885 (#321,787) "Side Slot Wooden Block"

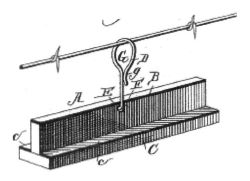

Figure 35. Chappell, M. B. 1889 (#401,133) "Hanging T Block"

Boone's design was classified as a "Visible Guard for Wire Fences" and Chappell's design was classified as a "Guard for Barbed-Wire Fences." These designs were developed when inventors were trying to make barbed wire fences more visible to reduce injury to cattle (for more discussion, see Chapter 5).

In 1868, Kelly (#74,379) incorporated the use of rope saturated with tar into his design to provide visibility to the barbed fence and proposed to attach his "thorns" or barbs to the rope when wire was not available (see letter "G" in Figure 36). He described the rope as being made of "twisted hay" (see Chapter 5 discussion on W. B. Vanvleet patent [#218,342] on unique barbs).

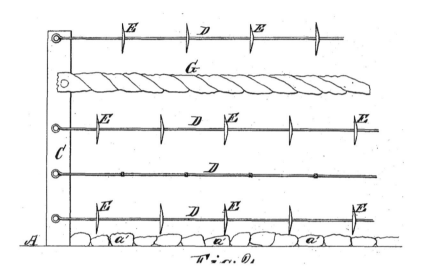

Figure 36. Kelly, M. 1868 (#74,379) "Thorny Single Strand"

# 4) INVENTORS, PATENTS, AND PATENT VARIATIONS

- » Number of Inventors, Patents, and Patent Variations
- » Change in Patent Designs Over Time
- » Why So Many Patent Designs?
- » Who Were the Most Successful Inventors of Antique Barbed Fencing?

## NUMBER OF INVENTORS, PATENTS, AND PATENT VARIATIONS

Developing a single, precise, and accurate number of barbed fencing inventors, patents, and patent variations is difficult for several reasons. First, the compilations of these numbers from published sources, such as Clifton, Hagemeir and Campbell, and Allison is difficult because these authors have used different criteria for identifying which inventors, their patents, and variations they include. For example, Hagemeier included the inventors, patents, and patent variations of metal strands, sheet metal strips, rods, bars, rails, and warning devices while Campbell and Allison included those but also added barbed fencing machines, dies for sheet metal barbs, and cattle guards. The common names they used were often different (see Chapter 6 on classification). Not all the authors included the same inventors, patents, etc., such as Meriwether because his design was not barbed or A. Dabb because his design (#63,482) was for a picket fence. Not all authors considered the same time period in their compilations and not all inventors were included in their compilations. Finally, as with any analysis, there were some discrepancies in the information presented so one-to-one comparisons of exact numbers was difficult.

In spite of the limitations, there was enough consistency in the information sources to develop reasonable estimates for the number of patents and patentees if one used qualifiers.

Based on available information from Clifton (1970), Hagemeier (2010), and Campbell and Allison (1986), the number of patents for all barbed fencing including wire strands, sheet metal strips, dies, tools, cattle guards, and barbed fencing making machines for livestock control from 1867 through 1914 is 948 patents. This number does not include variations that have been found. If one includes variations of only the strands, strips, barbs, and warning devices of Clifton (1970), then there are 992 patents and patent variations. For Hagemeier (2010), there are 1,666 patent and patent variations. No one has yet compiled information on variations in tools, dies, cattle guards, and barbed fencing machines. It is my opinion that the number of patent variations for dies, tools, cattle guards, and barbed fencing machines would increase the total number of patents and patent variations to over 2,000 for the period 1860 to 1914.

The number of inventors or patentees is more difficult to estimate. Clifton (1970) identified 311 patentees in his book for only barbed fencing and not inventors of other fencing items such as tools, die, etc. Hagemeier (2010) identified 397 inventors or patentees through 1914 for only the same limited types of barbed fencing (i.e., strands and strips but not tools, dies, etc.). Some double counting of inventors is likely in the estimates for inventors who teamed up for different patents, such as the Merrills, Gliddens, and Dodge & Washburn. Hagemeier identified 425 inventors. His number is a more recent compilation than Clifton and is a suitable estimate. If one adds the inventors for other barbed fencing devices (i.e., tools, dies, cattle guards), the total number of inventors responsible for antique barbed fencing would be considerably higher. In summary, there were nearly 1,000 antique barbed fencing patents, some 2,000 patents and patent variations invented by some 425 plus individuals. To generalize further, this means that the average number of patents per inventor was about 2 (1,000/425).

Hagemeier (2010) discussed the issue of barbed wire variations and made distinctions between variations, alterations, and modifications. He concluded that for a wire to be "true variation," the original patent design had to be intentionally changed for a specific reason. For example, railroads often ordered Glidden's patent (#157,124) be changed from round to rectangle shaped wires. These rectangular shaped wires were used as the strand or woven with a regular shaped round wire to identify their barbed fencing in case of theft.[32] These variations can be considered true to intentional variations. However, there are many other variations, modifications, or differences to the original patent designs that were identified by Hagemeier (2010, 2012), Clifton (1970), and others. It is likely many of these variations resulted when the barbed wire was fabricated by different authorized and unauthorized or "moonshiner" manufacturers (Hagemeier 2010). Called "moonshine," some barbed fencing was manufactured illegally by individuals, farm co-ops, and small manufacturing companies that did not own the patent rights or have a license to manufacture the barbed fencing they were producing.

Since it is impossible to differentiate between true variations from other variations, all design variations and known patent designs described in the literature are considered in this book, although emphasis is placed on patented designs. Some variations were unintentional from the lack of quality control in manufacturing. Some variations also resulted from farmers, ranchers, hardware men, carpenters, and blacksmiths assembling barbed fencing themselves.

---

32    http://www.rushcounty.org/barbedwiremuseum/bwhistory.htm

For example, early in the barbed fencing period, barbs were designed and manufactured for individual attachment to plain wire fences (see Chapter 2 discussion on transition from plain wire fencing to barbed fencing).

From reviewing the patent records most of the barbed fencing inventors were mail. Two female inventors have been found, American, Adeline Brock of Dunellen, New Jersey, in 1886 was granted a patent (#344,077) for flexible metallic fence; described as joining barbless sheet metal strips using ends of strips that were notched and locked with a washer. She was an owner of the Brock Flexible Fence Company of New York, New York. Hannah P. Willsey of Pasadena, California was born in Sweden in 1860 and died in California in 1941. She applied for a patent for fabric (woven-wire) fence in 1911 and it was granted in 1913 (#1,055,586). The purpose of the design was to provide a "fence wire structure" for "positively preventing the destruction or the uplifting of the same by such ground-rooting animals as pigs or the like." Although few women were granted patents it is important to point out that women likely had roles in barbed fencing design. Lucinda W Glidden, Joseph Glidden's wife, is recognized as highly influencing Glidden's first patent and the manufacturing of his design. (McCallum and McCallum 1985)

Foreign inventors were granted barbed fencing patents before 1915, including C. Westgarth in 1881 (#239,128) and I. Beresford in 1891 (#449,279), both from England, for metal rail designs (see Chapter 5) and T. Guilleaume of Germany in 1893 (#496,974) for four-point barb on two triangle-wire strands. In 1888, W. H. Rodden of Toronto, Canada, patented (#379,729) for a four-point half-round webbed wire barb twisted around the two-wire strand. A combination of US and Canadian inventors (e.g., A. B. Frost[33] of Ohio and

---

33    A. B. Frost was listed as a member of the Americans for the Advancement of Science (AAAS) in 1906. He appears to have been a recognized illustrator of agricultural and history books and hunting and fishing posters. His relationship to H. L. Frost is not known, but they were likely brothers given their similar ages. A Canadian Who's Who in Canada: An Illustrated Biographical Record of Men and Women in Canada published in 1916 indicated H. L. Frost was from Ohio and was president of several fence companies in Canada, including Frost Wire Fence Co. There was a Frost Wire Fence Company, Ltd. of Hamilton, Ontario, listed in the Canadian Industry, Commerce, and Finance book of 1915 by J. J. Harpell. A similarly named company was listed in the 1916 Farm Implement News Buyer's Guide. Robertson appears to have been a machinist.

H. L. Frost and A. Robertson of Welland, Canada) collaborated on the United States patent #777,662, a four-point mild steel barb on a single-strand mild steel wire with projections.

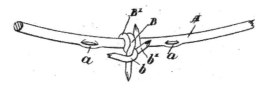

Figure 37. Frost, A. B., Frost, H. L., and Robertson, A. R. 1904 (#777,662), "Four Point"

The barb was designed so when an animal came in contact with it, it would "recede from the animal, although they (the barbs) will punish him sufficiently to make him keep way from it." It was classified as "Barbed Wire For Fences." It appears that the inventors made an application for their patent both in the United States and Canada in June 1903. Their Canadian patent (#106,079) was issued in December 1903 for the same design. The US patent was issued in December 1904.

In 1889, A. N. Pearson of Victoria, Australia, patented (#403,774) a two-point swinging barb woven fence design (see Figure 174).

In 1892, J. Beresford of Manchester, England, was issued a patent (#449,279) for barbed triangle rod (see later discussion in Chapter 5). Some inventors obtained patents for their designs both in the United States and in Canada. T. J. Barnes of Julesburg, Colorado, was granted a patent (#867,338) for woven-wire fence with rotating sheet metal barbs on October 7, 1907; the patent was classified as an "Improvement in Barbed-Wire Fence" (Figure 38). He was also granted a patent for the same design by the Canadian Patent Office in November 1907 (#108,419). Campbell and Allison identified it, but Hagemeier and Clifton did not.

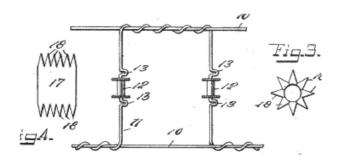

Figure 38. Barnes, T. J. 1907 (#867,338), "Parallel Strands"

Another example of a Canadian patent that was originally a United States patent and was subsequently assigned to three Canadians is a single mild steel wire strand with two wires twisted together forming a four-point barb. This was patented by G. W. Allen of Creston, Illinois, in 1876 (US #180,185), and three years later in 1879 (Canada #10,447) (Figure 39).

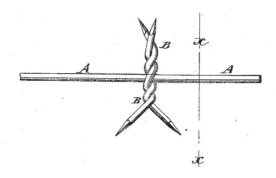

Figure 39. Allen, G. W. 1876 (#180,185) "Four-Point Twist"

The Canadian patent record showed the Canadian patentees being T. J. Clark, K. Forrest, and J. G. Short of Waterloo, Ontario, who apparently had been assigned the patent by G. W. Allen of Creston, Illinois.

## CHANGES IN PATENT DESIGNS OVER TIME

The exponential growth and peak in patent designs is seen in the number of barbed fencing patents issued by USPTO from 1860 to present day (Figure 40). Antique barbed fencing designs changed because of the economic opportunities for barbed fencing with most of the different designs or patents issued in the late 1870s through the 1880s. In the late 1880s and early 1890s, there was a sharp decline in patents issued; this is likely because of the litigation and decision of the Supreme Court in 1892 awarding Glidden and the Washburn and Moen Co. the primary patent rights (McCallum and McCallum 1985).

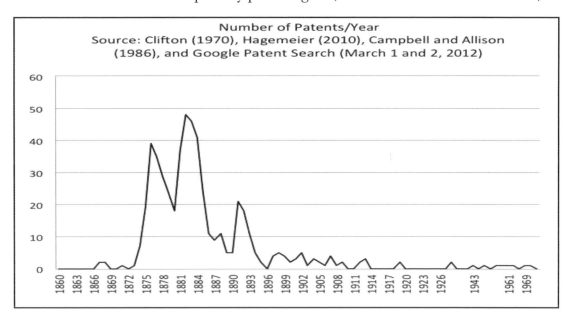

Figure 40. Frequency of Barbed Wire Patents Per Year

It should be noted that although the number of patents issued dropped, the production of barbed fencing continued to grow dramatically through the early 1900s (see following discussion on manufacturing).

In the beginning of the barb fencing patent design period, the barb designs tended to be sharp and long. In reaction to unacceptable injury to livestock, the designs changed to shorter and sometimes blunt designs to be less injurious (see Chapter 5 on barb length and sharpness). At the same time, new designs were patented in hopes of competing with the established designs and patent royalties. Other authors, such as McCallum and McCallum (1985) and Campbell and Allison (1986), have attempted to group the changes in barbed wire designs over time. McCallum and McCallum (1985) developed four "natural groupings" of designs, or temporal groupings, that reflected the evolution in designs, especially the changes in designs to avoid injury to livestock. Their four temporal groupings included:

1. **Early Varied Period** (1868 to 1877) – the first "uncoordinated attempts at patentable inventions."

2. **Vicious Period** (1876 to 1880) – types of wire fencing that were designed to "inflict injury so animals would stay away from fences."

3. **Obvious Period** (1879 to 1884) – wire designed to add visibility to fences to warn livestock on the danger of injury.

4. **Modified Period** (1879 to 1894) – incorporation of injury and modified with some form of helpful feature of the three previous types.

Campbell and Allison (1986) grouped the designs of barbed fencing chronologically into seven different periods reflecting not only an evolution in designs but manufacturing inventions and production:

1. **The Beginning Years** (1867-1875) – barbed wire patents included the use of wooden blocks, wooden rails with protruding metal spikes, as well as single stands of wire with barbs applied by the factory or by hand in the field.

2. **The Early Years** (1876-1878) – because of the injury caused to cattle, patent designs with blunt barbs and movable barbs were invented. Metal wooden warning devices to be attached to wires were also designed. Hand tools for applying barbs were issued patents. Commercial size barbed wire machines were patented.

3. **The Growth Years, Part** 1 (1879-1883) – more sophisticated barbed warning devices as well as barbed ribbon wire were patented to provide obvious or visible barbed fencing to address reaction to injury.

4. **The Growth Years, Part II** (1884-1887) – more sophisticated styles of barbs were invented, including more blunted and muted barbs to address unnecessary injury to animals. Barbed fencing machine inventions were more common. Multiple barbed fencing styles occurred.

5. **The Growth Years, Part III** (1888-1894) – during this period, the number of patents dropped significantly, likely because the success of the simplest designs persisted (e.g., Glidden, Baker, et al.) and litigation which made new designs less lucrative existed. Modified designs between injurious and more humane designs.

6. **Turn of the Century** (1895-1914) – lull in development of barbed wire styles but a high volume of manufacturing. It was a period of transition into modern uses.

7. **Modern Years** (1915-Present) – designs reflecting modern uses in war and protection of buildings and electric fences.

They also divided the Growth Years into three periods which reflected changes in barb designs and the increase in patented barbed fencing machines. They added a design period (Turn of the Century) to reflect a decline in barbed wire design and patenting and another period for the modern uses of barbed wire.

In looking at these groupings, one can find specific designs and patents that do not fit within a particular temporal period (e.g., some vicious barbs were patented during the "obvious" period and vice versa in McCallum and McCallum's groupings).

Dramatic changes in the frequency of patents can be seen if the cumulative frequency of patents issued is calculated (Figure 41). It can be seen that there was a slow beginning for inventions in the 1860s and early 1870s, then an exponential growth in the late 1870s and 1880s, and finally, a plateauing off in patents in the 1890s and beyond.

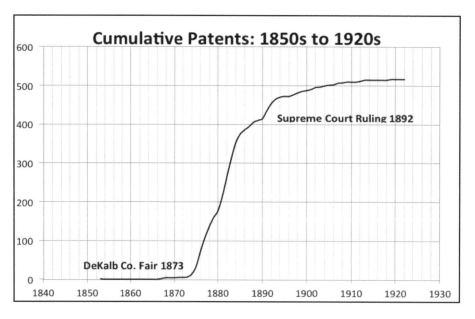

Figure 41. Cumulative Issuance of Antique Barbed Fencing Patents (1850s to 1930)

Therefore, a simpler timeline of three periods based on the frequency of patents issued is proposed. The antique barbed fencing design period is broken into:

1. **Initial Antique Barbed Fence Patent Designs** (1867 to 1874) – includes the initial patents to develop a more effective plain wire fence system with barbs starting with Smith's and Rose's patents and ending with Hunt's design which triggered the designs of Glidden, Ellwood, and Haish.

2. **Major Antique Barbed Fence Patent Designs** (1875 to 1893) – hundreds of patents and designs building upon the initial barbed wire designs of the first period, a nearly exponential growth of new patents.

3. **Decline of Antique Barbed Fencing Patent Designs** (Mid-1894 to 1914) – reflected in the decline of new patents applied for and issued.

A fourth period could be added to characterize modern patent designs for the uses of barbed fencing in war and for security after 1915.

### Initial Antique Barbed Fence Patent Designs (1867 to 1874)

As discussed in Chapter 2, no one person invented barbed fencing. The "invention" was the result of the thought processes of a number of farmers, blacksmiths, and others to improve plain wire fences in the United States after the Civil War. Between 1867 and 1873 and prior to the DeKalb County Fair in 1874, there were six barbed wire patents[34] from five inventors: (1) Lucian B. Smith, (2) William D. Hunt, (3) Michael Kelly, (4) Lyman P. Judson, and (5) Henry M. Rose. They addressed in various ways the common problem of cattle breaking fences by designing fences using barb-like attachments to repel livestock.

---

34    Not included is a patent by A. Dabb in 1867 (#63,482) for a sheet metal strip to be attached to picket fences.

Their patents included the basic design features of future barbed fencing designs (i.e., the use of longitudinal wire strands, sheet metal strips, and wire points or barbs).

The classification by USPTO of these early patents shows a transition in the patent classifications considered "Improvements in Wire Fences" in 1867 to designs considered "Improvement in Barbed Wire-Fences" in 1875 (Table 5).

Table 5. Transition of USPTO Classification of Plain Wire Fence Patents to Barbed Fencing Patents

### 1867 "Improvement in Wire Fence"
L. B. Smith of Kent, Ohio, in June 1867 (# 66,182) for an iron post fence design of two single-wire strands linked with wooden "spools" with projection points at two- to three-foot spacing.

### 1867-1868 "Improvement of Fences"
W. D. Hunt of Scott, New York, in 1867 (#67,117) for a single-strand wire using small spur wheels with serrated edges. He used the term "spurs" for barbs.

M. Kelly of New York, New York, in February 1868 (#74,379) for a single-wire strand "thorn fence" with "hard iron-tinned" thorns with holes placed on wire.

### 1868 "Improvement in Metallic Fences"
M. Kelly of New York, New York, in November 1868 (#84,062) for a single- and double-wire strand with double pointed "hard iron" thinned spike, called "thorn," passed through wire strand.

### 1871 "Improvement in Fences"
L. P. Judson of Rose, New York, in August 1871 (#118,135) for a sheet metal strip fence (called hoop or band iron) with sharp spurs and a sheet metal strip (called a "band") with sharpened edges. Designed for hogs and cattle. It was considered visible to animals.

### 1873-1874 "Improvement in Wire Fences"
H. Rose of Waterman Station, DeKalb County, in May 1873 (#138,753) for a design comprised of square strips of boards inserted with metal points six to eight inches apart.

J. Haish in January 1874, applied for in December 1873 (#146,671), for a double-wire strand fence with "S" barbs.

J. Glidden in November 1874, applied for in October 1873 (#157,124), for a two-point double-wire twisted strand.

**1874 "Improvement in Barbed Fences"** (first time this patent classification used)

J. Haish on February 17, 1874, applied for in December 1873 (#147,634), for using four-point sheet metal barbs on wooden rails.

I.L. Ellwood on February 24, 1874, applied for in January 1874 (#147,756), for sheet metal barb.

C. Kennedy on August 11, 1874, applied for on June 2, 1874 (#153,965), for multipoint sheet metal barbs for single-wire fences.

### 1875 "Improvement in Barbed Fence-Wire"
M. Mack on May 4, 1875, applied for on March 27, 1875 (#162,835), for a single-wire strand whose ends when twisted together formed a two-point barb.

### 1875 "Improvement in Barbed Wire-Fences"
C. Kennedy on June 8, 1875, applied for on January 30, 1875 (#164,181), for a single-wire strand with kinks and sheet metal barb.

Of these early pre-1874 designs, the 1868 patent of Michael Kelly of New York City, a single- and double-wire strand with a two-point barb design, turned out to be the most successful. The Thorny Hedge Co. manufactured his design for a number of years.

Rose used his fence at the DeKalb County Fair in 1873. It triggered the idea among other DeKalb farmers and merchants to use barbed wire for livestock control (Clifton 1970; McCallum and McCallum 1985). As mentioned earlier, Jacob Haish, Isaac Ellwood, and Joseph Glidden, who are purported to have attended the 1873 DeKalb County Fair and seen Rose's wooden square rails with spikes, all filed and were issued patents for three different designs the following year. Charles Kennedy, also from DeKalb County, was issued a barbed wire patent design in 1874. It is not known if he saw Rose's design or heard about it, but it can be assumed that he was aware of the experimentation of putting barbs on fences that was occurring in his Midwest region (see Chapter 2 for the discussion on early fencing in the United States). The following table provides a chronology of the first barbed fencing patents applied for and issued in 1874 after the 1873 DeKalb County Fair in Illinois.

Table 6. 1874 Chronology of First Barbed Fencing Patents Following the 1873 DeKalb County Fair

| Inventor, Patent #, Dates of Filing and Issuance | Barbed Fencing Design | Comment |
|---|---|---|
| J. Haish (DeKalb, Illinois), #146,671, Filed Dec 22, 1873, Issued Jan 20, 1874 | Double wire strand with ends twisted as "spikes" | First to use the word "strands" instead of wire. Classified by USPTO as "Improvement in Barb Fences" |
| J. Haish (DeKalb, Illinois), # 147,634, Filed Dec 27, 1873, Issued Feb 17, 1874 | Wooden rails with metal prongs attached six to twelve inches apart | Classified by USPTO as "Improvement in Wire Fences" |
| I. L. Ellwood (DeKalb, Illinois), #147,756, Filed Jan 7, 1874, Issued Feb 24, 1874 | Ribbon sheet metal or strip with metal "brads" or "pickers" or attached to sheet metal strip or rail | Classified by USPTO as "Improvement in Barbed Fences" |
| J. Glidden (DeKalb, Illinois), #150,683, Filed March 14, 1874 , Issued May 12, 1874 (Two reissues, #6,913 and #9,914 in 1876) | Double wire strand with "spurs" to stretch the wires to keep them in place | Drawing showed basic two-strand design with "spurs" of the same design as his later #157,124 patent. Purpose of this patent was for a fence wire stretcher. Classified by USPTO as "Improvement of Wire-Stretcher for Fences" |

| Inventor, Patent #, Dates of Filing and Issuance | Barbed Fencing Design | Comment |
|---|---|---|
| J. Haish (DeKalb, Illinois), #152,368, Filed Apr 18, 1874, Issued Jun 23, 1874 | Sheet metal strip (ribbon) twisted spirally with points | Classified by USPTO as "Improvement in Barbed Wire Fences" |
| C. Kennedy (Hinckley, DeKalb Co., Illinois ), #153,965, Filed Jun 2, 1874, Issued Aug 11, 1874 | Using sheet metal to make barbs to prevent cattle and horses from sticking their heads through wire fences | Barbs designed to attach individually to plain wire fence. Classified by USPTO as "Improvement in Barbed Fences" |
| L. & J. Merrill (Turkey River Station, Iowa), #155,538, filed Aug 28, 1874, Issued Sept 29, 1874 | Single wire strand with four-point "brads" designed as swinging fence with wires | Classified by USPTO as "Improvement in Wire Fences," allowed cattle to be pricked and encouraged them to move away |
| J. F. Glidden (DeKalb, Illinois) #157,124, Filed Oct 27, 1873, Issued Nov 24 1874 | Double wire strand with two-point barb wrapped around twice on one of the strands | A second wire was used to hold barb in place; this was a key distinction giving Glidden the Supreme Court decision, the wire was manufactured as "The Winner." It was classified by USPTO as an "Improvement in Wire Fences" |
| J. F. Glidden & P. W. Vaughan (DeKalb, Illinois) #157,508 Filed Oct 24, 1874 Issued Dec 8,1874 | Design was for a machine to make barbed wire | Machine was designed to make Glidden's two point double strand wire. First barbed wire machine patented. It was classified by USPTO as "Improvement in Machines for Making Wire Fences." |

Note: USPTO means US Trade and Patent and Trademark Office

What this table shows is that although Joseph Glidden filed the first patent application (on Oct 27, 1873) after seeing Rose's patent (#138,753) for wooden rail with metal barbs at the DeKalb Co. in 1873, Jacob Haish was issued the first patents for metal barbed fencing. It is important to point out that although he was issued the first patent for metallic barbed fencing he lost in later litigation between he and Glidden.

Jacob Haish's first patent (#146,671) was filed on December 22, 1873, and was issued a month later on January 20, 1874. It was for a double-wire strand with ends twisted as spikes. He was the first to use the term "strand." Until then, other patents referred to "wires." The patent office classified his invention as an "Improvement in Wire Fences." His second patent (#147,634) was filed five days later on December 27, 1873, and was issued two months later on February 17, 1874, for a wooden rail design with metal prongs attached six to twelve inches apart, a design similar to Rose's 1873 patent. This patent was classified as an "Improvement in Barb Fences." This was the first time the term "barb fences" was used. His third patent (#152,368) in 1874 was for a sheet metal strip. He seemed to be inventing designs that covered the various horizontal components of barbed fence designs (i.e., wire strands, sheet metal strips, and wooden rail fences) (Figure 42).

Haish 1874 (#146,671) Hooks (Double Wire Strand)

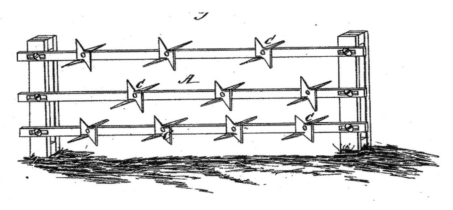

Haish 1874 (#147,634) Wooden Rail with Four Point Sheet Metal Barb

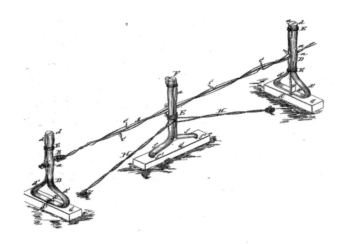

Haish 1874 (#152,368) Barbed Ribbon (Sheet Metal Strip)

Figure 42. Haish's Three 1874 Barbed Wire Fence Patents: Double Strand, Wooden Rails, and Ribbon Sheet Metal Designs

The second person after Haish to file a barbed wire patent was Isaac L. Ellwood, also of DeKalb, Illinois (#147,756, filed January 7, 1874, and issued a month and a half later on February 24, 1874). It was for a sheet metal strip design with metal "brads" or "pickers" attached to metal strip or rail. It was classified by the USPTO as an "Improvement in Barbed Fences" (Figure 43). Ellwood filed only one patent and then joined in partnership with Joseph Glidden and Washburn & Moen Co. of Worcester, Massachusetts in the manufacturing and distribution of barbed fencing (McCallum and McCallum 1985).

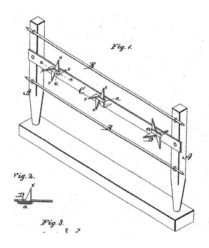

Figure 43. Ellwood, I. L. 1874 (#147,756) Centered "V" Barb

Joseph Glidden (DeKalb, Illinois) was the third inventor to be issued a barbed-wire-type patent (#150,683) issued on May 14, 1874. It was filed on March 14, 1874, two and three months after Haish's patent (#146,671 and 147,634) were issued. The purpose for his design was to hold "spurs" (barbs) at a proper intervals on a wire and provide uniform tension to the wire fence strand. It was classified by USPTO as an "Improvement in Wire Stretchers for Fences." This design included a "twisting key" for tightening the barbs if the wires became loose (Figure 44).

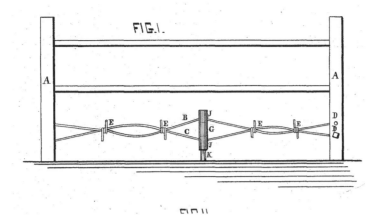

Figure 44. Glidden, J. 1874 (#150,683) "Wire Stretching"

The patent drawing shows barbs similar the barbs on to his later issued #157,124 patent (Nov 24, 1874) a double- twisted mild steel wire strand with two point barbs around one of the strand wires (Figure 45). This patent was for a double wire strand with "spur wires".

Figure 45. Glidden, J. 1874 (#157,124) "The Winner"

He applied for this patent on Oct 27, 1873 before he applied for the ire stretching patent (#150,683). The #157,124 patent was not issued until Nov 24, 1874, nearly 13 months after it was filed. This patent was filed on Oct 27, 1873 two months before Haish's first patent (#146,671) was filed.

Glidden did not claim the originality of the "spurs or prongs" in his #150,683 patent but "the means of holding the spurs at proper intervals on the wire." This description was a key distinction in awarding Glidden the Supreme Court decision in the early 1890s. This design was manufactured as "The Winner." The patent was classified as an "Improvement in Wire Fences." Joseph Glidden obtained patents for two designs, one for two-point and four-point barbs wrapped around single and double strands and one design for the barbed wrapped around one of the double-strand wires. This design (#157,124) was the most successful barbed fencing design and is found in hundreds of variations.

Coincidentally, in the same year (1874) two non-DeKalb County inventors, Luther and John Merrill of Turkey River, Iowa, were issued a patent design for a swinging wire fence with four-point barbs on a single-wire strand system. Their patent was filed on August 28, 1874, and it was issued a month later in September (Figure 46).

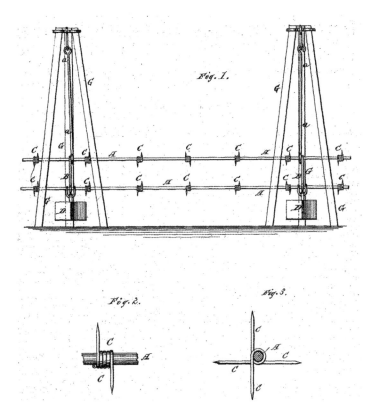

Figure 46. Merrill, L. and Merrill, J. C. 1874 (#155,538) Two-Wrap Four Point

It was classified as an "Improvement in Wire Fences." What influenced the Merrills to design a barbed wire product is not known. Had they heard or seen of Rose's barbed wooden fence at the DeKalb County Fair of 1873 or the patents of Haish, Ellwood, and Glidden issued several months earlier? As mentioned earlier, this part of the state had a number of unpatented barbed fences in use in the 1850s, 1860s, and 1870s (see Washburn & Moen Mgt. Co. versus Beat' Em All Barbed-Wire Co. [Barbed Wire Patent Case 143 US 265, 1892]).

The USPTO first used the term "barbed fence" in 1874 as patent classifications for the early barbed fencing patents of J. Haish, I. Ellwood, and C. Kennedy. USPTO classified J. Haish's 1874 patent (#152,368) as an "Improvement in Barbed-Wire Fence." The patent for a machine for applying barbs to fences was issued to J. F. Glidden and P. V. Vaughn on December 8, 1874 (#157,508). It was classified as an "Improvement in Making Wire Fences." The patent classification of "barbed wire" included not only barbed wire but also barbed metal strips. However, other more descriptive classifications for metal strip have been found, including "metallic fences," "metallic barbed striping," and "barbed fencing strips." In August 1874, C. Kennedy was the first to use the term "barb" in his patent description for the sharpened points attached to the wires.[35] Prior to that time, the early patents referred to barbs as "projecting points",[36] "spurs",[37] "thorns",[38] "metallic points",[39] "spikes",[40] "brads," or "pickers."[41] The term "strand" was first used in 1874 by J. Haish.[42]

It is interesting to note the differences in the date a patent was applied for and when it was issued. No explanation could be found on when a patent is filed and when issued.

---

35    C. Kennedy (#153,965) August 11, 1874

36    L. B. Smith (#66,182) June 25, 1865

37    W. Hunt (#67,117) July 23, 1867; L. P. Judson (#118,135) August 18, 1871; J. Glidden, (#150,683) May 12, 1874

38    M. Kelly (#74,379) February 11, 1868

39    H. M. Rose (#138,763) May 13, 1873

40    J. Haish (#146,671) January 20, 1874

41    I. L. Ellwood (#147,756) February 24, 1874

42    J. Haish (#146,671) January 20, 1874

Some patents were issued within a couple of months of filing (e.g. Merrill and Merrills (#155,538 patent design) while others took almost a year to be granted (e.g. Glidden's #157,124 patent design). The chronology of the patent numbers (when it was issued) does not always represent when the invention was thought of, applied for, or created.

This period of barbed fencing design was a transition from plain wire fence design to barbed wire fences (see discussion on plain wire fence as a forerunner to barbed wire). The transition is reflected in the various ways USPTO classified these patents from "Improvements in Wire Fences or Fences" (e.g., Smith, Hunt, and Kelly) to "Improvements in Barbed Fences and Barbed Wire Fences" (e.g., Haish, Ellwood, and Kennedy).

The inventions of these designs up to 1874 and 1875 shaped the subsequent patents and variations for the next twenty-five years. The most successful patents were Glidden's two-point round barb wrapped around one wire of a mild steel double strand patent (#157,124) and a later patent in 1883 by Baker (# 273,219) for a two-point flat metal barb also wrapped around one wire of mild steel double strand.

### Major Patent Design Period (1875 to 1893)

The most active antique barbed fencing design period was from 1875 to 1893. During this period, there were more than 451 barbed fencing patents[43] issued at a rate of twenty-four patents per year including modifications and elaboration of designs from the initial design period of 1867 to 1874.

---

43    Not including machines, dies, and cattleguards. The number is based on Clifton (1970), Hagemeier (2010), and Campbell and Allison (1986).

It was a time of innovation and creativity. Agricultural journals of the time endorsed the usefulness of barbed wire. In 1878, the *National Live-Stock Journal 8*[44] had several articles on the acceptance of barbed wire and how it could control cattle, especially bulls, along with advertisements for barbed wire manufacturers.

Barbed fencing designs and patents changed considerably during this period. Barbed fencing at the beginning of this period tended to have sharp and long barbs designed to deter livestock. Inventors attempted to adapt existing plain wire fences to barbed wire fences (see Chapter 2). This effort had the unintended consequence of causing unacceptable injury to cattle and other livestock.[45] There was pressure to design less injurious barbs (e.g., shorter barbs) and barbs supposedly more obvious to livestock (e.g., use of bigger sheet metal barbs). McCallum and McCallum (1970) presented an initial classification of barbed fencing not on the structural and material properties (see Chapters 3 and 5), but on the effects the different designs had on cattle and other livestock. Two classes were identified: (1) "vicious" designs causing unnecessary injury to livestock and (2) "obvious" designs developed to be less injurious and more visible to livestock so that they would avoid contact with fencing with barbs. The more injurious designs or "vicious" designs tended to be four-point wire barbs or sheet metal barbs with long and sharp points that easily penetrated the hides of cattle and other animals, causing rips or tears.

---

44      S. G. Brabook. Published monthly by The Stock Journal Company.
45      The issue of injury to livestock was so important that it was discussed in the agricultural journals, including The American Agriculturist 52 (1893). Numerous advertisements for treating barbwire cuts were found in these publications

The following are examples of injurious or "vicious" designs as characterized by McCallum and McCallum (1985):

» Billings 1878 (#205,234) *Four Point Two Staple* (long staples on double-wire strand)

» Brinkerhoff 1879 (#214,095) *Twist* (vicious because of twist, untwisted version obvious)

» Brotherton 1878 (#207,710) *Common Large* (two point; many variations, some with large barbs; common)

» Burnell 1877 (#192,225) *Four Point* (most successful four point, double strand)

» Glidden 1876 (Reissue #6914) *Four Point Coil on Round Strand* (large barbs on round single-wire strand)

» Merrill 1876 (#185,688) *Four Point Twirl* (single-wire strand with four-point barb, heavy gauge called "Buffalo Wire")

» Mighell 1878 (#199,924) *One Awhile, Two While* (two twisted strands with one strand cut to form a two-point barb)

» Reynolds 1878 (#203,779) *Necktie* (considered typical of vicious, single-strand four sharp points with thin barbs, hard to see)

» Ross 1879 (#216,294) *Four Point* (according to McCallum and McCalllum [1985], one of the six best patents for double-strand four-point wires; many variations using other metals [e.g., Al, Cu.])

» Scutt 1878 (#205,000) *Single Clip "H" Plate* (two twisted strands with "H" sheet metal plate clipped to one strand

» Shinn 1881 (#238,447) *Locked Four Point* (four-point barb twisted regularly around in four directions)

» Underwood 1878 (#206,754) *Double Tack* (three or four wire strands with double tacks inserted)

Figure 47 shows examples of the early barb designs considered injurious to livestock:

### Examples of Injurious Barbs

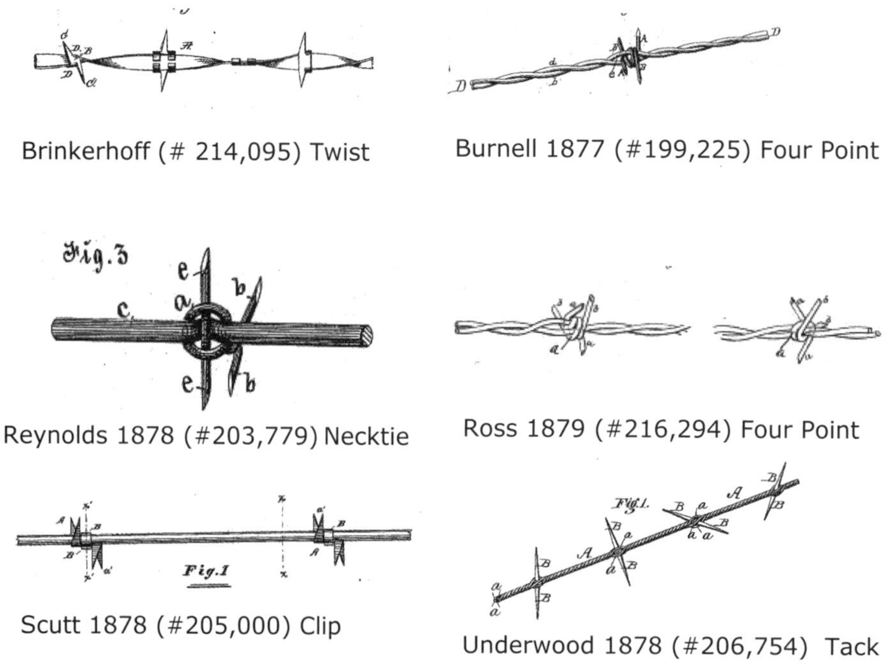

Brinkerhoff (# 214,095) Twist

Burnell 1877 (#199,225) Four Point

Reynolds 1878 (#203,779) Necktie

Ross 1879 (#216,294) Four Point

Scutt 1878 (#205,000) Clip

Underwood 1878 (#206,754)  Tack

Figure 47. Example of Injurious Barbed Wire Designs

In reaction to these "vicious" designs, barbs were invented or redesigned to be larger and blunt. An article in the 1889 *The Railroad and Engineering Journal*[46] described the use and construction specifications of barbed wire for railroad fencing. The article described how the barbs were originally very sharp. This design resulted in prejudices against barbed fencing by stockbreeders living along a railroad line. As a result, barbs were redesigned so they were not sufficiently sharp to seriously injure animals running against such barb. In addition, the horizontal component of barb fencing was designed to be more obvious

46      Forney, M. N. "Fences." *The Railroad and Engineer Journal* 63, no. 2 (1889): 69-71.

to livestock (e.g., replacing metals strands with sheet metal strips or adding more wires to a strand creating a more visible strand and sometimes using wood slats as an upper horizontal component). There is no data found in the patent records to show that the cattle acted differently to the more obvious designs. It was assumed that wider horizontal components (e.g., sheet metal strips) and the use of sheet metal plate-like barbs could be more easily seen by livestock, causing livestock to avoid this type of barbed wire. These types of barbs were called "obvious" barb designs (McCallum and McCallum 1985). Included in these "obvious" designs were:

» Allis 1881 (#244,726) *Buckthorn* (although twisted sheet metal had dull extruded barbs, this was the most popular ribbon wire)

» Brinkerhoff 1885 (#324,221) *Ribbon & Single Strand Wire with Barb* (mixed a single-wire strand with a two-point barb shielded by sheet metal strip)

» Crandal 1879 (#221,158) *Zigzag* (two twisted wire strands with interlocked multipoint sheet metal)

» Kelly 1885 (#322,108) *Twisted Loop Strand with Swinging Barb* (dangled two-point barbs from looped single-wire strand, described function of pricking rather than injuring)

» Hodge 1887 (#367,398) *Eight Point Rowel* (two twisted wire strands with eight-point sheet metal barbed rowel)

» Decker 1884 (#299,916) *Spread Twisted Strands* (wire spread apart by barb)

» Cline 1883 (#290,974) *Three Strand Rail* (three parallel wire strands with four-point barb around all strands)

» Stubbe 1883 (#287,337) *Stubbe Large and Small Plate* (double strand wire with 1" and 1 5/8th" plate, designed to be visible with slits in plates resulting in eight points)

» Brock 1884 (#293,412) *Brock Barbed Ornamental, Small Barb* (series of wire loops made of a single-wire strand with two-point barb providing elasticity, visibility, and allowing the barbs to move to limit injury)

» Blake 1891 (#446,607) *Looped Reverse Wrap* (two twisted strands with a reverse two-point barb loosely twisted on one strand)

Figure 48 presents examples of barbs with "obvious" designs that were intended to reduce injury to cattle:

**Examples of Obvious Barbs**

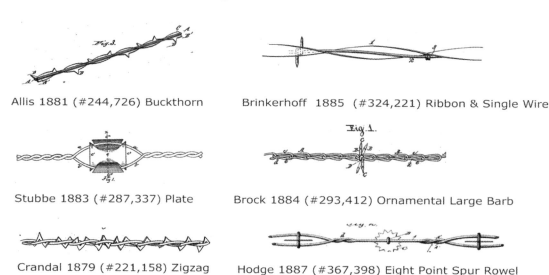

Allis 1881 (#244,726) Buckthorn

Brinkerhoff 1885 (#324,221) Ribbon & Single Wire

Stubbe 1883 (#287,337) Plate

Brock 1884 (#293,412) Ornamental Large Barb

Crandal 1879 (#221,158) Zigzag

Hodge 1887 (#367,398) Eight Point Spur Rowel

Figure 48. Examples of Obvious Barb Designs

In 1891, Blake described in his patent description (#446,607, "Looped Reverse Wrap") the injuries caused by traditional barbs. He claimed that his invention would provide a barbed wire for a fence so designed and manufactured that it would "…protect against and turn animals of all kinds equally as well as the barbed wire now made" and "will not cause loss of life or limb or other great injury when a person or animal comes in violent contact with it from dangerous angles of direction…"

During this period, there were designs with shorter barbs, blunt barbs, and flat sheet metal strips with and without barbs (see Chapter 4 discussion on shape of barbs). Longstreet's 1902 patent (#711,574) was for a "ball tipped barb" designed specifically to avoid injury to cattle, horses, and sheep and still repel them from "violent contact" with the fence.

Barb designs to minimize injury also included barbs that would bend when in contact with an animal, therefore reducing the likelihood of tearing hides and injury. Two inventors invented "shock absorber" barbs that yielded or bent rather than normal rigid barbs (e.g., Butler's 1881 [#248,999] "Shock Absorber" and Robinson's 1890 [#421,055] "Shock Absorber") (Figure 49).

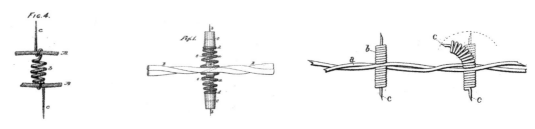

Gregg's 1879 (#221,300) Spread & Coil  Butler/s 1881 (#248,999) Shock Absorber  Robinson's 1890 (#421,005) Shock Absorber

Figure 49. Shock Absorber-Type Barbs

A fourth approach was to invent a barb that turned instead of remaining rigid, called "spur wheels." They were circular disks with multiple points that moved when rubbed against (see Chapter 4 discussion on circular plate barbs). One odd circular plate design to reduce injury was invented by two individuals. In 1881, Nealy and Marland from Pittsburg, Pennsylvania, designed and patented (#251,273) a sharpened metal disc barb that caused clean cuts and prevented the skin of cattle from being torn and made sore. Their design also prevented cattle from breaking the barbs off. (Figure 50).

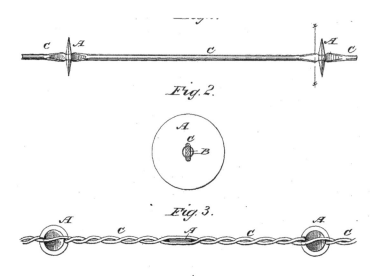

Figure 50. Neely, T. and Marland, A. 1881 (#251,273) One- and Two-Strand Knife Edge Discs

Medicines and liniments for the treatment of wounds by barbed wire were developed.[47] A 1902 publication (*Proceedings of the American Pharmaceutical Association at the Annual Meeting* 52: 542) provided a formula for use of these medicines by farmers. It included oil of turpentine, tar, carbolic acid, and fish oil. It recommended that the wound be washed with warm water and castile soap and liniment be applied once a day for a week, then two or three times a week until the wound healed.

Although only four years since the invention of barbed fencing in 1874, inventors were designing ways to repair barbed fencing. In 1877, G. G. Hunt of Bristol, Illinois, obtained a patent as an "Improvement in Barbed Fences" for repairing fences when "out of order" if one of the wire strands broke. His design was for a splice link consisting of a two-point barb. The barb piece could be hooked to two existing wire strands with the linking ends forming a two-point barb (Figure 51).

47      Fox, I. P. "Barbed Wire Liniments." *The Spatula: An Illustrated Monthly Publication for Druggists* 13 (1906): 409.

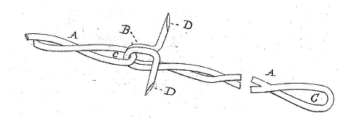

Figure 51. Hunt, G. G. 1877 (#189,861) "Link"

### Decline of Antique Barbed Fencing Patent Designs (1894 to 1914)

For the next twenty years, there was a rapid decline in barbed wire patents; only forty-nine patents were issued at a rate of two per year compared to a rate of twenty-four patents per year in the previous period (Table 7).

Table 7. Last Designs for One-, Three-, Four-Wire Strands and Sheet Metal Strips Through 1914

| Type of Horizontal Component | Date of Patent | Inventor | Patent Number | Design Comment |
|---|---|---|---|---|
| Single-Wire Strand | 1909 | V. Hoxie | 943,413 | Single undulating mild steel wire strand flattened with small knots to hold barb in place |
| Two-Wire Strand | 1913 | D. E. McAllister | 1,064,756 | Two twisted wires with a folded sheet metal plate clipped to both wires, making it more visible |
| Three-Wire Strand | 1893 | J. L. Riter | 506,258 | Corrugated three-wire strand with two points providing elasticity so fence won't break under pressure from cattle and return to previous shape |
| Four-Wire Strand | 1892 | T. J Ingraham | 496,062 | Four-wire strand with two-point bent barb separated by loops of strand |
| Sheet Metal Strip | 1914 | J. Luepker | 1,102,936 | Sheet metal strip with clamped sheet metal barb to be visible to cattle |

Of the forty-nine patents issued in this period, thirty patents were from the first nine years of this period. During this period, some of the last patents for one, two, three strand and sheet metal strand designs were issued. These patents addressed the same issues of earlier designs of holding the barbs in place, being visible to avoid injury to livestock, and providing elasticity in the wires so fence would return to its shape after pressure by livestock was applied.

Although the number of new barbed wire patents declined, this was a period for more barbed wire manufacturing machine patents, for patents for interconnected or woven barbed wire fences, and for patents for cattle guards for railway crossings.

Patent submittal and issuance dropped during this time, likely because the most successful and simplest designs had been invented and were being manufactured on a large scale and because of the litigations in the 1880s and 1890s that made the manufacturing of different designs with patent licenses more difficult (Hayter 1939). Barbed fencing litigation occurred almost immediately after the first patents were issued in the late 1870s and continued until reaching the Supreme Court in the early 1890s. It involved dozens of inventors, including Glidden, Haish, and Ellwood, and barbed wire manufacturing companies, including Washburn & Moen Company.[48] The litigation was over patent rights and royalty issues.[49] Resolving the royalty dispute in 1892, the Supreme Court stated Glidden's 1874 two-wire strand design as the legally standing "barbed wire strand design," thereby making further wire strand designing less of an economic opportunity. The Supreme Court did not consider sheet metal strip designs of the Brinkerhoff's as falling under its decision, but sheet metal designs were never as popular as wire strand designs. The Brinkerhoff's patents had already been assigned to Washburn & Moen Co. in the 1870s.

---

48    Forerunner of the US Steel Corporation.

49    McCallum and McCallum (1985) provided an excellent description of this litigation, including the various litigants and issues involved.

The Antique Barbed Wire Society defined antique barbed fencing as ending in 1925. However, based on the drop in frequency of new patents applied for and issued, the last patents for previously common barbed fencing designs (e.g., one-, two-, and four-wire strands and sheet metal strips), and the emergence of the use of barbed wire for other purposes than agricultural (e.g., war and security purposes), the antique barbed wire design era most likely came to end around 1914 the start of WWI. This also coincides with Campbell and Allison (1986) who considered 1915 the beginning of their "Modern Era" period for the above-mentioned reasons and the introduction of new fencing materials.

Two additional designs that could be considered antique barbed fencing designs were issued after 1914. In 1919, Braddock (#1,320,117), of Massachusetts, was issued a patent for a single-wire strand barb design used for livestock, and in the same year, Klenk (#1,294,677), of Idaho, was issued a patent for livestock fencing that could also be used for war and security (e.g., "entanglement to prevent entry into a territory"). No barbed wire designs were issued for the next nine years, but two patents were issued to J. E. Rayburn (#1,670,481), of Tennessee, in 1928 for a detachable barb and to O. Schmid (#1,654,837), a German inventor, in 1928 for a new method for manufacturing two-wire strand barbed wire.

As discussed earlier, there were more than four hundred inventors who had an average of two patents each. The creative interests of inventors in barbed fencing varied. P. Wineman applied for and was granted only one patent (#172,725) early in the barbed fencing design period (in 1876). His design was not a common strand design; it was a three-wire strand with cast iron three-point star-like barb. Other inventors kept on inventing after their first patent was accepted. The following are a list of inventors who were prolific and continued to invent barbed fencing designs for a period of ten or more years (Table 8).

Table 8. Examples of Inventors Who Continued to Develop Patents for Ten or More Years

| Inventor | Number of Years Active in Patenting | Number of Strand and Strip Patents (+ Other Fencing Patents) |
|---|---|---|
| Kelly, M. | 18 (1868 - 1885) | 5 |
| Allis, T. V. | 18 (1878 - 1895) | 18 (+ 2 barbed fencing machines and + 5 dies for sheet metal barbs) |
| Stover, D. C. | 11 (1875 - 1885) | 4 (+ 12 barbed fencing machines) |
| Haish, J. | 18 (1874 - 1891) | 11 |
| Edenborn, W. | 14 (1883 - 1896) | 4 (+ 3 barbed fencing machines) |
| Dobbs, J. | 13 (1875 - 1887) | 5 (+ 1 hand tool) |
| Bates, A. J. | 22 (1884 - 1905) | 0 (+ 11 barbed fencing machines) |
| Miles, P. | 11 (1878 - 1888) | 4 (+ 1 barbed fencing machine) |
| Curtis, J. D. | 11 (1884 - 1894) | 7 (+ 4 barbed fencing machines) |
| Upham, A. J. | 10 (1876 - 1885) | 19 (+ 2 barbed fencing machines) |
| Kettleson, O. O. | 10 (1877 - 1886) | 3 (+ 2 barbed fencing machines) |
| Jordon, E. | 10 (1884 - 1893) | 5 (+ 6 sheet metal dies) |
| Griswold, J. W. | 10 (1888 - 1897) | 13 |

Kelly and Allis, both from New York City, had the longest active barbed fencing inventing period of eighteen years. T. V. Allis He was the most prolific, with twenty-five patents that included eighteen sheet metal strip designs, two barbed fencing machines, and five for dies for sheet metal barbed strips. Although active in patenting for only ten years, Upham from Sterling, Illinois, had twenty-one patents, three of which were for barbed fencing machines. The other eighteen patents included wire strand and wire barb designs, sheet metal strips and barb designs, and a combination of wire barbs and sheet metal strand designs. A look at the patent issue frequency shows some inventors were issued a number of patents on the same day. For example, Allis was issued five patents on January 5, 1892, and Griswold was issued eight patents on December 22, 1891.

## WHY SO MANY PATENT DESIGNS?

The variations found in the designs of barbed fencing are due to different inventors with different designs and variations due to manufacturing.

### Different Inventors with Different Designs

To obtain a patent the design had to be "unique." Each inventor had to submit a patent description and a patent drawing. The USPTO[50] has three criteria that must be met to obtain any patent, including a patent for barbed fencing. First, the design must be useful or have a useful purpose (i.e., an improvement in wire fencing). Second, the design must be novel or new; the invention must not be known or described somewhere else in the world. The final criteria relates to the second criteria, novelty. The design must be "non-obvious," meaning the differences in this new invention are not obvious differences in the design already patented.

---

50    http://www.uspto.gov/patents-getting-started/general-information-concerning -patents

In regards to antique barbed fencing, all patented designs were deemed unique and novel. The following chapter on Designs and Patterns illustrate the numerous differences in the designs of the mild steel strands, sheet metal strips and in particular the extraordinary number of different types, shapes and attachment designs found in antique barbed fencing barbs that inventors patented. In reading the patent descriptions, a distinguishing or novel difference appeared to be a description of bend here or a certain twist there. If one reads the patent descriptions and sees how the inventors described their patents in the patent applications, some patent differences are obvious to see; however, in many cases it takes reading and re-reading of the patent application to determine how novel and non-obvious the invention was. The following is an example of a patent application description by M. Shinn of Burlington, Iowa, in 1881 where Shinn described his patent for four-point mild steel barb on a double mild steel wire strand design (Figure 52).

Figure 52. Shinn, M. C. 1881 (#238,447) "Locked Four Point"

Even with a picture, it is difficult to understand the unique differences of this design from other four-point mild steel barbs twisted on double mild steel strand. The picture helps understand the proposed design description, although it is not that obvious what is the "great advantage and novelty of this invention." M. Shinn ended his patent description with the statement that his design "…conspicuously indicates the great advantage and novelty of this invention."

This invention was designed to produce a metallic barb for wire fences that could easily be put on the wires, retain its position under all ordinary circumstances of wear and use, and be very durable.

In Figure 52, *A* denotes the fence-cable, preferably composed of two twisted strands or wires, *b* and *c*, and *D* the barb. This barb was made of the two short pieces of wire *d* and *c*. These two wires were of nearly equal length, and were closely wound interspirally around one of the cable-wires, and only crossing each other at one point, where they were made to interlock with each other for the purpose of being firmly united in one unchangeable barb. The ends, *d'* and *d"* and *e'* and *e"*, made the usual four-pointed barb. Thus, the four points of the barb would be at right angles to the cable and the barb-wires would be twisted firmly and securely on the cable. The cable wire *c* was twisted upon cable-wire *b* and the barb-wires, so as to bind the barb more firmly in place. This peculiar method of forming the barb by twisting each of its wires firmly and securely about one of the cable-wires and intertwisting them together, but only bending them on each other at the point of locking, conspicuously indicates the great advantage and novelty of this invention.

As discussed above, more than 400 inventors submitted designs for antique barbed fencing. Of these, a number of inventors had multiple patents for wire strand designs, including E. Crandal, J. Curtis, T. Dodge, E. Edenborn, F. Ford, J. Glidden, J. Griswold, J. Haish, H. Scutt, and A. Upham (Clifton 1970). The major inventors of barbed sheet metal strip patents include T. V. Allis, J. and W. Brinkerhoff, W. Brock, and F. Ford (Clifton 1970). Most patentees had one or two patents; however, thirteen inventors applied for and received five or more patents for their barbed fencing designs (Table 9).

Table 9. Patentees with Five or More Barbed Fencing Patents or Patent Reissues[51] Not Including Patents for Dies, Machines, and Cattle Guards (Campbell and Allison 1985; Clifton 1970; Hagemeier 2010, 2012)

| Inventor | Number of Patents and Reissues | Type of Designs Patented |
|---|---|---|
| Upham, A. J. (1876-1885) | 19 | · 13 wire strand and wire barb patent designs<br>· 3 sheet metal strips or ribbons and barb patent designs<br>· 3 combination wire barbs and sheet metal strand patent designs |
| Allis, T. V. (1878-1895; 7 patents in 1892) | 18 | All various designs of sheet metal strips and integrated barb designs |
| Griswold, J. W. (1888-1897; 8 patents in 1891) | 13 | · 10 wire strands and wire barb patent designs<br>· 2 sheet metal barbs and mild steel strands<br>· 1 woven-wire fence with barbs |
| Haish, J. (1874-1891) | 11 | · 7 wire strands and barb patent designs<br>· 3 sheet metal strips and wire barb patent designs<br>· 1 sheet metal strip and sheet metal barb patent design |
| Scutt, H. (1876-1885) | 9 | · 5 wire strands and barb patent designs<br>· 4 sheet metal plate (barbs) patent designs |
| Curtis, J. D. (1884-1894) | 8 | All wire strand patent designs |
| Crandal, E. W. (1876-1881) | 7 | · 4 wire strand patent designs (links)<br>· 3 combinations wire barbs and sheet metal strands and barb patent designs (zigzag design) |
| Brock, W. E. (1882-1884) | 7 | · 2 wire strand and barb<br>· 5 sheet metal strips and barb patent designs |
| Dodge, T. H. (1878-1883) | 6 | All wire strand patent designs |

---

*51*     An inventor could make corrections or changes to an early patent by obtaining a patent reissue.

| | | |
|---|---|---|
| Kelly, M. (1868-1885) | 5 | · 4 wire strands and barb patent designs<br>· 1 combination sheet metal strip and wire barb patent design |
| Ford, F. D. (1885) | 5 | · 3 wire strands and barb patent designs<br>· 2 sheet metal strips or ribbon patent designs |
| Jordan, E. (1884-1893) | 5 | All sheet metal designs, also five die patents |

Some of these inventors, and other inventors, patented mild steel wire barb making machines and sheet metal strip making machines. Included in this group are also inventors who patented different die designs for making sheet metal barbs. For example, A. J. Bales of Joliet, Illinois (1884 to 1905), patented eleven barbed fencing machines. The first four were for machines making sheet metal barbs. The last seven were for machines used to attach mild steel wire barbs to wire strands. J. H. Templin (1888 to 1893) was issued thirteen patents for one machine and twelve patents for sheet metal dies.

Eight inventors filed for barbed fencing patents that used a combination of metals (i.e., mild steel and sheet metal). Of those patentees with five or more patents, four patentees - Curtis, Decker, Dodge, and Glidden - invented designs using only mild steel. Allis used sheet metal for his design.

The most prolific barbed fencing inventor (not including dies and machines) was Andrew J. Upham of Sterling, Illinois. With nineteen patents (two machines) from 1876 to 1885, he had designs that included both mild steel wire, sheet metal barbs, and cast iron barbs. One of his more interesting designs was his 1881 patent (#239,891) for a slotted wire or rail design (Figure 53).

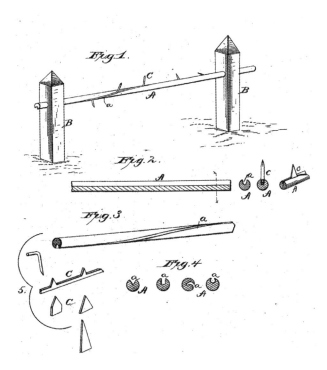

Figure 53. Upham, A. J. 1881 (#239,891) "Groove Rail and Square Sheet Metal Barbs"

His design involved a slotted or grooved metal rail that barbs were inserted into. They were then held in place by twisting the rail and the groove compressed the barbs in place. He showed more than five different kinds of barbs, from mild steel wire to sheet metal barbs, that could be used. His design was classified as an "Improvement in Metallic-Barb Fencing." The second most prolific inventor was T. V. Allis (1878–1895) from New York City, who had eighteen patents.[52] All were sheet metal strips with integrated barb designs. His earliest barbed design in 1878 (#209,790), named "Buckthorn," was a twisted sheet metal strip and rods which had the barbs integrated into the sheet metal strip or rod in different ways. It is found in the eastern and western United States. In addition, he had seven patents for machines and sheet metal dies. The following are the different designs he invented for sheet metal strips (Figure 54).

52    Not including seven machines.

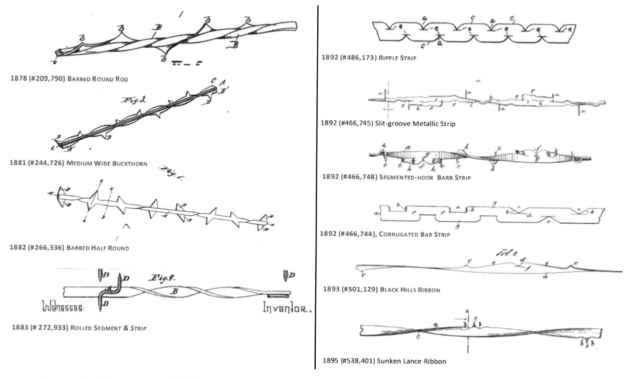

1878 (#209,790) Barbed Round Rod

1881 (#244,726) Medium Wide Buckthorn

1882 (#266,336) Barbed Half Round

1883 (# 272,933) Rolled Segment & Strip

1892 (#486,173) Ripple Strip

1892 (#466,745) Slit-groove Metallic Strip

1892 (#466,748) Segmented-hook Barb Strip

1892 (#466,744), Corrugated Bar Strip

1893 (#501,129) Black Hills Ribbon

1895 (#538,401) Sunken Lance Ribbon

Figure 54. Examples of T. V. Allis's "Buckthorn" Designs (Oldest 1878 to Most Recent 1895).

His "Buckthorn" designs involved a rod or narrow sheet metal strip with barbs stamped or punched out from a fin with a center rib. His various patent designs were variations of his early sheet metal barb designs. Overall, his designs appear to be mimicking the Buckthorn[53] vegetative hedge. The "Buckthorn" design was one of the most popular sheet metal strip designs (McCallum and McCallum 1985) and can still be found on old fence posts in the East and West (see earlier discussion, Chapter 2 Regional Patterns in Barbed Fencing). McCallum and McCallum (1985) indicated that it was expensive and "off the market" before 1900. He was issued five of his designs on January 5, 1892, which included (#486,173) "Ripple Strip"; (#466,744) "Corrugated Bar Strip"; (#466,745) "Slit-groove

53    Common or European invasive Buckthorn (*Ramnus sp.*) was first brought here from Europe in the mid-1800s as a popular hedging material. It escaped and has become a nuisance plant. (http://www.missouribotanicalgarden.org/PlantFinder/PlantFinderDe-tails.aspx?kempercode=c141

Metallic Strip"; (#466,748) "Segmented-hook Barb Strip"; and (#466,746) "Twisted & Corrugated Ribbon." Some of these designs were applied for in 1889 and renewed in 1891 before issuance. What motivated him to apply for this many patent designs is not known. They were classified as "Improvement in Barbed Fencing and Barbed Metallic Fencing."

J. W. Griswold of Troy, New York, received thirteen patents. His first two patent designs were for barbed fencing designs that used a sheet metal plate for the barb. He changed his next ten designs to mild steel wire linked designs (see Chapter 4). He applied for ten patents in June 1891 and eight were issued in December 1891. His other patent design was for a barbed woven-wire fence (#575,345) in 1897. He teamed with an A. G. Goldthwait in 1898 to patent (#604,041) for a wire-making machine for his barbed woven wire design (#575,345)[54] which was patented in 1897. It appears the Griswold family owned iron mills in Troy.

J. Haish of DeKalb, Illinois, one of the first inventors of barbed fencing, received twelve patents from 1874 to 1896 for different combinations of barbed fencing using mild steel wire strands and barbs and sheet metal strips and barbs. He invented one design for a woven-wire fence with barbs (Table 10).

---

54    His patent description referred to this patent as #375,345. It was issued on January 19, 1897. This appears to be an error in the referenced patent number.

Table 10. Summary of Haish's Patents

| Patent # | Patent Date | Design | Haish's Common Names[55] |
|---|---|---|---|
| 146,671 | January 20, 1874 | Short double-wire strands hooked together and forming barb | "Link Fence" or "Haish Hooks" |
| 147,634 | February 17, 1874 | Sheet metal strip with four-point sheet metal barb | "4 Pronged Sheet Metal Barb" (Flat Ribbon with Four-Point Sheet Metal Barb) |
| 152,368 | June 23, 1874 | Twisted sheet metal strip with one-point integrated and reinforcing core | "Briar Bush" or "Barbed Ribbon" |
| 164,552 | June 15, 1875 | Single round wire strand with two-point sheet metal barb crimped | "Stick Tight" (Spread Flat Sheet Metal Barb) |
| 167,240 | August 31, 1875 | Double-wire strand with two-point wire barb "S" shaped | "S Barb" or "Pioneer" ("S" Wrap) |
| 261,703 | July 25, 1882 | Single-wire groove strand with two-point wire barb pressed into groove | (Grooved Single Strand) |
| 261,704 | July 25, 1882 | Two half round wire strands twisted with grooved two-point sheet metal barb | (Half Round Two Strand) |
| 332,252 | December 15, 1885 | Double-wire strand with two-point offset sheet metal barb crimped to wires | (Offset Sheet Metal Barb) |
| 332,393 | December 15, 1885 | Concave sheet metal strip with two-point wire barbs crimped by strip | (Concave Rail & Crimp Barb) |
| 356,762 | February 1, 1887 | Single-wire strand corrugated with two-point half-round wire barb | "Ripple Wire" (Ribbed Barb on Ripple Wire) |
| 463,742 | November 24, 1891 | Double-wire strands twisted with flat sheet metal spear point on one wire | (Flat Barb Spear Point) |

Adapted from http://www.jacobhaishmfg.org/Barbed%20Wire.htm

---

55    Common names used by Haish (www.jacobhaishmfg.org). Common names given by Hagemeiger (2010) in parentheses. See Discussion on common names in Chapter 6.

His most successful patent was his "S" barb issued in 1875 (Figure 55).

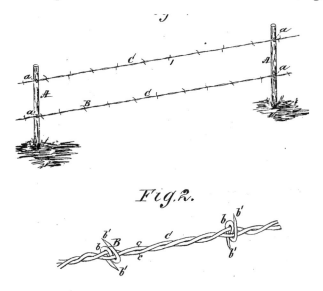

Figure 55. Haish, J. 1875 (#167,240) "S" Barb

This patent was classified as an "Improvement in Wire-Fence Barbs." The "S" barb could be attached to twisted strands of wire fence rails at the manufacturer or could be manufactured separately and attached to the rail or twisted plain wires afterwards. He recommended that the fence posts be twenty-five feet apart with "a rail formed of two wires twisted together." In 1896, he was issued an additional and last patent (#570,752) for a woven-wire fence design with sharpened projections of wire at the top and bottom of the fence. This design was classified as "Wire Fence."

Hiram B. Scutt was issued nine patents from 1875 to 1885 for different barb and fence designs, including two barbed machine designs using a combination of materials in the designs of wire strands, wire barbs, and sheet metal barbs (Figure 56).

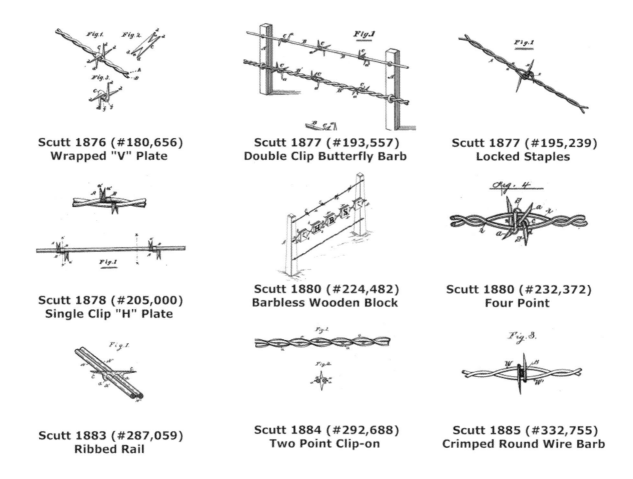

Scutt 1876 (#180,656)
Wrapped "V" Plate

Scutt 1877 (#193,557)
Double Clip Butterfly Barb

Scutt 1877 (#195,239)
Locked Staples

Scutt 1878 (#205,000)
Single Clip "H" Plate

Scutt 1880 (#224,482)
Barbless Wooden Block

Scutt 1880 (#232,372)
Four Point

Scutt 1883 (#287,059)
Ribbed Rail

Scutt 1884 (#292,688)
Two Point Clip-on

Scutt 1885 (#332,755)
Crimped Round Wire Barb

Figure 56. Examples of H. B. Scutt's Designs (1876 to 1885)

His first design was a fence design with Watkins in 1875 (Figure 57).

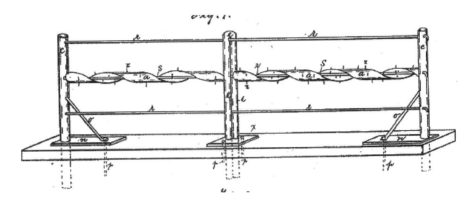

Figure 57. Watkins, W. and Scutt, H. B. 1875 (#163,955) "Half Round Rail"

This design was sheet metal strip pieced with two-point mild strand barb. They justified their design as being unique by referencing Rose's 1873 design (#138,763) without mentioning his name by saying they were aware "… sharp points or barbs have been used by being driven into a strip of wood, but never as passing entirely through, and sharp at either end, nor a metallic rod twisted around the wire for its support."

Some inventors patented several variations for the same barb patent design. For example, Charles Kennedy's 1874 patent (#153,965) included different styles for his four- and six-pointed star sheet metal barbs. These barbs could be attached by hand to single-strand plain wire fences with "pincers" (Figure 58). He patented a tool (called "pinchers") in 1876 for attaching Kennedy barbs (#180,351).

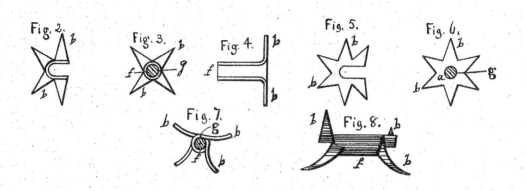

Figure 58. Kennedy, C. 1874 (#153,965) "Clamp on Barbs"

His designs were for barbs that could be attached to a barbless wire fence. An 1876 publication by Washburn & Moen Manufacturing Co.[56] promoted Kennedy's "efficient loose barb" to "improve old plain fence," saying that it would allow "arming" the hundreds of thousands of miles of plain fence wire not in use throughout the West, "transforming them into good and efficient barb fences." He considered it as an "Improvement in Wire Fences" and it was assigned to the classification of "Improvement in Barbed Fences." His design came in the same year as those of Glidden, Haish, and Ellwood. As mentioned earlier, he also lived in DeKalb County, Illinois, and may have been aware of Rose's design used at the 1873 DeKalb County Fair.

Kennedy apparently saw an opportunity to add barbs to existing plain wire fences and convert them into barbed fences. For wire fences with multiple strands, he made recommendations on how many strands should have barbs attached to them. For five-strand fences, he recommended that barbs be attached to the second and fourth wire strands.

56    Washburn and Moen secured the patent rights to Kennedy's patent and marketed it along with Glidden's barbed wire. The brochure referred to "Barb Fence Armor," a twelve-foot wooden strip with convolved circles of "Steel Barb Fencing" (circular strands attached to wood) that could convert ordinary wooden fence into a "formidable barrier."

For three-strand fences, it was suggested that barb be attached to all three strands. His design was considered as a new and useful "Improvement in Wire-Fence". He even designed a tool or "pincers" for attaching his barbs to existing plain wire fences (#180,351) in 1876.

Some inventors patented more than one barb design in a single patent. For example, Brinkerhoff patented four sheet metal barb designs (shapes and attachments) in 1879 (Figure 59).

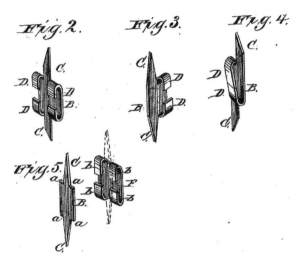

Figure 59. Brinkerhoff, J. 1879 (#214,095) Sheet Metal Barbs

(Fig. 2: Harrow Point, Fig. 3: Lugs Lance Point, Fig. 4: Lance Point, and Fig. 5: Spear Point)

The Brinkerhoffs (Jacob, Warren, and John J.) were a family of farm equipment inventors, including barbed fencing inventors. They obtained over forty-five patents from 1863 to 1890, which included patents for barbed fencing, milk churns, a corn sheller, washing machines, a potato digger, a cultivator, and a seeder and rake.

117

Not all the barbed fence designs that have been found were patented. Hagemeier (2010, 2012) identified more than eighty single-, double-, and three-wire strand designs and sheet metal strip designs with one to multipoint wire and sheet metal barbs whose origins are unknown. It is likely that these designs reflect handmade variations of wire where barbs were purchased in bulk and attached individually (Hagemeier 2010, 2012) or illegal, "moonshine" variations of legitimate patents (Hagemeier 2010, 2012; McCallum and McCallum 1985).

### Manufacturing Variations of Barbed Fencing Designs

As discussed earlier, manufacturing of barbed fencing was a major industry in the US in the late 1880s and has been characterized as contributing to the industrialization of agriculture. The economic opportunity in barbed fencing led to the monopolization of barbed fencing by Washburn and Moen Co. and I. L Ellwood Co., illegal manufacture of barbed fencing in response to its monopolization, e.g. Iowa Protective Farmers Association, and years of litigation. The economic opportunity in barbed fencing spurred the demand for new designs by individuals to invent designs and sometimes illegal variations (McCallum and McCallum 1985). McCallum and McCallum 1985 provide a detailed discussion on manufacturing of barbed fencing, its monopolization, the illegal manufacturing or "moonshining," and the resulting patent litigation.

Figure 60 shows the exponential increase in the manufacturing and sale of barbed wire immediately after its invention in 1874. In 1874, only five tons were produced and sold. By 1907, the production had increased to 250,000 tons. American Steel and Wire Company, one of the largest manufacturers, produced almost two-thirds of this production in 1901 (Hornberg 2009).

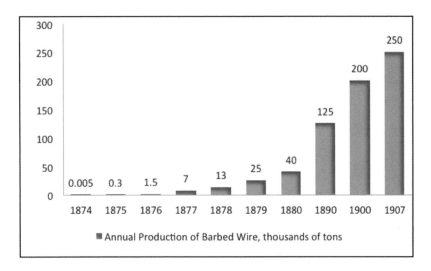

Figure 60. Annual Production of Barbed Wire[57] from 1874 to 1901 (Hornberg 2009)

In the 1880s, the manufacturing of barbed wire occurred primarily in the Northeast and Upper Midwest (Figure 61).

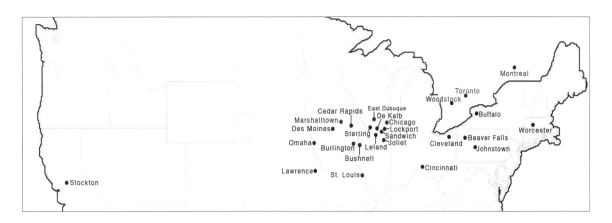

Figure 61. Production of Barbed Wire in the United States in 1881 (Adapted from Netz 2004 and The American Steel and Wire Records housed at Harvard Library in Boston).

---

57      Includes both barbed wire and barbed sheet metal strip fencing.

Initially, most of the manufacturing of barbed fencing occurred in Illinois (DeKalb)[58] and Massachusetts (Worcester).[59] Washburn and Moen Co. wasted no time in marketing barb fencing as an addition to its plain wire fencing. In 1876, within one year of Glidden's invention, the company published an advertising pamphlet entitled "The Utility, Efficiency and Economy of Barb Fence." The cover of the pamphlet stated that it was "A Book for the Farmer, The Gardner and The Country Gentlemen." In it, they advertised and extolled the virtues of Glidden's "Steel Barb Fence" and also the "Kennedy Barb Fence Wire," which they manufactured by placing Kennedy barbs on a single No. 9 wire strand. In the pamphlet, they listed the barbed fencing and machine patents and reissues they had rights to, including M. Kelly; J. Glidden; L. Smith; W. Hunt; C. Kennedy; I. Ellwood; J. Glidden and H. M. Vaughan; and H. Putnam.

It is not the scope of this book but there was an aggressive effort by Washburn and Moen Co. to obtain patent rights of other inventors and to enter into agreements with other barbed fencing manufacturing companies to manufacture Glidden's and other acquired patent licenses. Appendix A, Supportive Information, Table 1 provides a list of some four dozen companies with licences to manufacture Glidden's barbed wire.

---

58    The DeKalb County Manufacturer reported that 2,840,000 lbs. of barbed wire were produced in 1876; 12,863,000 lbs. in 1877; 26,655,000 lbs. in 1878; and 50,337,000 lbs. in 1879 (http://web.archive.org/web/20060712125058/http://www.ellwoodhouse.org/barb_wire/)

59    Washburn and Moen Factory had a wire manufacturing plant in Worcester, Massachusetts.

One interesting bit of information found in this pamphlet was a list of testimonials on the use of their wire. A testimonial from a M. F. Apolonio, President of the Boston Base Ball Association, stated that using the "Barb Fence Armor" (Figure 62) saved the Association $50 from having special police and $400 to $500 in admission fees. Boston Base Ball Club of the National Association formed in 1871 and was Boston's first professional baseball franchise, later becoming the Boston Braves and even later the Atlanta Braves.

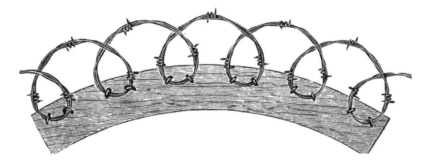

Figure 62. Picture of Barbed Fence Armor from Washburn and Moen Co. 1876 Brochure on Barb Fencing

It was described in the pamphlet as a series of "convoluted circles of steel barbed fencing, fastened upon strip of wood twelve feet long, which can be secured upon the upper edge of any wooden fence." This is the only reference found in this analysis promoting the use of early barbed fencing for security purposes. The advertisements of barbed fencing focused on farming and livestock management. Bennett and Abbott (2014) provided an in-depth analysis of barbed fencing advertising in the United States in the late 1800s. The major advertisers were Jacob Haish and Washburn and Moen Co. Their advertisements often focused on the beliefs and prejudices of the times, especially those of Jacob Haish who was in strong competition with Washburn and Moen Co.

Glidden, Ellwood, and one of the largest wire manufactures, Washburn and Moen Manufacturing Company of Worchester, Massachusetts,[60] collaborated to manufacture Glidden's barbed wire and Kennedy's barbed wire.[61] As mentioned earlier, by 1883, they had licensed more than four dozen companies to manufacture Glidden's patent (see Appendix A, Supportive Information, Table 1). J. Haish's "S Barb" (a two-point wire mild steel barb on a continuous double mild steel wire strand) was manufactured in DeKalb, Illinois, by Jacob Haish & Co. Other Illinois patentees who entered into manufacturing included HB Scutt & Co. of Joliet, Illinois. They had a plant in Pittsburgh, Pennsylvania. The Thorn Wire Hedge Company in Chicago manufactured Kelly's "Thorny Barb" from New York. The Doolittle & Co. in Bridgeport, Connecticut, also had licensees to manufacture Kennedy's sheet metal clamp on barbs for attachment to plain wire fences.

McCallum and McCallum (1985) and Netz (2009) provided more detailed descriptions of the manufacturing activities associated with barbed fencing; however, the manufacturing history of specific barbed fencing designs and patents has not been documented completely. The following is a list of companies manufacturing barbed fencing in 1888 as listed in *Farm Implement News Buyers Guide*.[62]

---

60    Later becoming part of the American Steel and Wire Company and in 1901, the US Steel Corporation.

61    (http://caselaw.lp.findlaw.com/cgi-bin/getcase.pl?court=us&vol=159&invol=423)

62    Farm Implement News Company Publishers. Chicago, IL (1888).

A. H. Shreffler - Joliet, Illinois

Ashley Wire Co. - Joliet, Illinois

Baker Wire Co. - Des Moines, Iowa

Baker Wire Company – Des Moines, Iowa

Buck Thorn Fence Company – Trenton, New Jersey

Cincinnati Barb Wire Fence Co. - Cincinnati, Ohio

Cleveland Barb Fence Co. - Cleveland, Ohio

Frentress Barb Wire Fence Company – East Dubuque, Iowa

Gautier Steel Department of Cambria Iron Co. - Johnstown, Pennsylvania

H B Scutt & Co. - Joliet, Illinois

H B Scutt & Co. - Ltd, Pittsburgh, Pennsylvania

Hawkeye Steel Barb Fence Co. - Burlington, Iowa

I. L. Ellwood & Co. - DeKalb, Illinois

Iowa Barb Steel Wire Co. - Marshalltown, Iowa

Iowa Barb Wire Company – New York, New York

Jacob Haish & Co. – DeKalb, Illinois

Janesville Barb Wire Co. - Janesville, Wisconsin

Joliet Enterprise Co. - Joliet, Illinois

Kelly Barb Wire Co. - Chicago, Illinois

Lambert & Bishop Wire Fence Co. - Joliet, Illinois

Lockport Wire Company - Lockport, Illinois

Lockport Wire Fence Co. -Lockport, Illinois

Lockstitch Fence Co. - Joliet, Illinois

Northwestern Barb Wire Company – Sterling, Illinois

Ohio Steel Barb Wire Fence - Piqua, Ohio

Oliver & Roberts Wire Co. Ltd - Pittsburgh, Pennsylvania

Rock Falls Barb Wire Co. - Rock Falls, Illinois

Superior Barbed Wire Company - DeKalb, Illinois

Thorn Wire Hedge Company, Chicago, Illinois

Washburn & Moen Manufacturing Co. - Worcester, Massachusetts

From this list, Illinois had the most barbed fencing manufacturing companies with fifteen; Iowa with five, and Ohio with three barbed fence manufacturing facilities. Northeastern states of Massachusetts, New York, New Jersey, and Pennsylvania had a total of six barbed fence manufacturing facilities each. Although reflecting geographical trends these numbers do not reflect the amount of barbed fencing produced.

Some of these manufacturers were associated with specific barbed wire inventors, such as Baker Wire Co. (G. C. Baker), Ellwood & Co. (I. L. Ellwood & J. Glidden), Frentress Barb Wire Fence Company (H. N. Frentress), HB Scutt & Co. (H. B. Scutt), Jacob Haish & Co. (J. Haish), Kelly Barb Wire Co. (M. Kelly), and Buck-Thorn Fence Co. (T. V. Allis)

Although information on who manufactured specific barbed fencing is not readily available, finding information from early manufacturing catalogues on specific barbed fencing products is sometimes possible. A review of these catalogues shows what patents and designs were for sale. These brochures or catalogues often provided specifications or intended manufacturing variations for barbed fencing products, including information on the gauge of the wire, barb separation, and coatings (e.g., galvanization). For example, The Dominion Barb-Wire Company (Montreal and Toronto, Canada), in a 1889 product brochure, advertised that it sold twisted sheet metal barbless wire or ribbon wire that was galvanized with a 3/8 inch wide ribbon. Along with the "E or "Thorn Ribbon Fencing" they manufactured and sold, it appears to be Allis' "Buckthorn," an integrated sheet metal barb strip with extended points. They named it "Lyman Thorn" and claimed it was the only ribbon wire made in Canada. They said the ribbon wire was preferred by some as a more visible top strand but that it would not take the place of barb-wire fencing. It too was galvanized. They provided instruction on constructing a barb- wire fence. Another design they sold, called "tablet fencing" (looks like a Stubbe Plate design, October 23, 1883

[#287,337]), a double mild steel wire strand wire with eight-point sheet metal warning plate barb. It sold in two sizes: "J" size was a one-inch tablet five inches apart and "K "size was a one-and-a-half inch square tablet nine inches apart. Dominion Barb-Wire Company had a licensing agreement with Washburn & Moen Co. to manufacture and sell the barbed fencing they advertised (Canadian House of Commons. "The Committee on Alleged Trade Combinations, Testimony of Thomas Workman." *Journal* 22, appendix 3 [April 20, 1888]).

In a 1915 product brochure, American Steel and Wire Company (formerly the Washburn & Moen Company) listed selling the following barbed wires under the American Barbed Wire Brand:

» American Glidden

» Ellwood Glidden

» Baker Perfect

» Waukegan 2-Point[63]

» Lyman 4-Point

» Waukegan 4-Point[64]

» American Special 2-Point

As mentioned earlier, the association of different patent designs with different manufacturers has not been sorted out. The following is a list of some initial patent designs described in the January issue of the 1880 *American Agriculturist* in which the manufacturers were identified.

---

63    Waukegan barbed wire was a design patented by J. D. Curtis, possibly the 1884 barb produced by his barb-making machine (#297, 679). Washburn & Moen Manufacturing Company of Worcester, MA, established a wire mill, the Waukegan Works, in Chicago along Lake Michigan. In 1892, the company, a principal manufacturer of Glidden Barbed wire, introduced Waukegan Barbed Wire invented by John D. Curtis.

64    Possibly J. D. Curtis 1894 (#494,326).

- » Kelly Steel Barb Wire – manufactured by Thorn Wire Hedge Co.

- » Crandal's Barbed Wire – manufactured by Chicago Galvanizing Co.

- » Sterling Barbed Wire – manufactured by North-western Barb Wire Co.

- » Glidden Steel Fencing – manufactured by Washburn & Moen Co.

- » Three-Pointed, Stone City Steel Barbed Wire – manufactured by Stone City Barb Wire Fence Co.

- » The Steel Barbed Cable Fence – manufactured by H. B. Scutt & Co.

- » Spiral Twist 4-pointed Steel-barbed Cable Fence Wire – manufactured by Watkins & Ashley

- » Quardrateed Barbed Fence – manufactured by Pittsburg Hinge Co.

- » Iowa 4-pointed Barbed Steel Wire – manufactured by the Iowa Barb Steel Co. (Iowa and New York)

- » Lyman Manufacturing Co. Barbed Wire – manufactured by Lyman Manufacturing Co.

- » American Barb Fence – manufactured by American Barb Fence Co.

- » Brinkerhoff Steel Strap and Barb and Brinkerhoff – manufactured by Washburn & Moen Co.

- » Scutt's Patent Tablet – manufactured by H. B. Scutt & Co.

- » Cord's Rotary Barb – No manufacturer identified.

Over time, licenses were bought and sold so a given patent design may have had different manufacturers. The names of the designs and manufacturers are the ones used in the article and don't reflect the common names identified by Hagemeier (2010, 2012). Some twenty-three designs were depicted in the journal, but the editor stated that since this invention was "new" the editor was not in a position to make recommendations on the best. The editor stated he would leave that opinion up to the readers.

A more thorough examination of these early catalogues is necessary to determine which manufacturers sold what specific barbed fencing products and what different variations were manufactured. Besides farmers and ranchers, the railroad industry was a large purchaser of barbed wire since many states required them to fence their right-of-ways if they expected to escape responsibility for damages to livestock. Farmers and cattlemen were losing livestock along unfenced tracks. For example, the Missouri, Kansas & Texas Railroad reported in 1876 that 1,948 animals had been killed in the three states where it operated at a cost of about $25,000[65] (Pryor 2005). According to Hayter (1939), in 1881, there were 93,671 miles of railroad tracks requiring a three- or four-strand fence on both sides of the right-of-way.

In 1879, Ellwood reported that he was furnishing fifty-nine railroads with the Glidden barbed wire. By 1885, the number of railroads had increased to over one hundred. The Western Fence Company of Chicago was devoted entirely to railroad fence construction, constructing thousands of miles of wire fence and employing from four hundred to five hundred men to erect fences. The company even provided men with equipment and sleeping and dining cars (Hayter 1939).

---

65 http://web.archive.org/web/20060712125058/http://www.ellwoodhouse.org/barb_wire/

As discussed in Chapter 2, barbed fencing took hold across the border in Canada, as exemplified by the number of barbed fencing manufacturing companies operating in Canada in the 1880s. Naylor (2006) listed seven of the Canadian manufacturers in 1889, including:

» Dominion Barb Wire Fence Co.

» Montreal Rolling Mills

» Ontario Tack Co.

» Pillow-Hersey Manufacturing Co.

» Canada Screw Co.

» Safety Barbed Wire Co.

» Ontario Lead and Barbed Wire Co.

In some cases, Canadian companies obtained licensing agreements with U. S. patent holders; in other cases they did not. For example, the Dominion Barb Wire Co. had a licensing agreement with Washburn & Moen Co. to manufacture and sell their barbed fencing. Washburn & Moen Co. placed advertisements in Canadian papers warning of the manufacturing and selling of American barbed fencing without obtaining a licensing agreement (Naylor 2006).

A final example of the aggressiveness of US barbed fencing manufacturers to market in Canada was seen in J. D. Curtis's April 1884 (#297,679) patent for a barbed wire machine that produced a two-point mild steel barb wrapped around two wire strands. The design was classified as a "Barb Fence Machine." The US patent was assigned to Washburn & Moen Co. of Worcester, Massachusetts. The same machine design is the Canadian patent #19,717, which was issued two months later in June 1884. The machine manufactured a two-point mild steel wire barb twisted around one or both the mild steel wires of the strand (Figure 63).

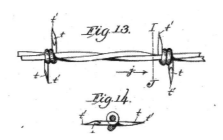

Figure 63. Curtis, J. O. 1884 (#297,679) Two-Point Barb Twisted Around One Or Both Twisted Wires Of The Strand (Barb design was shown in the patent described for the machine to make barbed fencing)

Some unique variations of patent designs for railroad companies were intentionally made to combat theft of their barbed fencing. It seems that some ranchers and farmers often stole this wire for their own use. Since the ownership identification of this stolen wire was impossible to determine, railroad companies started having wire produced that was unique to that railroad. They used variations of Glidden's "Winner" design. These variations often consisted of one or more square wire strands twisted among one or more traditional round wire strands. For many years, railroad companies were principal customers of The Barb Fence Company of DeKalb, Illinois,[66] who had the patent rights to the Glidden wire.

The variations found in antique barbed fencing designs occurred in two ways: (1) intentional variations in the designs during manufacturing such as special order variations (see above discussion on railroad variations) and (2) unintentional variations of specific designs from the lack of quality control in the wire steel stock purchased from steel mills, and illegal manufacturing.

---

66    http://www.rushcounty.org/BarbedWireMuseum/bwhistory.shtml#Railroads%20 and

Clifton (1970) and Hagemeier (2010, 2012) identified many variations for different patent designs, but the records are unclear as to who manufactured these variations, whether the manufactured variations were authorized or not, or when the variations were manufactured.

Figure 64 shows the number of patent variations associated with the years barbed fencing patents were issued. Based on Clifton (1970), a large number of variations were associated with the earliest patent period of 1874 to 1876 and again in the early 1880s. The least number of patent variations occurred from the mid-1880s on and associated with the decline in patent issuance.

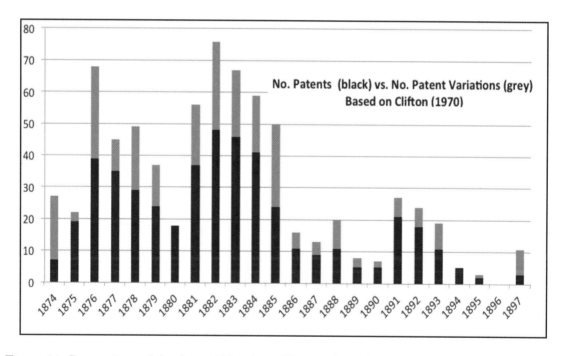

Figure 64. Comparison of the Annual Number of Patents Issued to the Number of Patent Variations Associated with Patent Issuing Years (Clifton 1970)

Unintentional variations resulted in flaws in barbed fencing made from crude manufacturing equipment that could result in changes in the shape of wire strands from the original patent designs. Wires in a strand could often vary in gauge and shape.

The manufacturing flaws found in barbed fencing occurred in two ways: (1) by use of hand tools and (2) by machine errors. Hand attachment of barbs occurred early in the barbed fencing period (Figure 65).

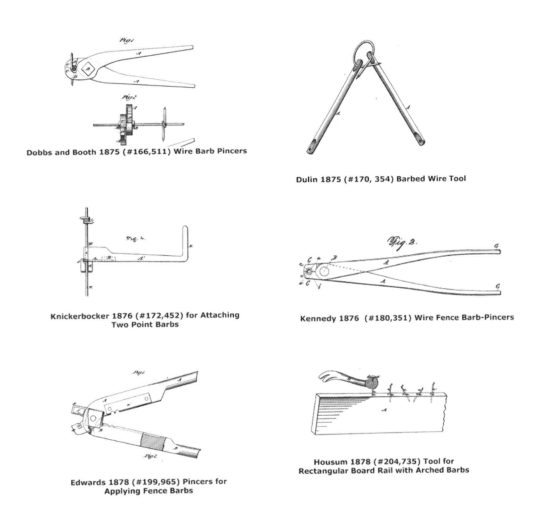

Dobbs and Booth 1875 (#166,511) Wire Barb Pincers

Dulin 1875 (#170, 354) Barbed Wire Tool

Knickerbocker 1876 (#172,452) for Attaching
Two Point Barbs

Kennedy 1876 (#180,351) Wire Fence Barb-Pincers

Edwards 1878 (#199,965) Pincers for
Applying Fence Barbs

Housum 1878 (#204,735) Tool for
Rectangular Board Rail with Arched Barbs

Figure 65. Examples of Barbed Wire Hand Tools

From 1875 to 1878, sixteen patents for hand tools, including hammers and pincers for attaching barbs, were issued. The attaching of barbs by hand by individuals led to considerable variation in shape, spacing, sharpness, and length of the barbs (see later discussion on barb design). In 1875, Dobbs and Booth patented the first tool for applying mild steel barbs to fence wire. The barb shown in their patent was a two-point barb on a single-strand that was patented four months later and was known as the "Non Slip Staple Barb."

From reading early patent descriptions and other literature, manufacturing of the barbed fence was often done in local factories and blacksmith shops with adapted equipment (e.g., Glidden's Coffee Mill barb machine). In other cases, the inventor described how to attach the barb (e.g., Kennedy 1874 patent [#153,965] by means of "pinchers with suitable jaws"). In his description, he mentioned that the barb did not have to be a "perfect star," but simply had to provide sharp points that cattle would rub against.

Three months later in November 1875, W. Dulin patented (#170,354) a very simple tool for hand applying barbs to existing plain wire fences. He described using old fence wire cut up to three-and-a-half inches long and using his tool consisting of two cast iron rods with holes in each end to twist these pieces of wire around existing plain fence wire. Patents for hand tools continued up until 1879, when manufacturing machines dominated the production of barbed wire fences and the conversion of unbarbed wire fences declined.

In 1879, J. Brinkerhoff and W. M Brinkerhoff patented (#216,779) a tool for attaching sheet metal barbs to sheet metal strips. Actual machines for manufacturing barbed fencing accompanied some of the barbed fencing patents. In Glidden's case, he started with a homemade machine. Glidden first produced his barb design of 1874 (a two-point wire barb [#157,124]) by adapting a hand-operated coffee mill to make his barb. This hand-operated coffee mill was quickly supplanted by the issuance of a specifically designed hand-operated barb-making machine patent, the Glidden & Vaughn machine in 1874 (#157,508). This patent was issued three months after Glidden's patent (#157,124) was issued.[67] The first patented power-driven machine for his barb was issued to H. W. Putnam of Bennington, Vermont, in 1876 (#173,667) (McCallum and McCallum 1985). This patent was used by Washburn & Moen Co. of Worcester, Massachusetts, to make Glidden's barbed fencing. In 1875, Doolittle and Elis (#165,661) were issued the first sheet metal strip manufacturing patent for a die for manufacturing sheet metal barbs.[68] This patent was described as a "device for making tabs for wire fences."

Some inventors patented their own machines. For example, Stover, an inventor of two-point sheet metal barbs for single-strand wire fences (1875, #164,947), patented a machine to make his barb two years later in 1877 (#196,313). Baker patented a machine to manufacture his 1883 (#273,219) two-point wire "Baker Perfect" barb for a double-strand wire fence a year later in 1884 (#295,513). In 1879, Stephen was issued a patent (#222,608)

---

[67]    It should be noted that spacing of the barbs was not stipulated either in the barb patent or in the machine patent.

[68]    This patent was not associated with a particular sheet metal barb patentee.

for a barb-making machine for his patent (#222,747), a four-point barb on twisted double strand called "X" Four Point. He filed his barb patent on July 19, 1879, and the machine patent a month later on August 19, 1879. Both were issued on December 16, 1879.

A real lag is seen in issuance of barbed fencing patents and/or machine patents for making the wire is seen in the Kelly "Thorny Barb" patented in 1868. A machine for manufacturing Kelly's 1868 "Thorny Barb" wire was not patented until 1876 by Mitchell and Calkins (#172,760).[69]

More often than not, others beside the inventor invented the barbed-making machines. For example, in 1882, Burrows from Illinois was issued a patent (#263,283) for a "Machine for Applying Barbs To Fence Wires." The machine was designed to apply Frentress's 1875 "Split Diamond Barb" (#171,008). Reflecting the unintended variation in barbed fencing in one of his claims was that his design allowed "imperfect barbs" to be detected and removed.

Given the potential profits to be made and the monopolization of the barbed fencing market in the 1880s by the Washburn and Moen Company and the Ellwood Company, illegal manufacturing and distribution occurred in an effort to avoid paying license fees (Hayter 1939; McCallum and McCallum 1985). Many unlicensed manufacturers sprung up; in Iowa for example, the Iowa Farmers Protective Association was formed in 1881 to manufacture and sell "free wire" to the groups members. Lawsuits resulted. [70] These groups intentionally varied the original patent design (McCallum and McCallum 1985; Clifton 1970; Hagemeier 2010). These activities resulted in "moonshine" and "bootleg" wires being produced which were copies and variations of fences from licensed manufacturers.

69    Patent was controlled by the Thorn Wire Hedge Co. and later by Washburn & Moen Co.

70    McCallum and McCallum 1985

As discussed in Chapter 2, barbed fencing took hold across the border in Canada as exemplified by the number of barbed fencing manufacturing companies operating in Canada in the 1880s. Naylor (2006) lists seven Canadian manufacturers in 1889, including:

» Dominion Barb Wire Fence Co.

» Montreal Rolling Mills

» Ontario Tack Co.

» Pillow-Hersey Manufacturing Co.

» Canada Screw Co.

» Safety Barbed Wire Co. and

» Ontario Lead and Barbed Wire Co.

In some cases, Canadian companies obtained licensing agreements in other cases they did not. For example, the Dominion Barb-Wire Co. had a licensing agreement with Washburn & Moen Co. to manufacture and sell barbed fencing, Washburn & Moen Co. placed advertisements in Canadian paper warning of the manufacturing and selling of American barbed fencing without obtaining a licensing agreement (Naylor, 2006).

A final example of the entrepreneurship of US barbed fencing inventors to market in Canada is seen in J.D. Curtis's April 1884 (#297,679) patent for a barbed wire machine that produced a two-point mild steel barb wrapped around two mild steel wire strands (Figure 66).

The US patent was assigned to Washburn & Moen Co. of Worcester, Massachusetts. The same machine design is the Canadian patent (#19,717) was issued in two months later June 1884. The design was classified as a "Barb Fence Machine."

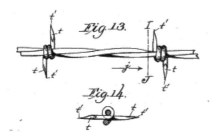

Figure 66. Curtis, J. D. 1884 (#297,679) Two-Point Barb Around One or Both Wires of the Strand (Design was for Machine to Make Barbed Fencing)

A review of early classified ads in papers and journals shows the patents were frequently offered for sale by the original patentee. In addition, some inventors assigned their patent rights to companies when the patent was first issued. As mentioned earlier the association of different patent designs with different manufactures has not been sorted out.

## WHO WERE THE MOST SUCCESSFUL INVENTORS OF ANTIQUE BARBED FENCING?

There are several ways of answering this question: the manufacturing volume or sales of a given patent, the number of patents issued, the number of copies or variations of a given patent, expert opinion, or some combination of these ways. Information on the manufacturing volume for a given patent is not ready available to make patent-to-patent comparisons. As discussed in the previous section (see earlier discussion on the number of inventors, patent, and patent variations), most of the more than four hundred barbed fencing inventors had one or two patents. However, there were groups of inventors with multiple patents. At least a dozen inventors applied for and received five or more patents each for barbed fencing designs. Upham (1876-1885) had the most patents of all inventors, with nineteen patents, including designs for mild steel wire strands and mild steel wire barb patent designs, sheet metal strips or ribbons, sheet metal barb patent designs, and patents for combination wire barbs and sheet metal strand designs. T. V. Allis (1878-1885) was the second most prolific inventor, with sixteen patents for sheet metal strips and barb patent designs. J. W. Griswold (1888-1897) had thirteen mild steel and sheet metal patents including seven patents issued in 1892.

However if one looks at the number of variations associated with a given inventor a different picture emerges. Figure 67 compares the number of patents versus the number of patent variations or copies that have been identified by Hagemeier (2010, 2012).

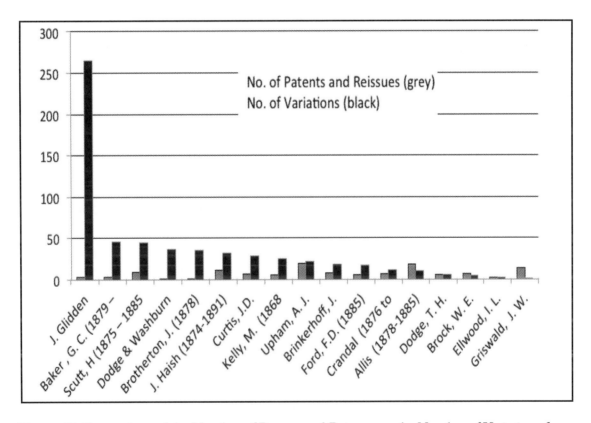

Figure 67. Comparison of the Number of Patents and Reissues to the Number of Variations for Selected Inventors (Hagemeier 2010; Clifton 1970; Campbell and Allison 1986)

The conclusion from this analysis is that, the inventors with the most patents were not the most successful as measured by the number of variations that have been identified. As discussed earlier, variations reflect not only unintentional variations, but also authorized and unauthorized differences in patent designs. If a patent design was effective and inexpensive to manufacture, e.g. J. Glidden's patent design, it was copied and widely varied. Upham, Allis, and Griswold had nineteen, eighteen, and thirteen patents, respectively, but few variations. On the other hand, Glidden, Baker, Washburn, and Brotherton had the fewest patents at three, three, one, and one, respectively, but had some of the largest variations. These variations included variations in the shape of the wires in the strand, different gauge wires, multiple strands (e.g., seven or more), barbs on different strands, etc. G. Baker (1880–1883) had only three patents. His two-point double-strand wire patent (#273,219) had forty-six variations.

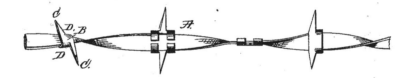

J. Brinkerhoff (1876-1879), who is known for his barbed sheet metal strip or ribbon wire, had eight patents and eighteen variations (Hagemeier 2010).

Dodge T. and Washburn C. (1882) had one patent (#252,746), a four-point round-wire barb twisted around one of the two wires of the strand; this has been found to have at least thirty-six variations:

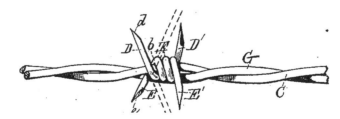

J. J. Brotherton's 1878 patent (#207,710) was for a two-point wire barb twisted around both wires of double-wire strand; this has been found to have at least thirty-five variations:

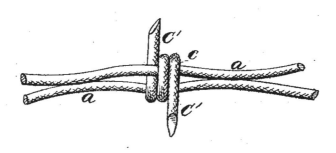

T. V. Allis had a large number of patents (i.e, eighteen), but only one of them can be considered successful based on the number of variations. His 1881 patent (#244,726) for a sheet metal strip "Buckthorn" design has at least seventeen variations:

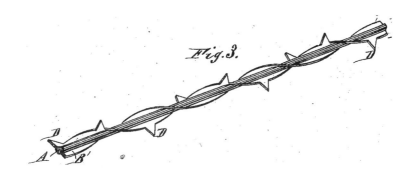

Glidden's 1874 two-point barb design (#157,124) and Baker's 1883 two-point barb design (#273,219) (Figure 68) are consider by most authors (e.g., Clifton [1970], Hagemeier [2010, 2012], and McCallum and McCallum [1985]) as the most successful patent designs.

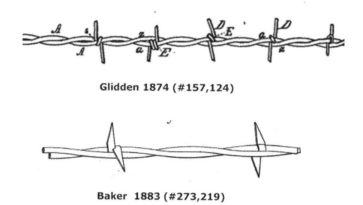

**Glidden 1874 (#157,124)**

**Baker 1883 (#273,219)**

Figure 68. Glidden and Baker Patent Designs

In reading the patent descriptions, it is apparent that different inventors had different and sometimes interesting business relationships. Often a patentee was associated with other inventors who helped in the patent application or the patentee referenced other inventors when pointing out how their patent was different from other inventor's designs. In the first case, H. Reynolds of Marshalltown, Iowa, in 1878, was issued a patent (#203,779) for his single-wire strand four-point barb, "Necktie." His attorney, who signed his drawing, was Thomas G. Orwig of Des Moines, Iowa, who himself patented two designs, one before Reynolds's patent and one after Reynolds's patent. The first Orwig patent in April 1876 (#201,890) was similar to the one designed by Reynolds for a wire strand design with a series of paired kinks in a single-wire strand that were meant to restrict lateral movement and allow barbs to revolve and reduce tearing of the flesh of animals if the barbs were made ridge. It showed three examples of barbs: a Kennedy-like three-point clamp on sheet metal barb and two Glidden-like two- and four-point steel barbs. His second patent (#225,717) was for a two-point barb driven through a wooden rail fence. Reynolds's patent shows two designs for barbs, two-point and four-point staple-form barbs, located in the bend or kink in the single mild steel wire strand. Where Orwig added the kinks to single-strand steel wire so that barbs could be attached to regions between kinks, Reynolds described producing the kink when the barbs were attached. A search of the history of these individuals revealed that Thomas Orwig was a Civil War veteran who moved to Des Moines, Iowa, and opened up a patent office. Hiram Reynolds was a farmer who invented a barb and a strand design and appears to have employed Orwig to help prepare the patent application.

Another example is found in J. W. Nadelhoffer patent application (#201,889) in 1878 for a double-twisted steel strand with two-point staple-shaped barb (Crossover "Z" Barb) in which he referenced O. H. Salisbury's 1876 patent (# 177,752). Nadelhoffer claimed his patent was different from Salisbury's design, which was also a double-twisted steel strand but used a two-point looped barb ("Looped Staple").

Although not often, some inventors did successfully team up. For example, T. Dodge and C. Washburn of Worcester, Massachusetts, teamed up and were issued a patent (#252,746) in 1882 for a "Two Wrap Round Barb," a four-point barb twisted around one of the strands of a two-wire strand design.

It was successful as measured by the number of variations (i.e., some thirty-six variations). T. Dodge was the corporate attorney for Washburn & Moen Co. and C. Washburn was the president of Washburn & Moen Co.; Washburn and Moen Co. engaged in the manufacture of barbed fencing nationally and internationally. Sometimes successful teaming inventors were family members, including the Merrills from Iowa for single and double mid-steel wire strands with four-point steel barb in 1876 (#185,688) and the Brinkerhoffs from Auburn, New York, in 1879 for their sheet metal strip and barb designs (#219,143).

# 5) DESIGNS AND PATTERNS

» Attachment Components: Barbs and Warning Devices

» Horizontal Component Designs and Patterns

» Unique Horizontal Component Designs

» The Number of Strands, Strips, Bars, Rods, and Rails in Antique Barbed Fencing

Barbed fencing designs and patterns were influenced by the materials used by the inventors (see earlier discussion in Chapter 3) and by the different ways inventors tried to improve the components of barbed fencing, especially the barbs (see Chapter 5).

## ATTACHMENT COMPONENTS: BARBS AND WARNING DEVICES

As discussed in Chapter 1, one of the two major components of barbed fencing are the attachments to the horizontal component. Based on the materials used, four types of barbs and two types of warning devices are found. (Figure 69).

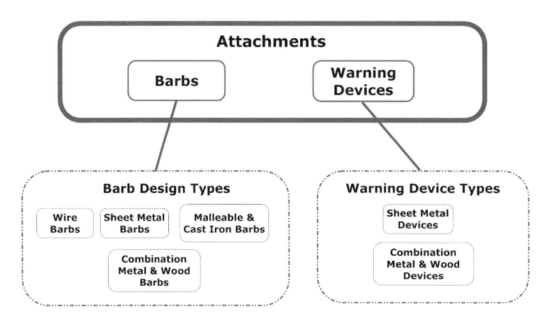

Figure 69. Type of Attachments Based on Type of Materials

## Barb Designs and Patterns

The defining components to antique barbed fencing are the pointed projecting attachments or barbs. The first impression is often that barbed wire fences are a series of "knots" of short pointed wires projecting from a strand or strip and regularly spaced apart. In comparing barbed wire fences, one will notice that these projections are not "knotted" the same way along the strand or strip. Most of the more than four hundred patents and more than 1,500 patent variations are variations in design of barbs. The differences seen in barbed fencing are more differences in the designs of the barb itself rather than the design differences in horizontal components (i.e., wire strands or sheet metal strips). For barbs, the primary design features involve the number of points on the barb, their appearance (shape and form), and their mode of attachment to the strand or strip. There are also a number of secondary design features, including spacing, sharpness, length, and gauge (Figure 70).

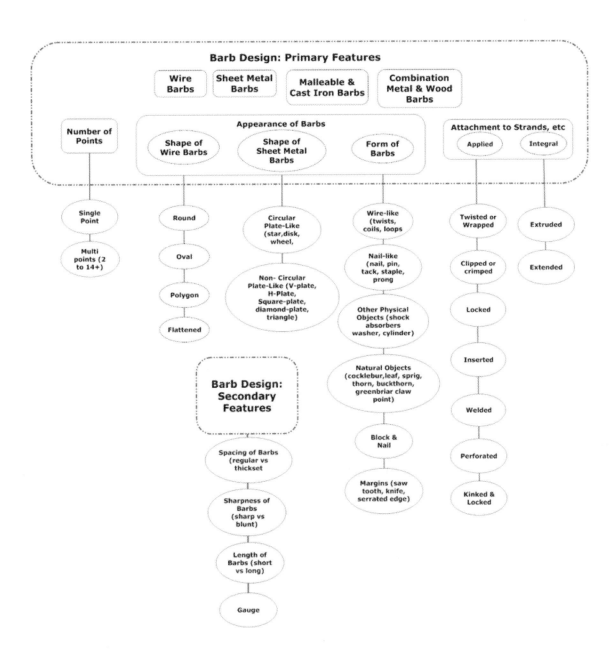

Figure 70. Design Classification for Barb Attachments

## Primary Barb Designs

*Number of barb points.* One of the obvious design differences in antique barbed fencing is the number of barb points. For wire strands, two-point barbs are the most common design found on wire strands followed by four-point barbs. Two- and four-point barbs are the most common designs, comprising more than 94 percent of the number of point designs found in wire strands. Two and four point barbs are the most common designs found on one single- and double mild steel wire strands comprising 84% of the different number of points found on these strands. A few single-point barb designs (21) along with three-point barb designs (6) and multiple-point barb designs (9) have been identified by Hagemeier (2010, 2012) and Clifton (1970).

Table 11. Comparison of the Different Number of Mild Steel Barb Points on Mild Steel Wire Strands

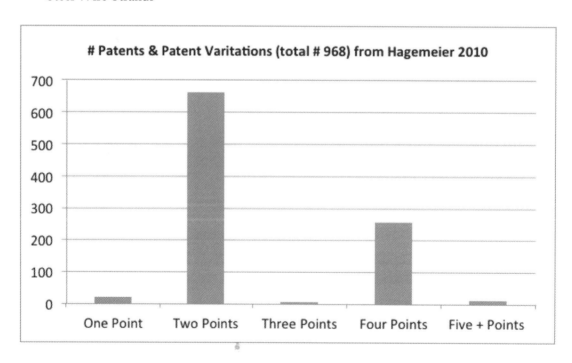

**Examples of Single and Multiple Point Wire Barbs**

Kelly 1868 (#84,062) Tack Ribbon

Glidden's 1874 (#157,124) Two Point "Winner"

Baker's 1883 (#273,219) "Baker Perfect, Two Point Flat Barb"

Merrill's 1876 (#185,688) Four, Six and Eight Point Coil Barbs

Figure 71. Examples of Single- and Multi-Point Wire Barbs

For sheet metal barbs, one-, two-, four-, and other multiple-point barbs are also found on sheet metal strips. Most sheet metal barbs (sixty-four percent) are multi-point design and were designed to be manufactured as an integral part of the sheet metal strip as either extended from the strip or extruded from the strip. Two-point sheet metal barbs are the next most common patented sheet metal design (twenty-nine percent) followed by four-point barbs **(**Figure 72).

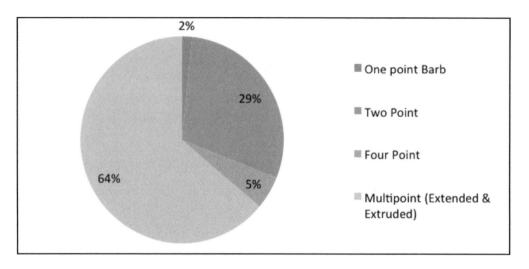

Figure 72. Percentage of Sheet Metal Point Barb Designs (Patents and Variations)

*Appearance of barbs (shape and form).* As mentioned above, the appearance of barbs can be influenced by several design features, including the type of materials and the method of attachment. In addition, barbs can be characterized by shape and form. Shape is a two-dimensional characterization and form is a three-dimensional characterization. Two general shapes are found in antique barbs: (1) round barbs and (2) flat barbs. The round shape is the most common shape barb and is associated with wire barbs. The flat shape is associated with sheet metal barbs but can be found with mild steel wire strands. For example, Baker designed a simple two-point flat wire barb (1883, #273, 219) (Figure 74).

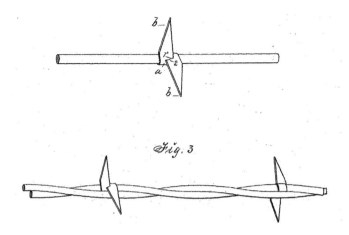

Figure 73. Baker, G. O. 1883 (#273,219) "Baker Perfect" Two-Point Flat Barb

The form of the barb, or its 3-D characteristics, has been used to characterize the appearance of the barb. Clifton (1970) and Hagemeier (2010, 2012) characterized the appearance of antique barbs in different ways. The varied appearance of barbs is reflected in the way Clifton characterized barb design patterns.

He identified more than four dozen patterns based on the differences in shape and form, including:

» Arrow Plate

» Block and Nail

» Bur

» Chipped Wire

» Clip and Nail

» Cut Edge

» Cylinder

» Diamond Plate

» Disc

» Double Saw Tooth

» Double Tack

» Dropped Loop

» Fence Strap

» H Plate

» Knife Edge

» Knob

» Leaf

» Nail

» Pin

» Prong

» Punch Out

» Rider

» Rod

» Saw Tooth

» Segmented Edge

» Serrated Insert Strip

» Shock Absorber

» Spinner

» Spiral Fin

» Split Panel

» Split Point

» Spreader Plate

» Sprig

» Square Plate

» Star

» Strand Mounted Barb Strips

» Tack

» V Plate

» Wheel

» Wheel Rowel

» Wire and Barbed Washer

» Zigzag Strip

These patterns are grouped into six simpler patterns based on their form (Figure 75):

1. Wire-like barbs

2. Nail-like or staple barbs

3. Circular barbs

4. Non-circular plate-like barbs

5. Looped barbs

6. Strips with edges (integral barbs)

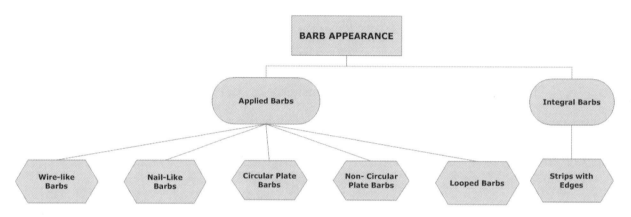

Figure 74. Barb Appearance Designs

The first five barb designs are all applied barbs. The one integral barb is the "Strip with Edges" design; it is manufactured at the edge of the sheet metal strip with a saw tooth-like edge pattern.

*Wire-like barbs.* Most barb designs used short pieces of sharpened mild steel wire. These barbs were twisted around a strand in various ways (see later discussion on modes of attachments). The most commonly found barbs are two- or four-point wire-like barbs. The most successful and early wire-like barbed designs were Glidden's "The Winner"[71] in 1874

---

71    Named the "Winner" by Glidden and Washburn & Moen Co. for the Supreme Court decision of 1892.

(#157,124), Baker's "Perfect" in 1883 (# 273,219), Haish's "S Barb" in 1875 (#162,240), and Brotherton's 1878 design (#207,710). (Figure 75). Wire-like barbs include Clifton's "Coil", "Single Turn", "Sprig", and "Twist."

**Two Point Wire-Like Mild Steel Barbs**

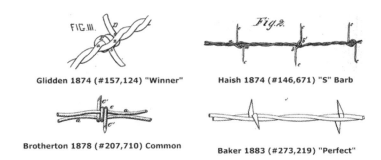

Glidden 1874 (#157,124) "Winner"          Haish 1874 (#146,671) "S" Barb

Brotherton 1878 (#207,710) Common          Baker 1883 (#273,219) "Perfect"

**Three Point Wire-Like Mild Steel Barbs**

Edenborn 1884 (#299,763) Webbed Barb

**Four Point Wire-Like Mild Steel Barbs**

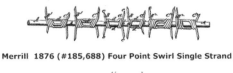

Merrill 1876 (#185,688) Four Point Swirl Single Strand

Dodge & Washburn 1882 (#252,746) Two Wrap Round Barb

Figure 75. Examples of Wire-Like Barbs

A unique wire barbed design is T. Lord's 1884 design (#293,584), which was a four-point split wire barb which was characterized as a "Caltrop" design (Greer 2014). The barb as designed presents four points in different directions. It can be attached to double-strand wire to rotate or not rotate (Figure 76). The non-rotating variety on a wire strand with the rotating variety was thought to be a manufacturing error.

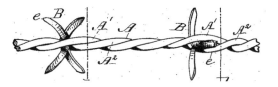

Figure 76. Lord, T. C. 1884 (#293,584) "Split Wire Barb"

*Nail-like barbs.* These designs used common nail-like materials (e.g., nails and other ordinary pointed metal materials such as wire fence staples and tacks for barbs) to form the barb. Some of these patented barbed fencing designs were manufactured to be applied to existing nail-like materials, such as staples and tacks to be attached to wire fence or individual strands of wire. Figure 77 provides examples of nail-like barb designs. They include Clifton's "Clip & Nail", "Double Tack", "Nail", "Pin", "Prong", "Staple", and "Tack".

**Examples of Nails and Staple Designs**

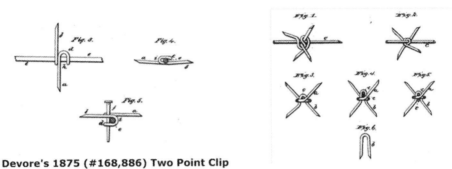

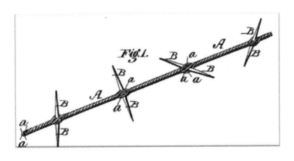

**Devore's 1875 (#168,886) Two Point Clip**

**St. John's 1878 (#199,330) Locked Staples**

**Underwood's 1878  (#206,754) Double Tack**

Figure 77. Examples of Nail Barb Designs

*Looped barbs.* The looped barb design includes Clifton's "Loop" and "Dropped Loop" designs. Two types of looped barbs were found: (1) loops as part of the strand and (2) barbs that are looped on the wire strand. Some single- and double-wire strands formed barbs from loops in the wire in the strand (Figure 78). The looped barb was formed by sharpened loops as part of the wire in the strand (e.g., Miles 1883 [#277,916]).

153

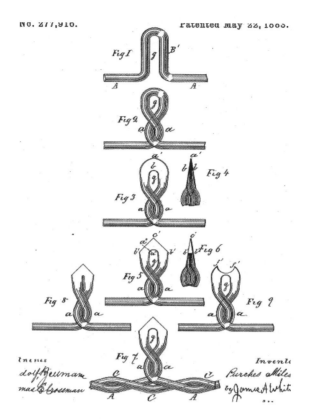

Figure 78. Miles, P. 1883 (#277,916) Open Diamond Point

The second type of design used a short piece of sharpened looped wire inserted between two wires of a double-wire stand (e.g., Brainard 1882 [# 268,453]) to form a loose barb (Figure 79).

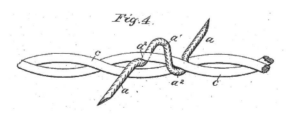

Figure 79. Brainard, C. B. 1882 (#268,453)

In 1875, Devore patented (#168,886) a wire barb that could be attached to existing single-strand plain wire fence by looping the short pointed wire and securing it with a nail to create a three-point barb (Figure 80).

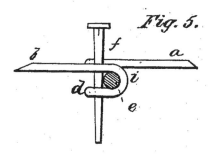

Figure 80. Devore, L. M. 1875 (#168,886) "Nail Lock"

*Circular plate barbs.* These barbs have a circular plate design using sheet metal or cast iron. Some circular plate barbs were fixed in place while others could spin. C. A. Hodge's "Spur Wheel" is an example of the rotating sheet metal plate multi-point design (Figure 81). The rotating movement was considered to reduce injury to livestock. Hodges twelve-point sheet metal barb rotated on a wire shaft attached to either a single-wire strand or a double-wire strand.

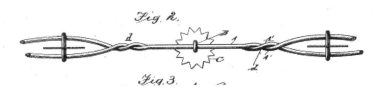

Figure 81. Hodge, C. A. 1887 (#367,398) "Spur Wheel"

This group often represents different forms and includes Clifton's "Bur", "Disc", "Cylinder", "Wheel", "Wheel Rowel", and "Wire & Barbed Washer."

G. E. Barker's 1881 (#251,505) "Hanging Spur Wheel" is a complicated example of a circular plate design (Figure 82).

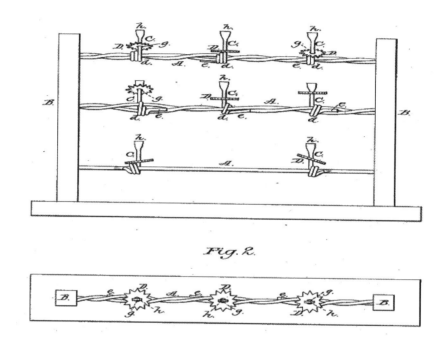

Figure 82. Barker, G. E. 1881 (#251,505) "Hanging Spur Wheel"

As mentioned earlier, some inventors had specific reasons for their designs. Nealy and Marland designed a knife-edge disk barb that would prevent "the skin and flesh of cattle being torn and being made sore" (Figure 83). They claimed there invention "will make a small clean cut in their skins, which will readily heal and the pain of which will cause the said cattle to keep out of contact with the fence."

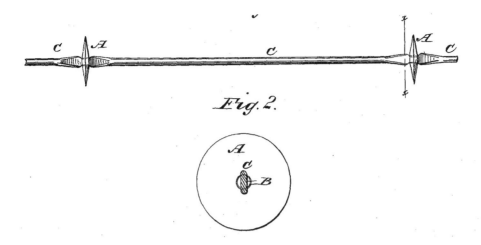

Figure 83. Nealy, T. and Marland, A. 1881 (#251,273) "Knife Edge Disc"

*Non-circular plate barbs.* Non-circular plate-like barb designs are larger barbs made of sheet metal that were invented to be more visible and cause less injury to livestock. They have distinctive forms or shapes reflected in Clifton's "Arrow Plate", "Diamond Plate", "Fence Strap", "H-Plate", "Spreader Plate Square Plate", "V- Plate", "Leaf", and "Spinner."

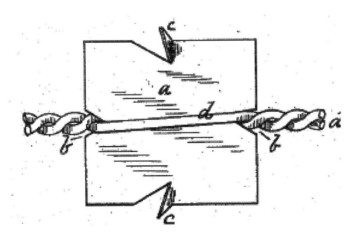

Figure 84. Barr, C. H. 1883 (#289,207) "Edge Cut Warning Plate Barb"

157

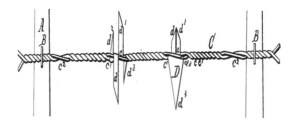

Figure 85. Armstrong, F. 1876 (#176,262) "Split Diamond Barb"

*Integral barbs.* There is one category of barbs where the edges of the sheet metal strip, or in one case a mild steel wire, is manufactured to form a barb-like condition as part of the strip or wire. These are known as integral barbs. The sharpened or pointed edge creates an avoidance reaction when animals encounter it. These integral barbs were part of the individual sheet itself (e.g., Woods 1879 patent where one edge of the strip was serrated and the other edge rolled) (Figure 86).

Figure 86. Woods, F. 1879 (#214,860) "Saw Tooth and Roll"

T. Allis, discussed earlier, had several designs called "Buckthorn" with lance points on one edge. "Buckthorn" had a central reinforcing core. It was a popular design used to contain sheep since the barbs did not entangle their wool. This design has been found by the author in California, New York, and Vermont.

These integral designs include Clifton's "Chipped Wire", "Cut Edge", "Double Saw Tooth", "Knife Edge", "Perforated", "Punch Out", "Saw Tooth", "Serrated Edge", "Serrated Insert Strip", "Spiral Fin", "Sprig", and "Zigzag Strip."

**Attachment of Barbs**

Barbs were attached in two basic ways: (1) attached as part of the strand, strip, etc. and called "integral barbs" or (2) attached separately to the strand or strip as either part of the manufacturing process or by local farmers, ranchers, or farm supply merchants and called "applied barbs." The type of attachment integral vs applied also influenced the type of sheet metal strip types (See later discussion on Sheet Metal Strips). The majority of barb designs are applied barb designs. Many of the early barbed fence patents were for barbs that could be applied to existing plain wire fences and wooden rails (see Chapter 2). Hagemeier (2010, 2012) organized sheet metal barbs this way. Clifton (1970) provided more detailed descriptors based on the mode of attachment that accounted for both applied and integral barbs. These descriptors conveyed both a general and specific mode of attachment. Clifton identified nineteen types of applied attachments for mild steel wire and sheet metal barbs, including the following:

- » Clip
- » Coil
- » Crimped Locked
- » Horizontal Strand Locked
- » Hitch
- » Inserted
- » Joint Locked
- » Kink Locked
- » Loop Locked
- » Perforated
- » Plate Locked
- » Riveted
- » Single Turn
- » Strand Clutched
- » Tie
- » Twist
- » Washer Locked
- » Welded
- » Wrap

Two integral attachment designs unique to sheet metal barbs are found: barbs that were extended and barbs that were extruded from the sheet metal strip.

These applied and integral attachment designs can be grouped into eight simpler attachment designs:

1.  Clipped or crimped on the strand or strip

2.  Inserted into the strand or strip

3.  Perforated to attach to the strand or strip

4.  Locked in various ways to the strand or strip

5.  Twisted, wrapped, and coiled around the wire strand or sheet metal strip

6.  Riveted or welded to the strand or strip

7.  Extended barb from the sheet metal strip

8.  Extruded barb from the sheet metal strip

For mild steel wire barbs, "twisting, wrapping, and coiling" attachment designs were the most common (seventy-six percent). (Figure 87) For sheet metal strips, "extended" designs were the most common (forty-six percent) (Figure 88).

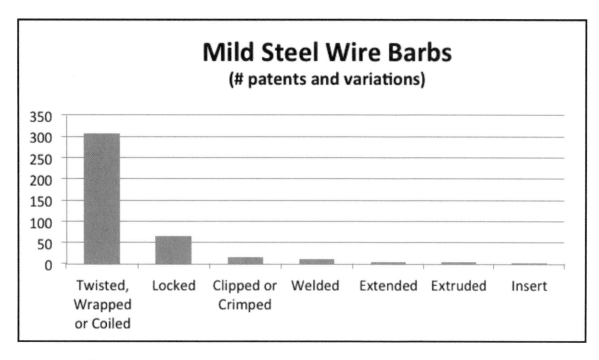

Figure 87. Comparison of Barb Attachment Groups for Mild Steel Barbs
(n= 404) from Clifton 1970

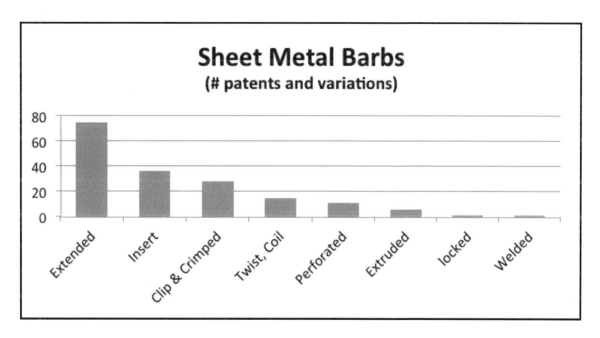

Figure 88. Comparison of Barb Attachment Groups for Mild Steel Barbs
(n= 162) from Clifton 1970

161

*Twisting or wrapping of barb around a strand or strip.* Twisted or wrapped wire barbs are the most frequent patent designs and patent variations found in antique barbed fencing (see Figure 87 ). The differences in attachment may have appeared subtle, but were sufficiently different to warrant a new patent for different inventors. According to Clifton (1970) and Hagemeir (2010, 2012), different designs and variations included single and multiple twists around a single-strand or around or through multiple wires of a strand. For example, C. H. Baker (#273,219) and J. O. Curtis (#470,746) twisted or wrapped their two-point barbs <u>once</u> around a wire in a strand. J. Glidden (#157,124) wrapped his two-point barbs <u>twice</u> around a wire in a strand. The location of the wrap (e.g., center wrap, end wrap, etc.) are variations that are found.

Figure 89. Example of Twisted Barb - Allen's, G. W. Twist 1875 (#180,185)

Another example of a "twist" attachment design to be used on existing barbless plain wire fences was Pooler and Jones's 1876 patent (#181,537). Their design was a three-point wrought-iron steel (or sheet metal) barb twisted around a single plain-wire strand (Figure 90). They referred to cutting the barb with an increased "rusting surface" for securing the barb to the wire.

Figure 90. Pooler, R. H and Jones, W. T. 1876 (#181,537) "Three Point on Single Strand"

*Clipped or crimped barbs.* Barbs were also designed to "clip-on" or be "crimped" to a wire strand or sheet metal strip. Over forty "crimped or clipped-on barb" designs were patented, especially for attaching barbs to barbless wire strands and converting them into barbed wire strands (see discussion in Chapter 2 on converting plain wire fences to barbed fences in the 1870s and in Kennedy's patents). These barb designs were manufactured and sold separately to farmers, ranchers, and hardware men for use on existing barbless single-strand wire fences. A number of these were clip-on mild steel barbs (e.g., Nelson's Clip-on Barb) (Figure 91).

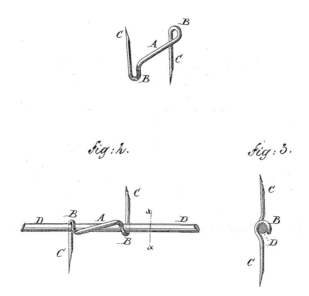

Figure 91. Nelson, J. 1876 (#185,346) "Clip-On Barb"

Ford's "Offset Barb" is an example of "crimple-on" design for sheet metal (Figure 92).

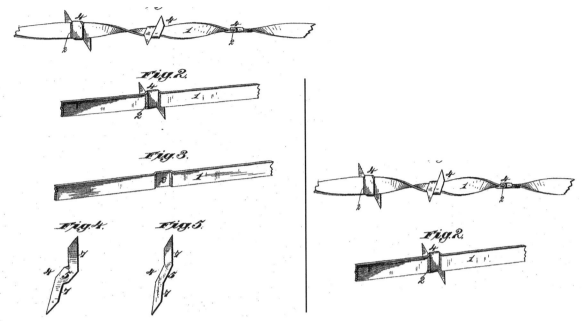

Figure 92. Ford, F. O. 1885 (#319,807) "Offset Barb"

In 1874, C. Kennedy (#153,995) had seven different sheet metal clip-on designs for mild steel strands described in his patent (Figure 93).

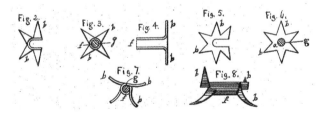

Figure 93. C. Kennedy, C. 1874 (#153,995) "Four- to Six-Point Star Barbs Clamp On"

Clip-on attachments for the cast iron barb designs were found early (1875) in D. Stover's (#164,947) patent (Figure 94). He developed a two-point barb for single-strand fencing and designed several variations on the "clip" design. His design was classified as an "Improvement in Wire-Fences."

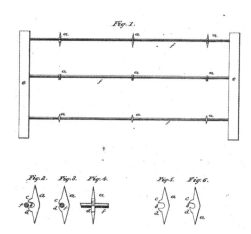

Figure 94. Stover 1875 (#164,947) "Clip On Barbs"

A clip-on design example for a barbless sheet metal fence is found in the sheet metal strip design of Nellis's 1877 patent (#191,011) with spring-like clip (Figure 95).

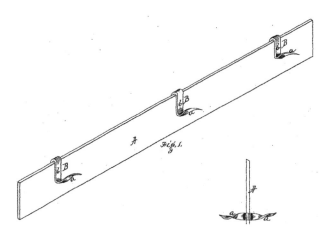

Figure 95. Nellis, A. J. 1877 (#191,011) "Ribbon with Spring Clip Barb"

*Locking barbs.* One of the major problems with early barbed fencing was that early barbs tended to bunch up on wire strands, especially on single-wire strands. Glidden's design using a second strand to hold the barb prevented this from happening. However, some inventors attempted to solve this problem of single-strand wires with barbs designed to hold the barbs in place by "locking" the barb to the strand. These locking barbs were twisted and looped in such a way that made them less likely to move or slip on a wire. Duncan's 1879 design was such a barb attachment design (Figure 96), which was classified as an "Improvement in Barbed Fence-Wire." This single wire strand was looped to receive the barb. He showed the same barb design in his patent description for a two-wire strand.

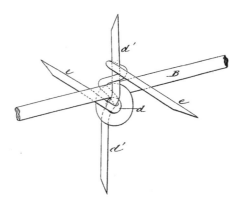

Figure 96. Duncan, J. A. 1879 (#281,506) "Looped Strand"

Variations of the "locked" design were identified by Clifton (1970), including "kink locked" design, "horizontal strand locked", "joint locked", "loop locked", "plate locked", and "washer locked" designs.

J. Haish, as discussed earlier in Chapter 4, was one of the original DeKalb inventors with his successful "S" mild steel wire barb for wire strands; he had twelve patents over the years. In 1885, he patented (#332,393) a concave sheet metal strip that was crimped to hold two-point and four-point wire barbs (Figure 97).

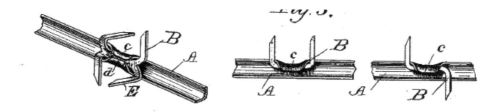

Figure 97. Haish 1885 (#332,393) "Concave Rail and Crimp Barb"

Many patentees promoted their designs in their patent applications. Haish acknowledged that, although more visible to animals, sheet metal barbs were not as satisfactory as steel barbs. Haish claimed that his crimping design using steel barbs was the most simplistic design for attaching wire barbs to sheet metal strips and provided a barb that was "recognized having many advantages, the defects applying entirely to the want of permanence and strength of a barb of this construction, and to the weakening of the metal by the cutting of the edges, as which are weakened with barbs are cut from the strip."

*Inserted barbs.* Many of the early inventors used tacks, nails, or staples as barbs and attached them by inserting them into the mild steel wire or sheet metal strip. Many of these attachment designs involved inserting sheet metal wire barbs into sheet metal strips. Clifton (1970) identified some two dozen sheet metal strip designs besides Kelly's design.

One of the earliest barbed fencing designs was the inserted design by Kelly (Figure 98).

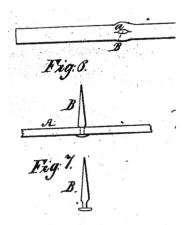

Figure 98. Kelly, M. 1868 (#84,062) "Tack Ribbon"

This attachment design by Kelly was an "Improvement in Metallic Fences" and in particular, an improvement in the manufacturing of his first design, the "Thorny Hedge" (#74,379) of 1868. He also designed perforated barbs (see discussion below).

*Perforated barbs.* Besides inserting barbs into strands and strips, some inventors perforated the barb so it could be attached to a strand. Initially, these perforated barbs were associated with single mild steel wire strands (e.g., Kelly's 1868 [#74,379] diamond-shaped sheet metal barbs for single- and double-wire strands) (Figure 99).

Figure 99. Kelly, M. 1868 (#74,379) "Thorny Common"

Other perforated designs included S. Gregg's 1879 (#221,300) two-point sheet metal barb on a two-strand mild steel wire (Figure 100). Circular and non-circular barb designs commonly used the perforated barb attachment.

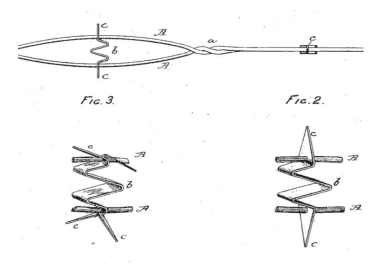

Figure 100. Gregg, S. 1879 (#221,300) "Drilled Sheet Metal Barb"

*Riveted or welded barbs.* Besides twisting, clipping, and other modes of attachment, inventors designed barbs that could be riveted or welded to the strand or strip. Clifton identified only twenty of 506 patents and patent variations using this method of attachment. One of the earliest welded designs was by T. D. Stetson of New York City for "Thorny-Wire Fences" (#192,468) in 1877 (Figure 101). His designs were concave-headed barbs or thorns that could be applied by hand or machine. Without specifically mentioning Kelly's 1868 design, he said his design was an improvement to the "Thorny-Wire Fences" design that was being manufactured and distributed at that time.

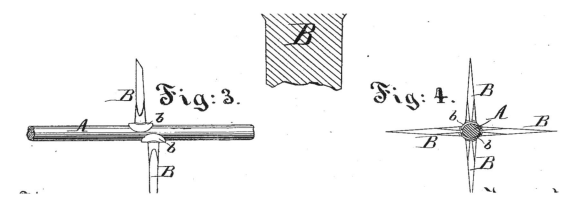

Figure 101. Stetson, T. D. 1877 (#192,468) Welded Pin Two Point"

The Stetson design is another example of a design that mimicked natural occurring thorns (see later discussion on unique barb designs).

J. C. Perry's patent of 1897 (#588,774) is an example of an inventor patenting the welding process for a particular kind of barb. It was classified as an "Improvement in Wire Fences." Specifically, Perry's objective was to permanently attach barbs to plain wire fences to economize the use of existing barbless wire fences. The design involved eight different kinds of two-point mild steel barbs that could be attached by "electric welding" to single-strand and two types of double-strand mild steel wire (Figure 102).

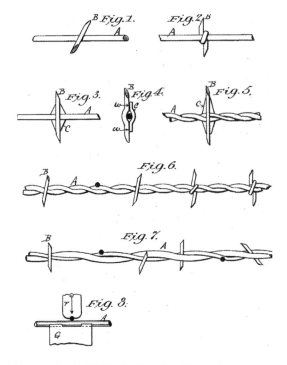

Figure 102. Perry, J. C. 1897 (#588,774) Welded Barbs (Pins, Staples, Plates)
on Single- and Double-Wire Strands Including Different Gauge Wire Strands

In 1875, Dobbs and Booth designed a staple barb that they subsequently modified by welding spurs to it (Figure 103).

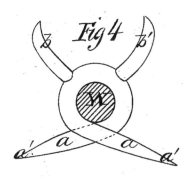

Figure 103. Example of Welded Barb - Dobbs, J. and Booth, F. 1875 (#171,104)
"Curved Point Horn Barb"

They had two patents in December 1875: (1) #171,104 and (2) #171,105. Although the #171,104 patent had a lower number, it was filed in October 1875, three month before the #171,105 patent that was filed in August 1875. The August design was a staple that could be added to barbless wire fences, creating a two-point barb that could be attached to plain wire fences. The #171,104 patent design was also a staple that could be attached to barbless fence wire, however, it had two welded spurs on the staple creating a four-point barb (see Figure 89104). This design was considered more effective in keeping cattle from resting their heads on the fence and breaking the fence down. Dobbs and Booth commented that resting the heads of horned cattle was common and resulted in breaking through post-and-rail fences or worm-rail fences. This design was classified as an "Improvement in Barbed-Wire Fences." The barbs could be used on plain wire fences (see Chapter 2 discussion of adaptation of plain wire fences to barbed fencing).

One of Haish's designs in 1874 (#147,634) involved riveting a two-point or four-point sheet metal barb to sheet metal strips or metal rails (Figure 104).

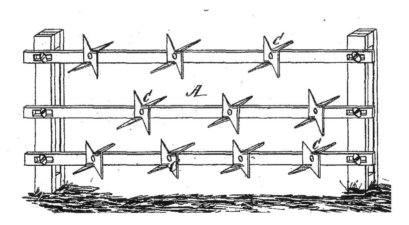

Figure 104. Haish, J. 1874 (#147,634) Flat Ribbon with Four-Point Sheet Metal Barb

*Extended and extruded barbs (integral barbs).* Patent designs for barbs that were part of the mild steel wire or sheet metal strips are integral barbs. There are two integral barb attachment designs: (1) extended barbs and (2) extruded barbs. They are only found with integrated barb sheet metal strips. Extended barbs were formed by cutting into the edge of the strip and forming sharp edges along the edge of the strip or in the middle of the strip and bending the sharp cut portion outward to form a barb. Clark's 1876 (#179,268) "Flat Rail" design is an example of an extended barb design (Figure 105).

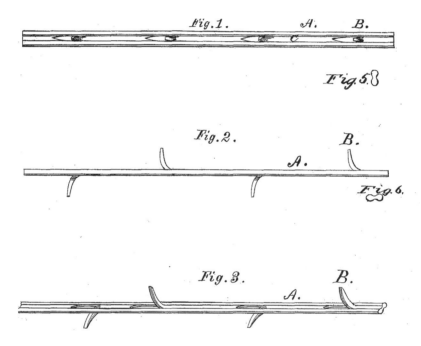

Figure 105. Clark, N. 1876 (#179,268) "Flat Rail"

The object of his invention was to form barbs from "flattened wire, with somewhat concave sides …deliver the wire to cutters… to cut barbs from the center… and turn them right or left in a curved form…" Figure 106 is an example of this extended barb design process by Bates in 1882 (#254,904).

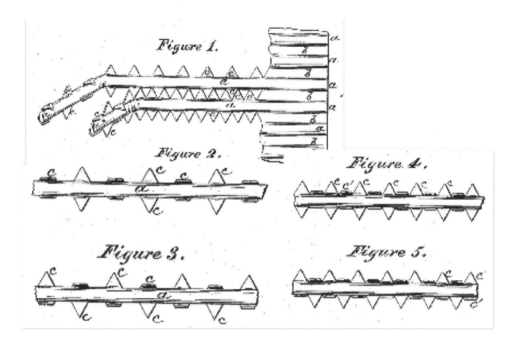

Figure 106. Bates, W. S. 1882 (#254,904) "Multi-Point Barb Strip"

Bates's patent was for a "Process of Producing Barbed Fencing Material," or more particularily, a new manufacturing processs for creating barbs on two sides of a sheet metal strip. The strip could be twisted so the barbs occurred on opposite sides of the strip.

Within the extended barb group, several distinct types of extended barbs have been identified by Clifton (1970), including:

- » Cut Edge
- » Double Saw Tooth
- » Knife Edge
- » Prong
- » Punch Out
- » Saw Tooth
- » Segmented Edge
- » Split Pane

The extruded barbs is a barb design which involved manufacturing the barb by "extruding" or shaping a piece of the sheet metal strip into a barb during the manufacturing of the strip. The idea was to integrate them in a sheet metal stip as extrusions of the strip itself. Only a few barb designs were patented (e.g., Allis 1883 [#272,933], Howell 1884 [#299,072], and Roop 1886 [#345,259]) (Figure 107) .

**Examples of Extruded Barb Designs**

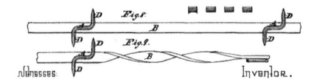

Allis's Rolled Rod and Strip 1883 (#272,933)

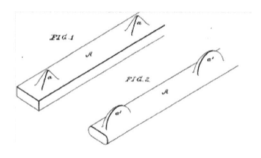

Howell's Pyramid and Round Knob Barbs 1884 (#299,072)

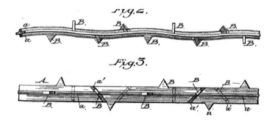

Roop's Fence Stripping with Spurs 1886 (#345,259)

Figure 107. Examples of Extruded Barb Designs

Allis's patent described the manufacturing process of his "Rolled Rod and Strip" design. Howell described his design as an "Improved Fence Rod." The rod could be twisted with the sharp edge and fin-like projections extending from the middle portion of the rod. Roops claimed his invention as an "Improvement in Barbed Fence Strips."

### Secondary Barb Designs

Besides appearance, other secondary design characteristics were found, including sharpness, spacing intervals on the strand or strip, and length of the barb. Some of these secondary designs were specifications described in the patent or were legal or illegal artifacts (see Chapter 4 on manufacturing).

*Sharpness of barbs.* The sharpness of the point of the barb found in barbed fencing also varies. Some of this sharpness or dullness is due to weathering over time. However, many barbs were purposely designed with different degrees of sharpness, some sharper and some blunter. Hagemeir (2010) identified more than half dozen variations of Baker's "Perfect Design" (#273,219), including "needle point", "notched-point", "blunt", "fish mouth" and "blunt-fish mouth" designs. Other examples of specifically designed sharp barbs include Greene's 1888 (#380,884) "Taper Barb" (Figure 108).

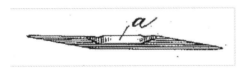 

Figure 108. Greene, M. 1888 (#380,884) "Taper Barb"

Greene discussed in his patent description that his design was more economical in wrapping around one of the wire strands, and said his design would hold the barb in place and be unyielding to pressure. His design focused on "Improvement in Wire-Barbs," not the barbed wire strand itself.

Haish's 1891 patent had three sharp-design barbs: (1) "Spear Point", (2) "Cleat", and (3) "Notched Spear Point" (Figure 109).

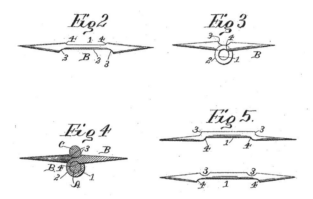

Figure 109. Haish, J. 1891 (#463,742) "Spear Point", "Cleat", and "Notched Spear Point Barbs"

His designs were also to improve wire barbs that were coiled between fence wires. The barbs were sharp and were designed not to rotate. These barbs were considered vicious or injurious type barbs (see Chapter 4).

When unacceptable levels of injury to livestock started to be observed, there were attempts to design barbs that were not as sharp, such as Haish's spear-point barb, by purposely making them blunt (e.g., Longstreet's 1902 [#711,574] balled-tipped barbs). Shuman's "Blunt Two-Point Barb" (#215,404) was designed to be obvious to cattle and yet be sharp enough that they would resist pushing through a fence. Figure 110 provides examples of the different sharpness designs found in barbed fencing:

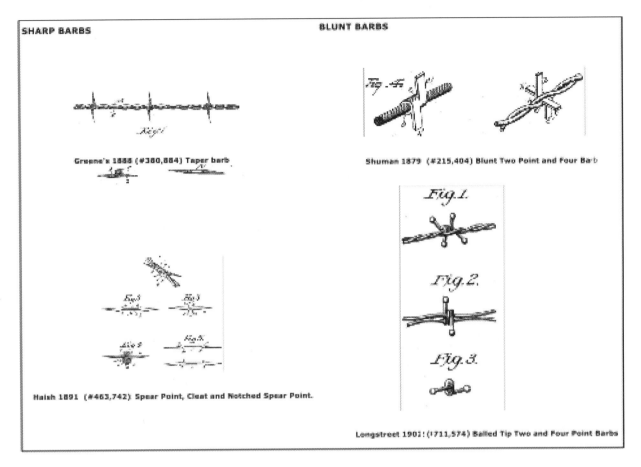

Figure 110. Examples of Different Barb Sharpness Designs

*Length of barbs.* There are also design variations in the lengths of the barbs. These design variations can also be intentional and unintentional manufacturing variations. In his 1868 patent (#74,379), Kelly specified that his "Thorny Barb" be "five-eight of inch the entire length" but could vary. The length of barbs was an early topic in agricultural journals. The 1880 *American Agriculturist*[72] discussed correspondence with two unnamed manufacturers regarding their readiness to provide barbs of any length or shortness and bluntness. The journal was addressing its opposition to the placement of long and sharp

---

72    Volume 39: 134.

barbs along travelled highways that humans might use, resulting in tearing clothes and skin. The editor was not in opposition to long and sharp types of barbs on interior fences. The editor indicated that in the East, the public would not accept long and sharp barbs along travelled highways. He indicated that according to manufacturers (in 1880), the long and sharp barbs were preferred in the West.

A review of my collection shows variable lengths of barbs for the same design. For example, I have a Kelly "Thorn Wire" with short thorns one inch in length and other pieces with 1 3/8 inch long thorns. A Dodge & Washburn "Two Wrap Round Barb" (1882, #252,746) has wire barbs that are 3/8 inch, 1/2 inch and 5/8 inch long .

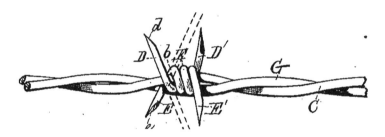

Figure 111. Dodge, T. H. and Washburn, C. G. 1882 (#252,746) "Two Wrap-Around Barb"

Variations are found in the spacing intervals of wire barbs along a strand or sheet metal strip. Also in my collection are wires of the same patent with different spacing in the barbs. One Dodge & Washburn (see above) "Two Wrap Round Barb" wire sample has regular spacing of 2 ½ inches between barbs along the wire stand. I also have six samples with different spacing variations of the same Dodge & Washburn patent design (#252,746) of 2 ½", 3", 3 ¼", 5 ½", 6", and 7 ½" spacing between barbs. These wires are from two different collecting locations.

The spacing of wire and sheet metal barbs at various distances along a strand or strip could be intentional (i.e., part of the patent design or part of manufacturing specification). For example, Haish in his 1874 patent (#147,634) for wooden rails did specify that the metal prongs (barbs) attached to the rail be six inches to twelve inches apart. Some manufacturers sold wire offering different spacing intervals of the barbs. In the 1880 *American Agriculturist,*[73] an advertisement by the Iowa Barb Fence Company Limited for "Four Point Barb Steel Wire Fencing" stated that barb wire six inches apart was available and not three-and-a-half inches apart as shown in the advertisement. An 1882 brochure for wires offered by the California Wire Work described "The Scutt Patent"[74] with sheet metal barbs six inches apart. The 1889 brochure by the Dominion Barb-Wire Co. of Montreal, Canada, stated that it was the sole manufacturer of Lyman Steel Fencing. In its brochure, it listed the following designs: Lyman two- and four-point steel barb fencing. The two-strand twisted barbed wire was described as four-point wire barb available in two designs or sizes – barbs six inches apart and recommended "for use on pastures and railway fences to turn horses, cattle etc." and four inches apart for use with "sheep, hogs and small stock." The barbs appeared to be Ross's four-point design (1879, #216,294). They also offered Glidden's two-point barb (under a special arrangement with The Washburn & Moen Mfg. Co.). It came in two designs or sizes: (1) "G" with barbs five inches apart and (2) "H" or "thickset" with barbs two-and-a-half inches apart. In their 1882 catalogue, Washburn and Moen Co. provided pictures of normal and thickset Glidden two-point two-strand wires (Figure 112). Thickset or short spacing barbs were manufactured for smaller animals like hogs and sheep. Regular spacing of barbs were manufactured for larger animals like cattle.

---

73    Volume 39: 134.
74    Assumed to be Scutt 1876 (#180,656).

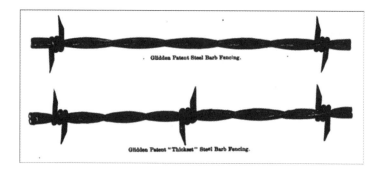

Figure 112. Ad from Washburn and Moen Co. 1882 Catalogue Showing Regular and Thickset Varieties of Glidden Two Point

The 1922 catalogue of the American Steel & Wire Company (formerly Washburn & Moen Co.) advertised two spacing choices for Baker Perfect wire, Waukegan, American Glidden, and Lyman four-point wires: (1) "Thickset or Hog" wire with barbs three inches apart and (2) "Regular or Cattle" wire with barbs six inches apart.

Variations in barb spacing could also unintentionally result from lack of quality control in manufacturing or in "moonshine" manufacturing variations. Variation in spacing was likely quite common with barbs that were designed to be hand applied. Wilkes, in his 1879 staple patent (#216,637), indicated that the attachment of his barbs "could be at any desired intervals." For most patents, the spacing interval of barbs was not specified in the patent description. In an 1878 history of Marshall County, Iowa, an example of how manufacturing variations in spacing could occur from lack of quality control was provided. The article discussed a new barbed wire manufacturing plant, The Iowa Steel Barb Co., that initially used hand labor to attach the Burnell patent (#192,225, a four-point double-strand wire) and was waiting for an automatic machine that Burnell had invented that would attach barbs, cut off the wire, and spool the wire (Western Historical Co. 1878). In addition, spacing variations likely resulted from barbs that were invented to be attached by hand (see Chapter 2 discussion on Kennedy barbs). Hand tools were used and in all likelihood, there was great variation in the spaces when barbs were attached.

Apparently, several states in the 1890s[75] actually stipulated how many barbs should be found in a barbed fence. Iowa law defined barbed fencing as strands with no less than forty barbs to the rod (16.5'). Similar definition was found for Wisconsin and Minnesota of forty barbs/rod of strand length. No information was provided on why the numbers of barbs were stipulated. It might be coincidental that these upper-Midwest states with similar regulations adjoin each other. There may have been similar political interest in stipulating the number of barbs on barbed fencing.

### Unique Barb Designs

The preceding discussion on the appearance of barbs provides numerous examples of barb designs that can be grouped by appearance. There are a few designs that don't fit into these broad appearance categories and are unique in appearance themselves. An early example of a star-shaped barb is a design by Brown and Tubbs from Dunlap, Iowa, in 1875 (#170,518); their design was comprised of a four-point barb made of two interlocking iron isoscoles triangles (Figure 113).

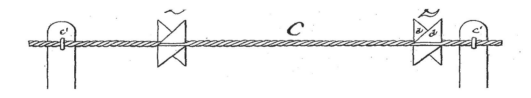

Figure 113. Brown, W. L. and Tubbs, L. G. 1875 (#170,518) "Joined Triangles"

---

75    *American Agriculturist* 49 (1890): 87.

Other inventors used refuse metal for making barbs. Milligan (1882, #268,264) invented a novel way of using waste sheet metal scraps (refuse metal) from spoon making into both sheet metal strips and barbs (Figure 114).

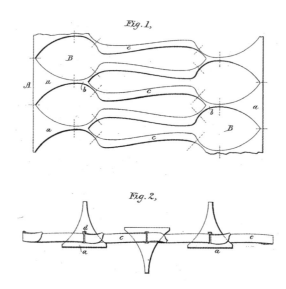

Figure 114. Milligan, J. C. 1882 (#268,264) "Scrap Metal Fencing Front Clinch"

Where most barb designs involved common wire point designs, some inventors attempted to mimic nature in their barb designs (i.e., thorns and other thorny vegetation) (Figure 115).

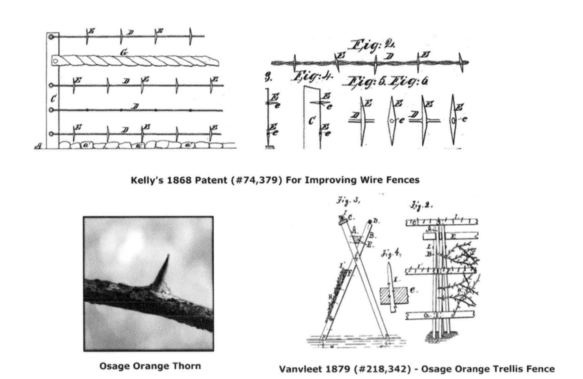

**Kelly's 1868 Patent (#74,379) For Improving Wire Fences**

**Osage Orange Thorn**

**Vanvleet 1879 (#218,342) - Osage Orange Trellis Fence**

Figure 115. Thorny Hedge-Like Patent Designs

This approach is not surprising since thorny hedges[76] were used to control livestock, especially in the Midwest in the 1850s and 1860s (Humphries 1916; Hornbeck 2007). Thorny hedges were commonly planted as fences to control cattle (McCallum and McCallum 1985).[77] [78] [79] The earliest and most successful thorny hedge mimic was Kelly's barb design (see Figure 115), which predated the DeKalb inventions by six years. This patent was unique in attempting to design a barbed wire that mimicked the common vegetative thorny hedge fences using Osage Orange[80] in common use in the Midwest (see Figure 115). The barb was a thorn-shaped two-point elongated diamond-shaped sheet metal barb. Called "Thorny Fence" or "Thorn Wires" by Kelly, it was first patented for a double-wire-strand fence. It was classified by USPTO as an "Improvement in Fences." Some additional comments Kelly made in his patent description included the recommendation of adding a rope or "twisted hay" saturated with tar to make the fence smell more recognizable at night to cattle. He suggested that thorns could be attached to rope and a second wire could be used to hold thorns in place. This barbed wire was manufactured by several successive

[76]    Thorny hedge was also known as Osage Orange (*Macular pomifera*). In 1871 a special report on immigration by Edward Young, chief of the Bureau of Statistics, recommended "thorny hedges," in particular Osage Orange, as the best least expensive and most effective for fencing. (House documents, otherwise publ. as Executive documents: 13th congress, 2nd session-49th congress, 1st session)

[77]    *Burke's Texas Almanac* 143; *Democratic Leader* (Cheyenne, Wyo.), 6 March 1884; Osgood, E. S. "The Cattleman in the Agricultural History of the Northwest." *Agricultural History* 3 (July 1929): 129; "Kansas Had Seven Times More Hedge than Wire Fence in 1878." Kansas State Board of Agriculture, Biennial Report 1 (1877-78):526-527. http://xroads.virginia.edu/~UG99/cook/barb2.html

[78]    The 1893 *American Agriculturist* 52: 163 discussed the limitation of hedges, including Osage Orange. It stated that it was limited in states where temperatures fell below zero, required pruning, and took up more space as a result of barbed wire taking its place.

[79]    The idea of the thorny hedge fence was introduced to the United States by England (Humphries 1916).

[80]    http://www.stateoftheozarks.net/NaturalHeritage/Trees%20%26%20Shrubs/Osage-orange.html

companies and had commercial success throughout the antique barbed fencing era. Peacock (1879, #215,719) was issued a patent for a machine to manufacture "Thorny Fence." Kelly's "Thorn Fence" can be found today.

Also attempting to capitalize on thorny hedges was W. B. Vanvleet in 1879, who was issued a patent (#218,342) for a fence with a trellis-like structure where one could attach Osage Orange "trimmings" (see Figure 115). He claimed it was an "Improvement in Fences."

In 1893, Phillip patented a thistle-like design, "Thistle Burr" (Figure 116), which was classified as an "Improvement in Barb-Fences." It was a cast metal multipoint design that had channels to secure to the wire strands. It was designed to be a barb that was more visible and less harmful to cattle.

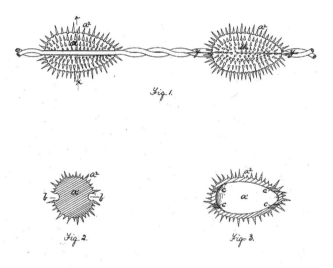

Figure 116. Phillip, O. D. 1882 (#280,857) "Solid Cocklebur"

In 1893, Delff patented a leaf-like design (Figure 117). He claimed his design was less injurious to cattle because it was more visible than other barbed wire fences. His design was classified as an "Improvement in Barb-Fences." This type of large barb design and other similar designs (e.g., plate designs discussed earlier) were considered more visible to cattle and considered a way to reduce injury (see Chapter 4 on changes in designs over time).

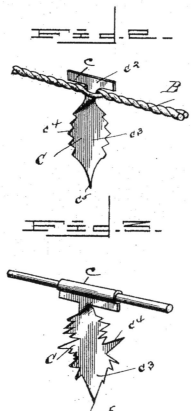

Figure 117. Delff, A. 1893 (#490,187) "Tattered Leaf Single Strand"

One unique barb and strand design is a vegetative mimic by Hallner in 1878 (#199,538), which is an extended barb design discussed later under "Unique Strand Designs. It is a combination mild steel wire and sheet metal strip cover with a double row of projecting barbs twisted around an ordinary wire (Figure 118). Called "Greenbrier," the design appears to be adapted from greenbrier vines *(Smilax spp)*, a woody vine or shrub with thorns commonly found in the United States.

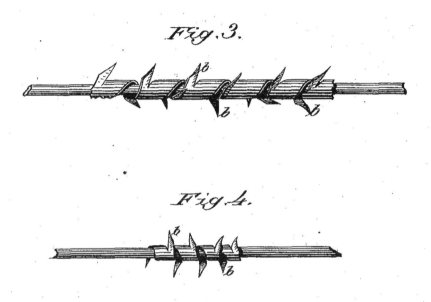

Figure 118. Hallner, J. 1878 (#181,433) "Single-Cut Greenbrier"

## Summary of Barb Designs

As discussed in the preceding section, hundreds of different barb designs were invented. The following figure provides a depiction of the various barb design features found in antique barbed fencing, including primary and secondary features (Figure 119).

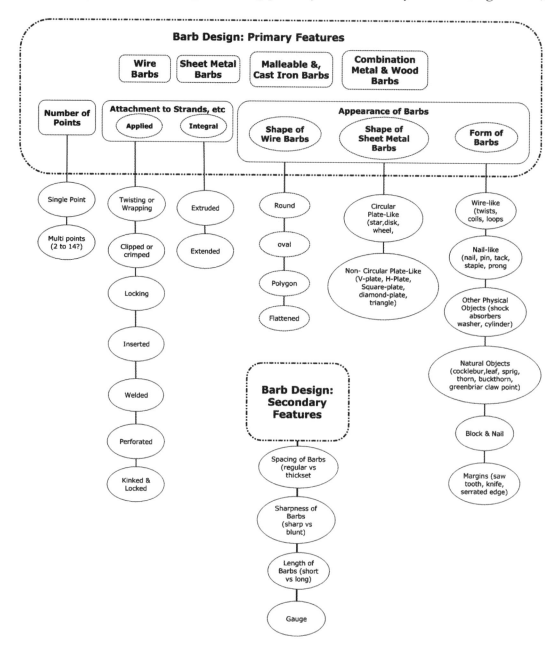

Figure 119. Primary and Secondary Barb Design Features

In reviewing over 350 patent descriptions for barbed fencing, the overall rationale for designing a certain type of barb with a certain type of wire strand or sheet metal strip was to better solve the problem of containing livestock from breaking fences. All designs were considered an improvement over other designs. Soon after the early designs and patents, the common purposes stated for the barb designs changed in emphasis to reducing injury caused by early barbed fencing designs and to invent new designs that were less expensive and easier to maintain than previous designs or patents. Some sheet metal barb and strip designs claimed to be more visible to livestock. Mild steel wire barbs are primarily associated with wire strands, but sheet metal barb, cast iron barb, and a few wood/metal combination barb designs are also found. Sheet metal barb designs are primarily associated with sheet metal strips. Some mild steel wire barb designs are found with sheet metal strips. Metal rods, bars, and rails only have integral barbs or extended and extruded barbs. Wooden rails have both applied mild steel wire barbs and sheet metal barbs. The following table summarizes the different materials associated with barb designs along with the different horizontal components, types of attachments, appearance, and number of barb points. The relative frequency of one type of characteristic over another is shown (Table 12).

Table 12. Association of Different Barb Material Properties with Different Horizontal Components, Types of Attachments, Barb Appearance, and Number of Barb Points

| Barb Appearance (Materials) | Types of Attachments | | Number of Points on Barb |
| --- | --- | --- | --- |
| | General Attachments | Specific Attachment Types | |
| Wire-like > Nail-like, Circular Plate, Non-Circular; Plate, Looped, Formed Edges (Mild Steel, Sheet Metal, Cast Iron) | Applied Barbs > Integral Barbs | Twist, Wrap, Coil; Locked; Clip or Crimped; Extended; Extruded | Single to Multiple |
| Circular Plate, Non-Circular; Plate, > Wire-like, Formed Edges > Nail-like (Sheet Metal, Mild Steel) | Applied > Integral | Extended, Inserted, Clip & Crimped, Twist & Coil, Locked, Riveted | Single to Multiple |
| Formed Edges (Sheet Metal, Mild Steel) | Integral | Extended, Extruded | Multiple |
| Nail-like, Non-Circular Plate (Wood and Metal) | Applied | Inserted, Clip or Crimped | Single to Multiple |

Mild steel materials were the most commonly used material by inventors followed by sheet metal and cast iron materials. Most antique barbs were applied barb.

## Warning Devices, Designs, and Patterns

The second group of attachments to antique barbed fencing is "warning devices." Their purpose was to make barbed fencing more visible to livestock and humans. They were called "barbed wire signals", "indicators", "warning plates", and "cattle protectors." The warning devices could be hung on barbed fencing. According to Clifton (1970), they were primarily barbless, made of paper, wood, and metal, and had various shape designs. He grouped these warning devices into five different designs: (1) plates, (2) strips, (3) blocks, (4) balls, and (5) tags. These devices could be attached at the factory or attached later as the fence was being erected. Clifton identified more than a dozen different patents and variations. Hagemeier (2010, 2012) identified some forty patents and variations. Some obvious barb designs were designed to act as warning devices (Figure 120).

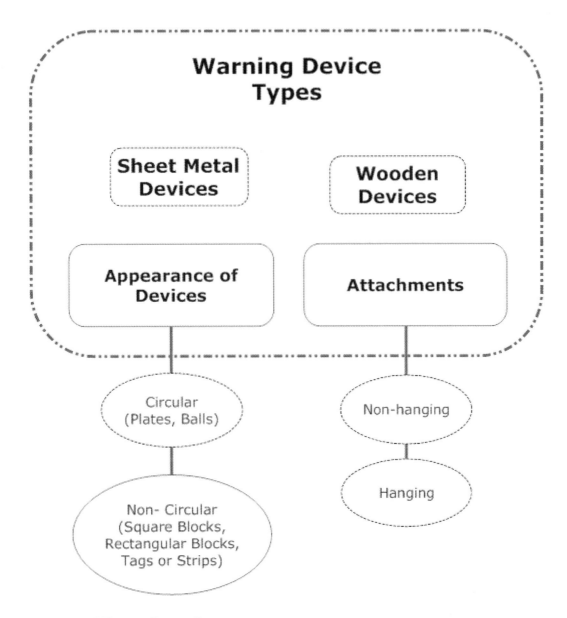

Figure 120. Warning Device Designs

There are two types of warning device attachment designs: (1) hanging attachments which were hung to a wire strand or sheet metal strip, allowing it to move and (2) non-hanging or fixed attachments that were attached to two or more wire strands. None of these warning devices were designed for sheet metal strips since it was presumed these strips were in themselves visible to cattle. The patenting of warning devices came as a delayed reaction to the injurious nature of the early barbs with these designs of the mid-1870s (see Chapter 4) with the peak of warning device patents occurring in the mid-1880s. By the 1890, at least five states – Florida, Idaho, Michigan, West Virginia, and Texas, - passed fence laws stipulating the requirement of warning type devices in the form of boards or metal strips placed above the top strand. Florida in 1885 required metal or "wood tablets" on the top strand of barbed fences. Idaho stipulated that a barbed wire fence shall consist of not less than two barbed or three plain wires with a board or rail on that top of these fences. Michigan stipulated the use of barbed wire and boards for barbed fences and a six inch board for strand barbed wire fences. West Virginia required that for five strand fences two-inch square blocks be placed no more than two feet apart on a fourth strand or one could use a "board" or "plank" as the fourth strand. Texas required for three strands of barbed wire a four-inch board not less than four inch wide and a half-an-inch thick be hung on the top wire or a board or rail on a two-strand fence. The design period for warning devices was relatively short compared to the barbed wire and strip fencing period lasting occurring mostly in the 1880s (Figure 121).

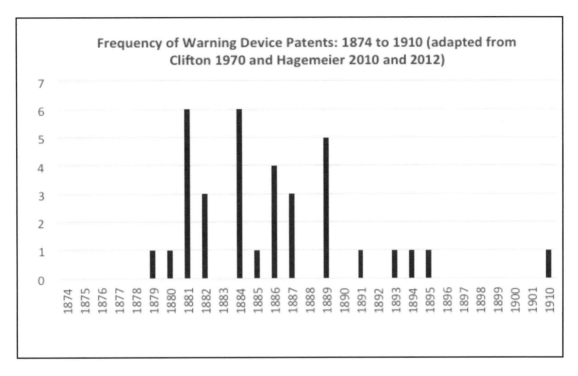

Figure 121. The Number of Warning Device Patents Issued Per Year: 1874 to 1910

The appearance of the warning devices could be circular in the form of balls or plates or non-circular in the form of square or rectangular blocks or tag or strip shapes. The following are examples of these warning devices. Note how the inventors addressed the injury issue.

Scutt's 1880 (#224,482) design was classified as a "Warning-Plate for Barbed-Wire Fences" (Figure 122). The plates could be made of wood or metal with barbs. He referred to his design as a "cattle protector." Two unique features he described were that: (1) the plates could be painted in colors to make them "more prominent" and (2) "paper, pasteboard" could be affixed to the plates to make them an "excellent form of advertising."

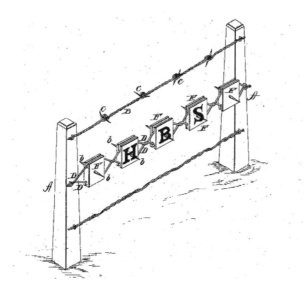

Figure 122. Scutt, H. B. 1880 (#224,482) "Warning Plate"

In 1882, Smith patented a design using two-point wire barbs to attach the wooden warning devices ("tags") to the horizontal wire (Figure 123). He described the invention relating to a class of fences to which swinging tags were attached to "indicate to the stock the location of the fence and thus prevent the stock from accidentally running into the barbs." His design was classified as an "Improvement in Wire Fences."

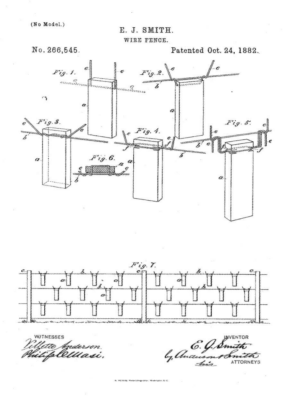

Figure 123. Smith, E. J. 1882 (#266,545) "Hanging Warning Blocks"

J. J. LaFleur (#249,777) used different forms of sheet metal plates as warning devices (Figure 124) that could be hung on not only the top strand but other strands. He recommended that the warning devices be hung on the top strand for cattle and horses.

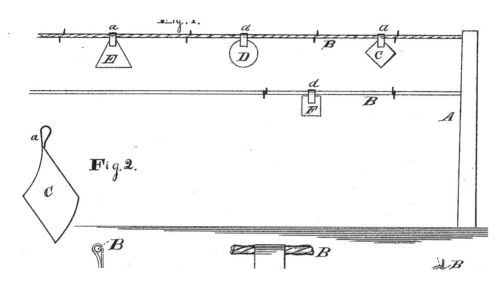

Figure 124. LaFleur, J. 1881 (#249,777) "Clip Plate"

The purpose of his design was to make cheap, convenient, and conspicuous means for marking barbed wire fences. LaFleur's design was classified as an "Improvement in Tags for Barbed-Wire Fences."

In 1910, MacIntosh (#970,524) used a thin longitudinal fabric such as thin sheet metal attached to upper wire strands of a fence (Figure 125). It was the last warning device patented in the antique barbed fencing era.

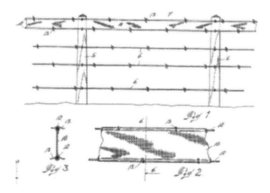

Figure 125. MacIntosh, W. 1910 (#970,524) "Top-Member Strip"

MacIntosh claimed the top row of wire with the warning device could have rough barbs on it since the device would make the fence conspicuous. The purpose of the device was to prevent injury to animals coming in contact with harsh wires. The patent was classified as "Visible Warning Attachments for Barbed-Wire Fences."

An exception to the invention of barbless warning devices is S. Forrester (1882, #298,193), who was issued a patent for a warning device with barbs with the objective to design a combination warning plate and barb that not only provided warning but also acted as a barb for cattle not paying attention (Figure 126).

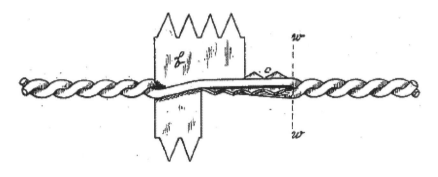

Figure 126. Forrester, S. 1882 (#298,193) "Vertical Cut Sawtooth Plate"

## HORIZONTAL COMPONENT DESIGNS AND PATTERNS

The second most obvious component of barbed fencing is the wires of the horizontal component. As discussed earlier, the term wire is a misnomer because not all the horizontal components are wire or wire-like. Based on the type of materials used in the horizontal components, there are four groups of horizontal components: (1) wire strands, (2) sheet metal strips, (3) bars and rods, and (4) rails (Figure 127).

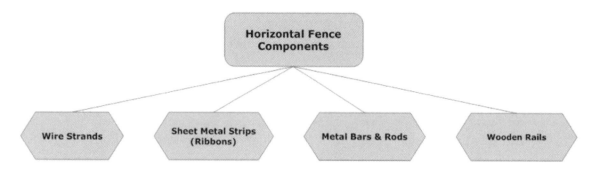

Figure 127. Horizontal Components of Metal Barbed Fencing

### Mild Steel Wire Strand Designs: Configure and Appearance

Wire strand designs can be broken down into several common designs based on their configuration or arrangement, appearance of their form and shape, and other more specific wire design features (Figure 128). There are three types of wire strand configurations: (1) continuous-wire strands, (2) linked strands, and (3) interlaced-wire strands or woven-wire strands. The appearance of the wire strand designs (i.e., the shapes and forms) can vary considerably. Many of the variations in the shape of the wire had the functional purpose of securing the barb, especially in single-wire strands.

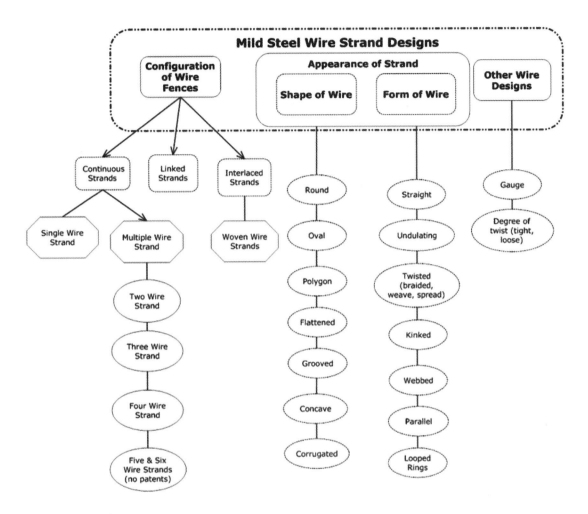

Figure 128. Basic Barbed Wire Strand Designs

Variations in wire strands are also found in whether the wires of the strand were twisted or not twisted, the tightness of the twist (i.e., loose or tight), and the direction of the twist (i.e., right twist [wire strands or barbs twisted in a clockwise direction] or left twist [wire strands or barbs twisted in a counter-clockwise direction]).

Part of a patent by N. Morford of Waynesville, Illinois (#9427,321), in 1909 was a tool for reversible twisting fence wires. It was classified as an "Improvement in Wire Twisters." Morford said that his design could be used for applying stays to line wire of fence, for spacing wire, and for applying tie wires to posts.

Mild steel wire strand designs could be barbless, reflecting their origin in plain wire strands invented before the 1850s (see Chapter 2), or barbed wire strands. As discussed earlier, plain wire strands were the forerunner of barbed wire. Hagemeier (2010, 2012) identified over ninety barbless wire strand patents and variations that were invented during the barbed fence period. A look at these designs indicates the designs were the result of both patents and likely manufacturing variations of plain fence wire. Some inventors patented designs of barbless wire that were strictly ornamental. Other patented designs that had the purpose of looking like barbed wire to livestock with twists in the wire resulting in barbless projections (i.e., loops) that looked like barbs to livestock (e.g., Reynolds [1883, #287,391]) (Figure 129).

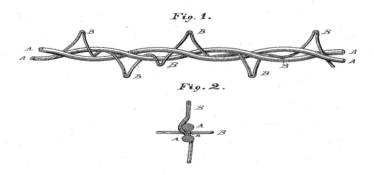

Figure 129. Reynolds, W. R. 1883 (#287,391) "Three-Strand Web"

Reynolds's design was classified as an "Ornamental Fence-Wire." It was designed as an attractive alternative to wire fences but with the appearance of barbed wire. Other inventors (e.g., Grosvenor in 1891 [#453, 272]) patented ornamental designs that were claimed to be as "effective as ordinary barb-wire in retaining stock without the disadvantages attending the use of ordinary barb-wire" (Figure 130).

Figure 130. Grosvenor, G. H. 1891 (#453,272) "Loop and Bend"

Another example of the use of ornamental wires with barbed implications was by Ingraham in 1892 (#469,062), who patented an ornamental barbless strand design on which barbs could be attached (Figure 131).

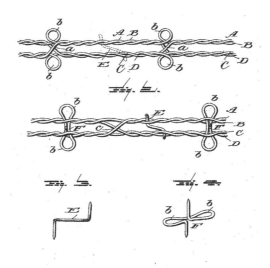

Figure 131. Ingraham, J. J. 1892 (#469,062) "Barbed Looped Parallel Ornamental"

**Configuration of Wire Strands**

There are three basic types of wire strand arrangements or configurations found in antique barbed fencing (Figure 132).

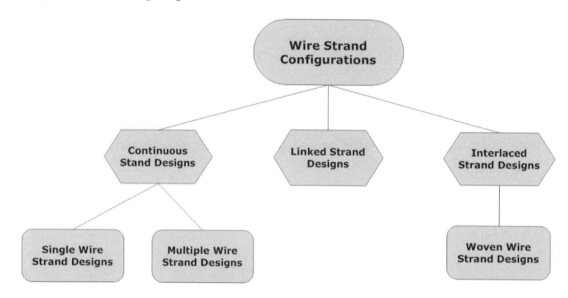

Figure 132. Wire Strand Configurations

The first type of wire stand configuration is continuous strand designs with the individual strands stretched between posts. The steel wire strands can be made up of one to six wires twisted together with attached barbs. The second configuration is a linked strand design where single- or double-wire strands are linked together to form a chain and are then connected to a post. The third type of configuration is the interlaced stand design where horizontal and vertical sections of mild steel wire strands are interconnected and the whole system is connected to fence posts. The interconnected wires often form a barb with barbs at the top and/or bottom of the wire strands. This configuration design is referred to in the patent literature as woven fences or fabric fences. Clifton (1970) and Hagemeier (2010) referred to these woven fence designs as mesh and interlaced fences.

*Continuous strands designs.* Most barb fencing designs are continuous-wire-strand designs. The patent designs for a continuous strand can range from one to four wires in a strand (Figure 133).

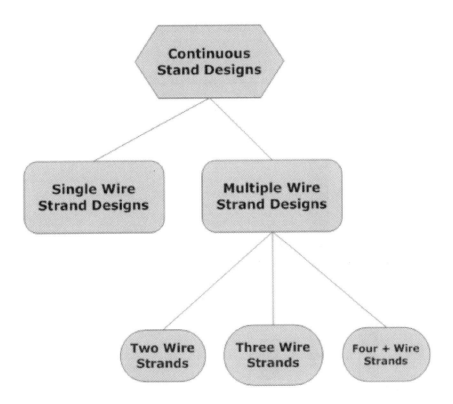

Figure 133. Continuous-Wire Strand Designs

Multiple-wire-strand patents and patent variations (two to six wires) are composed of mostly twisted mild steel wire, although some parallel wire strand designs occur. Inventors, manufacturers, and other fabricators more often used single- and double-wire strands for attaching their barbs than other numbers of wires in a mild steel strand (eighty-eight percent of the continuous barbed strand designs) (Figure 134). The greatest numbers of wire strand designs (771/1180 or sixty-five percent) are with two-wire strand designs followed by single-wire systems (twenty-three percent). The two-wire strand design was recognized as the most effective way to secure barbs in place.[81] Although there were six-wire strand design variations (also called "cables"), only the two-strand wire design was successful based on the number of patents and patent variations and the fact that this is the preferred design manufactured today for modern livestock fencing.

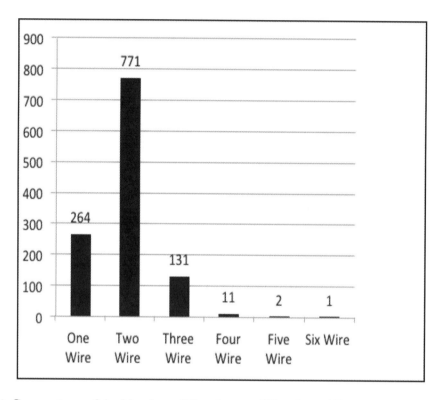

Figure 134. Comparison of the Number of Continuous-Wire Strand Patents and Patent Variations (Based on Hagemeier 2010, 2012) (n=1,180)

---

81      See earlier discussion on Glidden's 1874 patent (#157,124).

Single-wire strands. Over 250 variations in single strand systems have been identified (Hagemeier 2010, 2012). Originally, wire fencing was designed as single-barbless-wire strand (i.e., plain wire) (see Chapter 2 discussion on plain wire fences as the forerunner of barbed wire). The first barbed wire fence designs were also single-wire strands classified by USPTO as "Improvements of Plain Wire Fences." In June 1867, L. B. Smith of Kent, Ohio, patented (#66,182) the first single-strand wire (Figure 135).

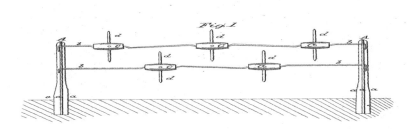

Figure 135. Smith, L. B. 1867 (#66,182) "Wood Spool Four Point"

One month later, W. D. Hunt of New York City was issued the first patent (#67,117) for a single continuous-wire strand design comprised of sheet metal spur wheels on single-wire strand[82] (Figure 136).

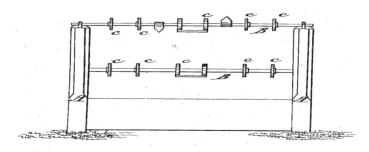

Figure 136. Hunt, W. D. 1867 (#67,117) "Spur Wheel"

---

82    His patent was actually for a complete barbed fence with cast iron posts and two single-wire strands.

The first commercially successful design was for a continuous single-wire strand; this was designed by M. Kelly from New York City in February 1868 (#74,379) (Figure 137).

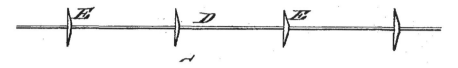

Figure 137. Kelly, M. 1868 (#74,379) "Thorny Single Strand"

Kelly stated that the design imparted the character "approximating a thorn hedge" and was "… produced as a thorny fence." He called his barbs "thorns" attached to single[83] "galvanized iron wires." The barb was manufactured by the Thorn Wire Hedge Co. and later by Washburn & Moen Co. According to McCallum and McCallum (1985), although his design had good qualities, the spurs were rigid and caused injury to cattle.

The major barbed fencing limitation in early designs was that in the single round-wire-strand designs, the barbs tended to slide together along the wire and bunch up. This limitation was addressed within a very short time by designs that varied the shapes of the round wire (e.g., Glidden's 1876 [#181,433] "Twisted Oval") (Figure 138). (See later discussion on shape of wires of strands).

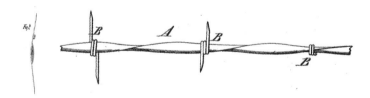

Figure 138. Glidden, J. F. 1876 (#181,433) "Twisted Oval"

---

83    Kelly also described a two-wire-strand version (see two-wire-strand discussion).

Kelly recognized this serious limitation and attempted to fix it with his 1868 patent (#84,062), where he proposed to piece holes by hand or machinery in a flattened wire and inserting his "thorny" barbs. He recommended that the barbs be placed six inches apart on single-wire strands and proposed to produce twelve-, fifteen-, and twenty-foot lengths.

In spite of the limitation of single-wire-strand designs, a large number of single-wire-strand patents were applied for and issued at the beginning of the antique barbed fencing period in the late 1870s, with inventors attempting to invent different types of barbs for attaching to existing plain single-wire fences (see earlier discussion on barbs). The last single-strand design in the antique barbed fencing period was in 1909 by V. Hoxie (#943,413). It was a single undulating preferably non-round wire strand with small knots to hold a two-point barb in place (Figure 139).

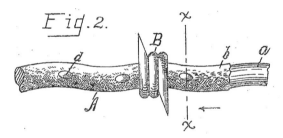

Figure 139. Hoxie, V. 1909 (#943,413) "Corrugated Flattened Knot Strand"

The purpose of his design was to prevent "… rotary and longitudinal movement of the barbs on the wire." His patent was also unique in describing the formation of the knobs or "protuberant portions or lugs." They were formed from compressing a galvanizing coat applied to the wire. He stipulated that the galvanizing coat should be "… from 6/1000 to 10/1000 of an inch in thickness and then compressing it approximately one-half…" to make sufficient prominence to stay a longitudinal movement of wires.

*Multiple wire strands.* Besides altering the shape of the wire, inventors almost immediately designed barbed wire fences with two or more wires in a strand. The purpose of these multi-strand designs varied from better securing the barbs to the strand to increased strength and increased visibility of the strand. Up to six wire strand variations have been identified. However, patents have only been identified for strands with two-, three-, and four-wire strands (Hagemeier 2010, 2012).

*Two-wire strands.* As stated above, two-wire strands are the most common multi-wire-strand design compared to other multi-wire-strand designs (see Figure 135). Hagemeier (2010, 2012) has identified more than 750 patents and variations. The two-wire-strand design was the earliest multiple-wire-strand design patented. The two-wire-strand design was the earliest multiple-wire-strand design patented. M. Kelly in 1868 patented the first two-wire strand (#74,379). However, his patent was subject to ligation by J. Glidden and Washburn & Moen Co. who succeeded in arguing that Glidden's 1874 two wire strand patent (#157,124) was the primary design (McCallum and McCallum, 1985). A few of the early two-wire strands designs were referred to as cable (e.g., Armstrong [1876, #176,262]). Today, the two-wire-strand design is the primary modern barbed wire design manufactured. Most of the different patent designs and variations for antique two-wire barbed strand designs are differences in the barb designs such as the types of barbs, their appearance, and means of attachment.

The first two-wire-strand design patents occurred a year after Smith and Hunt's single-wire-strand designs by M. Kelly from New York City in February 1868 (#74,379) (Figure 140). This patent also included a single-wire-strand design with a thorny barb. His two-strand design was part of this single-wire-strand design as an alternative to the single-wire-strand design and involved adding an additional wire to his single-wire-strand design to provide "additional strength" and "regularity in the distribution of the points (barbs) in different directions."[84]

Figure 140. Kelly 1868 (#74,379) "Thorny Two-Strand System"

The next two wire designs were by J. Haish in January 1874 (Figure 142) and J. Glidden in May 1874 (Figure 142).

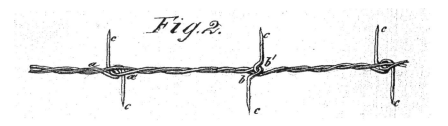

Figure 141. Haish, J. 1874 (#146,671) "Two-Strand System"

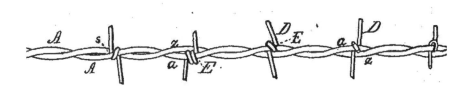

Figure 142. Glidden, J. 1874 (#157,124) "The Winner"

---

[84] If he had more specifically mentioned in his patent description that the two wires held the barb in place like Glidden, he might have been recognized by the Supreme Court as the primary inventor of barbed wire.

Glidden's (#157,124) twisted two-wire-strand patent design was important not only from a commercial success point of view, but from a legal point of view by the Supreme Court in 1892 as the primary barbed wire patent. The Supreme Court awarded Glidden as the originator of the idea for two-wire-strand barbed wire because he specifically stated in his patent description that the purpose of twisting two wires together was to hold barbs in place. His patent expired in the 1890s. This design and numerous variations are still manufactured today.

Haish's design, although issued a few months earlier than Glidden's, did not explicitly state that the purpose of two wires was to hold the barb in place (nor did Kelly's 1868 patent). He lost in a long litigation battle against Glidden that went to the Supreme Court. Glidden assigned his patent to Washburn and Moen Co. in 1876. They also acquired other Glidden patents, including Kelly's and Kennedy's patents (McCallum and McCallum 1985).

Nearly all two-wire-strand designs involved some form of the twisted two-wire design. One variation to the twisted-wire design was a design for two parallel wires held in place by a longer barb. In 1882, A. Ellwood, brother of Isaac, was issued a patent (#253,022) for a two-parallel wire three-quarters-of-an-inch apart with a two-point spread barb securing the parallel wires (Figure 143) as an "Improvement in Barbed Fences-Wire Devices." His patent showed two ways of wrapping the barbs around the parallel wires. He also patented a three-wire-strand parallel design. He claimed that his designs were both less injurious to livestock, in particular horses and colts from lacerations caused by sticking their heads between the wires, and were more visible.

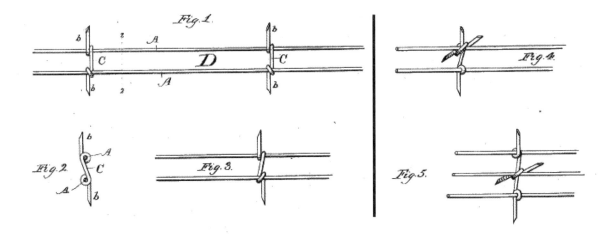

Figure 143. Ellwood, A. 1882 (#252,022) "Parallel Strand with Twist Wrap Barb"

Another double-parallel-wire design was by P. Miles of Brooklyn, New York, in 1883 (#277,917) for two parallel wires "braced" by a short "oblique" wire with "points" which had the purpose to provide increased strength and performance against "vertical strain" (Figure 144).

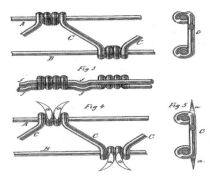

Figure 144. Miles, P. 1883 (#277,917) "Parallel and Claw Points"

A third parallel design was an early patent that came just as the barb-fencing era was getting under way and reflecting the growing objection to the injurious nature of barbed wire. This patent was in 1878 by W. Frye (#204,312). His design was a barbed fence (almost looking like a picket fence) that could be used in a field or barnyard and was made visible by inserting "palings" between the two steel-wire strands. Two-point wire barbs were attached to the stands between slats or palings (Figure 145). Frye said the "palings" could be painted as an "effectual aid in making the fence visible. This also is of great consequence, since now it has come to be a common objection to simple barb on a wire cable that, by reason of the difficulty in observing the same, oftentimes cattle are seriously injured by coming suddenly and violently in contact with it." It appeared more as an ornamental fence than an ordinary livestock fence. It was classified as an "Improvement in Wire Fences."

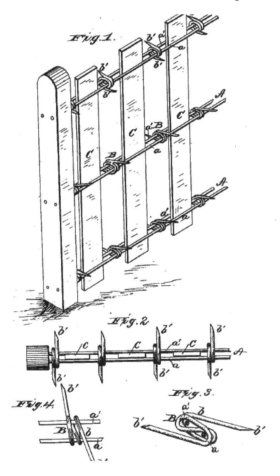

Figure 145. Frye, W. H. 1878 (#204,312) "Frye Parallel Strands"

Another variation to the two twisted-wire-strand design was D. Smith's patent in 1897, which was for a series of two-strand fence wire with loops. One of his designs had two-point barbs between the loops (Figure 146). The purpose of his design was for visibility and elasticity of fences.

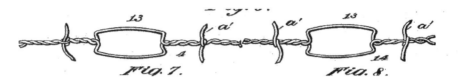

Figure 146. Smith, D. C. 1897 (#578,032) "Loops and Two-Point Barb"

Another variation of the two-wire-strand design is the loop-spreader design. This was exemplified by Decker (1884, #299,916), who used two-point barbs to create a loop spreading the two wires at various intervals (Figure 147), which he claimed gave greater stiffness without increasing its weight. It was classified as an "Improvement in Barbed Fencing."

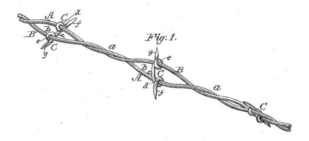

Figure 147. Decker , A. C. 1884 (#299,915) "Spread, Twisted Strands"

Clifton (1970) named this type of barb a "Spreader" (see later discussion on types of barbs). Less than a dozen patents for the parallel designs and for loop designs have been identified.

One of the more unique two-wire-strand designs was by Edenborn (1885,#313,929) for a two-wire strand with a thin, flat web connection. Two- and four-point barbs were twisted around the two wires of the strand and a perforated thin metal or web between the two wires held the barbs in place (Figure 148). The design was considered an "Improvement in Barbed Fence-Wire" by better securing the barbs in place.

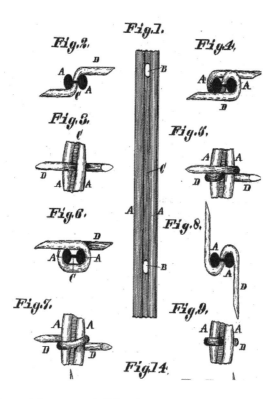

Figure 148. Edenborn, W. 1885 (#313,929) "Two-Wire Strand Web and Various Barbs"

*Three-wire strand.* Three-strand wires are the third most common, with over one-hundred-thirty patents and variations (eleven percent of all continuous-wire strands). Three sub-designs are found: (1) three twisted wires or cable-like strands, (2) three braided or loose twisted-wire strands, and (3) three wires parallel to each other forming a strand (Figure 149).

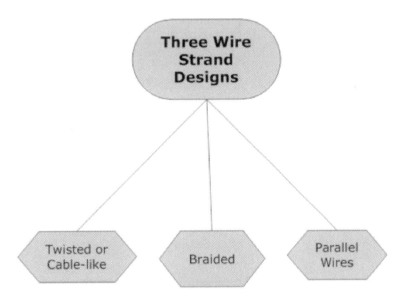

Figure 149. Three-Wire Strand Designs

The three-wire-strand designs are twisted wire or cable-like designs with barbs inserted on the central wire. P. Wineman of Rock Island, Illinois, in 1876 (two years after the DeKalb County Fair), designed and patented the first three-wire-strand system (Figure 150). It was classified as an "Improvement in Barbed Fence-Wire." Wineman called his design a "fence cable."

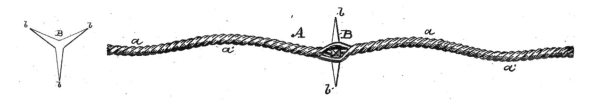

Figure 150. Wineman, P. 1876 (#176,725) "Three strand with Three-Point Star"

The second three-wire patent was a twisted-wire design with a five-pointed sheet metal star by McGlin and Hart from Shabbona Grove, Illinois, in September 1876 (Figure 151).

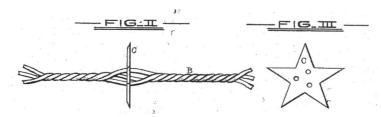

Figure 151. McGlin, J. C. and Hart', T. E. 1876 (#182,212) "Five Point Star"

In some patent descriptions, the inventor often stated the design was for a three-wire system, but it could be used for more than three wires (e.g., Preston's "Braid and Wrap Barb" [1881, #248,348] is an example of a braided three-wire strand) (Figure 152). Preston stated that the purpose of his design was to provide visibility and be strong and durable. He called his strand a "braided rail."

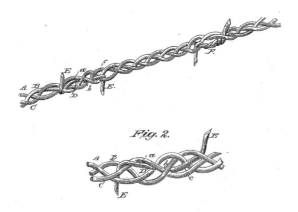

Figure 152. Preston, O. 1881 (#248,348) "Braid and Two-Point Barb"

Two family members from Cedar Rapids, Iowa - S. H. and J. M. St John - patented a three-wire strand with sheet metal barbs (Figure 153).

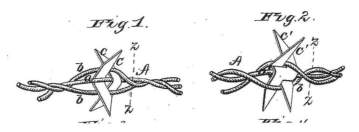

Figure 153. St. John, S. H. & St. John, J. M. 1878 (#205,697) "Double V Barb"

They claimed their design not only increased the strength and durability, but also added the "beauty of appearance, with a perfect and secure retention of barbs in place."

Three-parallel-wire designs are found. In 1882, A. Ellwood[85] was issued a patent (#253,022) not only for a two-parallel-wire strand, but also for a three-wire parallel-strand design where the wires were spread three-quarters-of-an-inch apart by a four-point spread barb (Figure 154).

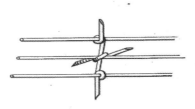

Figure 154. Ellwood, A. 1882 (#253,002) "Three Strand Parallel"

He claimed his design as an "Improvement in Barbed Fence-Wire Strand" by being stronger, preventing cattle from sticking their heads through the wire, and being less likely to have the galvanization loosen and peel off than in twisted wires.

---

85    A relative of Isaac Ellwood, one of the original inventors of barbed fencing.

In 1883, J. B. Cline patented a three-parallel-wire strand with four-point barbs (Figure 155). He referred to his design as a "cable." He claimed that the vertical shape of the strand and the attachment of the barbs provided visibility, stiffness, and longer distances between posts. The design was classified as an "Improvement in Barbed-Fence Wires."

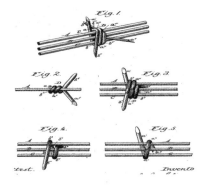

Figure 155. Cline, J. B. 1883 (#290,974) "Three-Strand Rail"

In addition, he claimed his design allowed itself to be more easily painted and was less likely to lose its tensile strength than twisted wires experienced in winding and unwinding.

A design of three untwisted and unbraided wires held closely parallel to one another was patented by Clark in 1882 (Figure 156). It had two variations for attaching a two-point barb. One variation was with the barb around the central strand and the other variation was the barbs alternating wrapping around two of the three stands (see earlier discussion on twisting or wrap attachment of barbs).

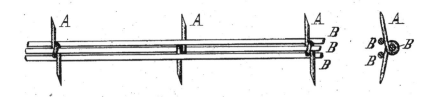

Figure 156. Clark, N. 1882 (#260,844) "Inside Wrap Rail"

The object of his design, as with other similar designs, was to provide a fence where the barbs did not move and a strand was strong, flexible, and long lasting. He said his design provided an advantage if galvanizing was used because the strand wires were not bent and galvanizing cracking would not occur. This was the second patent in 1882 to mention the issue of galvanization of the wires cracking when twisted. The first was A. Elwood (#253,002) for a two- and three-parallel-wire design.

One of the unique three-wire-strand designs incorporated the barb as part of the three twisted-wire strands. M. Mighell in 1878 was issued a patent (#199,924) for a three-wire strand with two continuous-twisted wires and a third wire twisted with the first two wires but with a regular cut in the third wire and its ends bent out to form a single-point barb (Figure 157). He also patented a similar two-strand design with one of the wires also cut and bent. He indicated that the three-strand design was stronger than other designs.

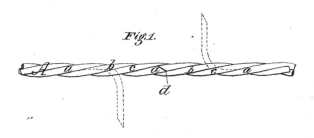

Figure 157. Mighell, P. 1878 (#199,924) "Two Awhile, Three Awhile"

More than thirty three-wire-strand variations of Glidden's 1874 two-point wire-barb patent have been identified (Hagemeier 2010, 2012).

*Four-wire strand.* Hagemeier (2010, 2012) identified two-dozen four-wire-strand patents and patent variations. Of these only three actual patents have been identified. H. Underwood in 1878 was issued a patent for a four-wire strand using tacks (Figure 158).

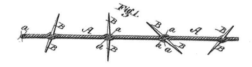

Underwood 1878 (#206,754) Four Strand Double Tack

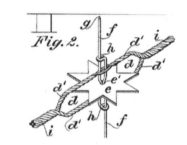

Evans 1883 (#287,261) Four Strand Rowel

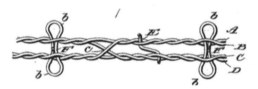

Ingraham 1892 (#469,062) Barb and Visible Loop Wire

Figure 158. Examples of Four-Wire-Strand Patent Designs

In 1883, Evans was issued a patent for a "Four Strand Rowel" (#287,261). He stated that his design would be less injurious to cattle because the rowel would move and not pierce or puncture the hide of the animal. Ingraham's "Looped Parallel & Barb Ornamental" (#469,062) in 1892 was a four-wire-strand ornamental-wire system that had a two-point barb. This design was considered more visible because of the size of the strand. Ingraham also called his barbed wire a "cable."

Most of the four-wire strands identified are some variation of Glidden's two-point patent (#157,124) (Hagemeier 2010, 2012).

*Five- and six-wire strands.* Two five-strand variations with two-point wire barbs and one six-strand variation with two-point wire barbs have been identified (Hagemeier 2010, 2012). These are variations of Glidden's 1874 two-wire-strand patent (#157,124). According to Hagemeier (2010, 2012) and Clifton (1970), no specific patents were issued for five- and six-strand systems, but a number of variations have been identified. Some patentees often indicated the multiple wires could be used but no specifics were given.

*Linked barbed strands.* Where most individual single- and multiple-wire strands are continuous and attached to posts, some inventors designed short single or double mild-steel-wire strands that were linked together by folding and/or twisting single- or double-wire strands forming a "chain-like" strand that would be attached to a post. Linked-wire systems were considered more easily transportable than rolls of standard barbed wire because they could be laid on top of each other rather than in rolls of wire. The linked ends of these shorter strands were designed to form a wire barb or were linked to each other with a sheet metal barb. These designs could be made of single-wire strands or double-wire strands (e.g., A. E. Bronson [1877, #189,994]) to form a continuous connection between posts or could be inserted into a discontinuous (broken) single- or double-wire strand (Figure 159).

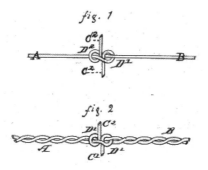

Figure 159. Bronson, A. E. 1877 (#189,994) "Double-Loop Barb On Single- And Double-Wire Strands"

Both Clifton and Hagemeier identified two types of linked designs: (1) "link wire" and (2) "sectional link wire." A review of these designs and the patent descriptions do not clearly distinguish what the major difference is between "link wire" and "sectional link wire." For this analysis, these two designs are grouped as "Linked Barbed Strands." Some three- or four-dozen patents and patent variations have been identified by Clifton (1970) and Hagemeier (2010, 2012). The stated purpose of this type of design varied from providing barbed fence wire that could be folded (e.g., E. Crandal [1876, #174,664]) (Figure 160).

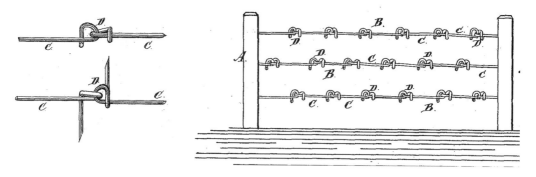

Figure 160. Crandal, E. M. 1875 (#174,664) "Small-Loop Link Wire"

Crandal patented four-link barbed strand designs. His second linked-barbed design was his 1876 patent (#184,844), which he called an "Improved Barbed-Wire Chain-Cable and Barbed Wire Fence" and was classified as an "Improvement in Barb Fence-Wires" (Figure 161).

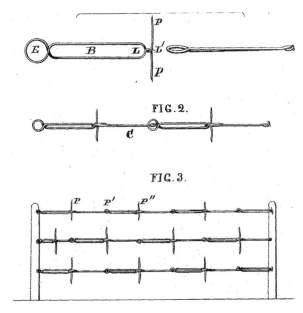

Figure 161. Crandal, E. M. 1876 (#184,844) "Double-Twisted End or Barb- and Ring-Link"

It was a link design that involved a single strand that was folded to form a two-point barb. His last two-linked barbed strand designs, including two in 1881 (#240,388, #241,791), were classified as a "Link Fence."

One very early lined barbed strand patent was by P. Hill in 1876 (#182,928); Hill designed a barbed wire link that could be used to convert barbless wire fences into barbed wire fences by inserting barbed sections (Figure 162). It was classified as an "Improvement in Barb Fence Wire."

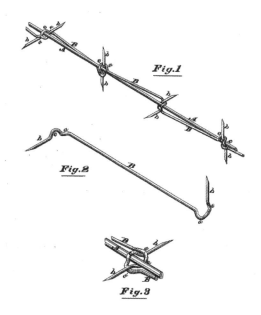

Figure 162. Hill, P. P. 1876 (#182,928) "Crossed-Strand Hooked Link"

A year later, a patent by Hunt (#189,861) was issued for a design that could be used for repairing barbed wire fences or for allowing temporary gaps in double-wire-strand fences to be made and reattached with this linked design (Figure 163).

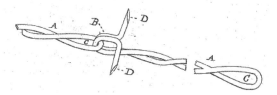

Figure 163. Hunt, G. G. 1877 (#189,861) "Link"

In 1881, Crandal received a third patent (#241,791), which was classified as a "Link Fence" (Figure 164). When twisted, the barbed links formed a strand that looked and acted like the "plain" wire portion of the strand.

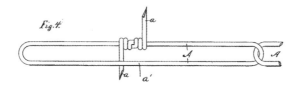

Figure 164. Crandal, E. M. 1881 (#241,791) "Parallel Link"

In 1882, Cook was issued a patent that related "to that general form of barbed fence-wire known as linked fencing." It consisted of a barbed fence-wire composed of short links of single-wire strands linked by a sheet metal star barb (Figure 165).

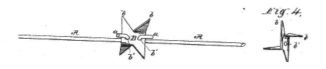

Figure 165. Cook, J. T. 1882 (#265,025) "Perforated Double-Fin Link Wire"

In 1888, Freese designed a link system with sheet metal barbs (#383,804) of twisted and straight links (Figure 166). Freese said his design allowed the sheet metal barb to turn in the direction of the length of the fence, minimizing injury to animals. It was classified as an "Improvement in Wire Fences."

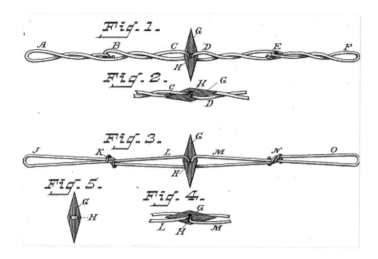

Figure 166. Freese, P. C. 1888 (#383,804) "Parallel Link Diamond Plate"

In 1886, Whitney and Hubbell designed a linked system (#344,428) using circular "rotatory barbs" of sheet metal that would reduce injury to cattle (i.e., allowing the barb to turn). It linked a double-wire strand system (Figure 167).

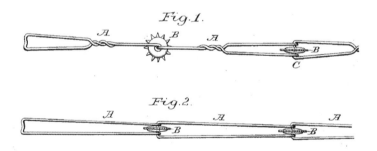

Figure 167. Whitney, J. F. and Hubbell, M. R. 1886 (#344,428) "Spur Wheel Link"

J. W. Griswold of Troy, New York, was the most prolific designer of linked barbed strands and patented slight variations for a single design (see Chapter 4 discussion on USPTO criteria for obtaining a patent). He applied for ten patents in June 1891, and eight of them were issued in December 1891. The other two were issued in 1892. All were just slightly different twists to his first 1891 design (#465,638), a two-point twisted barbed link (Figure 168).

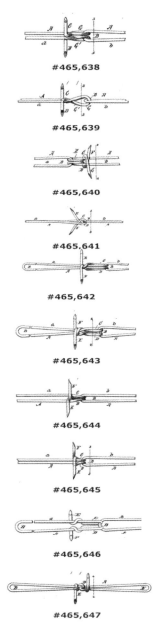

Figure 168. Griswold, J. W. 1891 and 1892 "Twisted Linked Designs"

A unique linked barbed design was by L. Evans of New York City in 1876 (#183,552) for a link wire made of "hard iron or semi steel" (Figure 169).

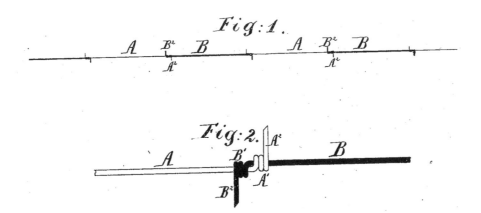

Figure 169. Evans, L. E. 1876 (#183,522) "Twisted Barb Link Wire"

His design included painting alternating single wires as well as having the size of the wires different for increased visibility. It was classified as "Improvement in Barbed Fence-Wires." He referred to his barbs as "thorns," as did Kelly in 1868. Evans recommended to "'japan'[86] it with a suitable coating to defend it from the weather" (see Chapter 3 discussion on barbed wire materials).

*Interlaced strand designs (woven wire).* The third strand design configuration is the multiple horizontal wire strands interconnected to one another vertically, generally by single-wire strands. These designs are called "woven wire," also referred to as "fabric wires." These interlaced wire systems are attached to posts to form a fence.

---

[86] "Japanning" refers to painting metals with a black lacquer.

Clifton (1970) divided interlaced barbed strand designs into link, sectional, mesh, and interlaced designs. Hagemeier (2010, 2012) did not make a major distinction between linked and sectional strands and did not identify the same number of patents as Clifton (1970). Both authors seemed to focus on the barb design, not the interconnection of horizontal and vertical strands. Recent fencing literature provides a better definition of mesh versus woven-wire fences (Virginia Cooperative Extension 2003). Mesh fence differs from woven-wire fence in the interconnection methods of the horizontal and vertical strands. In mesh fences, a separate wire wrap (a stay knot) joins the horizontal and vertical wires. Hagemeier (2010) referred to these fence systems as "Barbed Net Wire." Clifton's interlaced wire fencing designs were mesh-like wire fences. In woven fences, the horizontal and vertical wires can be joined by wrapping the vertical strand around the horizontal strand. These groups do not appear to be significantly different structurally or functionally.

Horton (1916) described different types of connections for woven fences and identified two types of woven fences, wide and narrow, depending on the presence or absence of barb. Narrow-woven wire is woven wire no more than forty-two inches in height that has two or more barbed wire strands attached to the top. Wide-woven wire is taller but does not have barb strands attached. For this analysis, given the unclear distinction between mesh and interlaced fences of Clifton and Hagemeier and woven fence descriptions of other authors, mesh and interlaced barbed strands are lumped into woven barbed strands with designs.

According to Horton (1916), woven-wire fences were an outgrowth of the three-wire strand barbed fencing of A. C. Decker of Bushnell, Illinois, who was granted the first patent (#186,716) for square-wire-mesh barbed fence in 1877 (Figure 170). This design was patented three years after the invention of the individual continuous-wire strand designs of DeKalb inventors Glidden, Haish, and the Merrills in 1874.

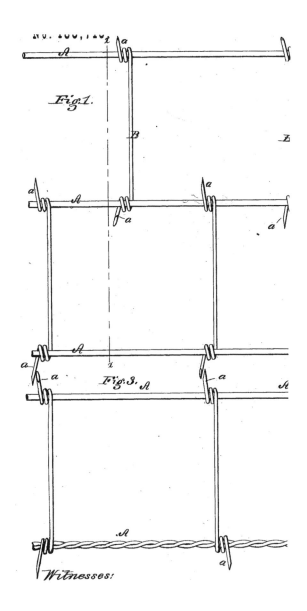

Figure 170. Decker, A. C. 1877 (#186,716) "Spaced Three Strand and Spaced Two Strand"

His design involved two or more horizontal wires connected by a series of vertical wires that extended beyond the vertical wires and were sharpened. Decker's design was a departure from the horizontal continuous-strand designs of barbed fencing and the plain wire common at the time. In the previous year, and on the same date Decker applied for the patent he was issued, a patent for single mild-steel-round-wire strand with beads or ribs to hold barb (#178,605) was issued. He had a later invention in 1884 (#299,916), which was a two-point barb that acted as a "spreader" for two-wire strands. Decker referred to his design as a "netted" or "reticulated" type fence with the feature of sharpening the ends of the wires which formed the body of fence, "…that they serve to repel animals and thereby protect the fence from injury." It was classified as an "Improvement in Barbed Fence-Wires."

It is unclear from reading the patent description of M. Kelly (1878, #208,399) (Figure 171) why it was not considered a woven-wire-type design, or at least an early version of the barbed woven-wire design like Decker's 1877 patent.

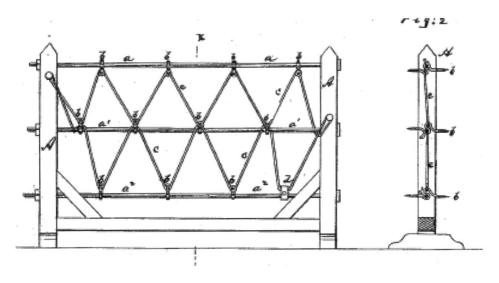

Figure 171. Kelly, M. 1878 (#208,399) "Hanging Barb"

Clifton (1970) did not identify the patent and Hagemeier (2010) only described the barb. Kelly described his design as horizontal wires with barbs with zigzag wires connecting the barbs on the horizontal wires so that barbs are connected above and below each other in a mesh or woven fashion. His barbs were "three-sided bayonet-points." This type of barb would be considered as a "vicious" barb design (see earlier discussion on barb design).

In the 1890s, more barbed and barbless woven-wire patents were issued than during other time periods (Campbell and Allison 1986) and barb wire use increased in farming (see Chapter 2 on regional patterns in barbed fencing).

Woven wire or "fabric" patents of the 1890s and early 1900s with barbs included:

G. M. Depew, 1893 (#495,029)

A. J. Bates, 1896 (#561,193)

J. W. Griswold, 1897 (#575,345)

P. W. and W. M. Dillon, 1909 (#908,757)

H. P. Willsey, 1913 (#1,055,586)

By the beginning of the 20th century, woven fences had become quite popular, especially in the Midwestern states of Ohio, Indiana, Michigan, Illinois, and Missouri. In Missouri, woven wire was more common than barbed wire. An article in the 1906 *Hardware Dealers' Magazine* 26: page 58 stated that woven wire was rapidly displacing barbed wire. Table 13 provides a detailed state-by-state comparison of specific fences, including wide- and narrow-woven-wire fences (Humphries 1916).

Table 13. Percentage of Different Fence Types in Various Regions and States in the Midwest (Adapted From Humphries 1916)

| Regions and States | Types of Fencing | | | | | |
|---|---|---|---|---|---|---|
| | Woven (Wide) | Woven (Narrow) with Barbs | Barbed Fencing and Smooth Wire Fencing (Plain Wire) | Hedges | Wooden Fences (Different Types) | Stone Fences |
| Western Dakota, Nebraska, Kansas, & Northern Minnesota | 5.5 | 10.2 | 84.0 | 0.03 | 0.3 | 0.0 |
| Eastern Dakota, Nebraska, Kansas, & Southern Minnesota | 8.8 | 20.0 | 63.0 | 6.4 | 0.6 | 0.6 |
| Iowa | 8.0 | 45.5 | 43.5 | 2.1 | 0.9 | 0.0 |
| Missouri | 13.8 | 49.4 | 27.2 | 5.6 | 3.8 | 0.04 |
| Wisconsin | 13.5 | 33.4 | 49.8 | 0.04 | 2.3 | 0.8 |
| Illinois | 11.4 | 41.7 | 29.0 | 12.4 | 5.5 | 0.0 |
| Michigan | 55.9 | 11.8 | 11.9 | 0.6 | 19.7 | 0.0 |
| Indiana | 53.3 | 18.0 | 12.9 | 1.6 | 14.1 | 0.05 |
| Ohio | 59.8 | 3.8 | 7.0 | 1.2 | 27.9 | 0.05 |

In the western portion of the Upper Midwest in 1916, eighty-four percent was barbed and smooth wire and nearly sixteen percent of the different types of fencing included woven wire. A different pattern was seen as one went east. The eastern portion of the Upper Midwest had sixty-three percent of its fences as barbed and smooth and approximately thirty percent as the two kinds of woven wire. According to Humphries (1916), this pattern may have been explained by the different kinds of farming found in those areas. In the eastern Midwest (e.g., Ohio), farms had wooden fences and hedges before barbed fencing came on the market and did not use barbed fencing as much as farmers in the western Midwest where there was less of the other kinds of fencing at the time. When woven wire came on the market in areas with wooden fences and as prices of woven wire went down, it was adopted as the preferred fence type because of limitations of wood fences and hedges (e.g., maintenance and loss of cultivatable land associated with wooden fences).

This trend was seen in Hornbeck's data in more detail with predominance of wire-like fences, especially barbed and smooth wire fences and narrow woven wire with barbed wire in the western Dakotas, Nebraska, Kansas, and northern Minnesota. The continued importance by the diminished proportion of traditional fences (e.g., wooden and hedges) in the eastern Midwest (e.g., Ohio and Illinois) was reported. Horton (1916) provided a detailed discussion on the construction and use of woven fences on farms in the Midwest and discussed how farmers were transitioning from all barbed fencing to various types of woven-wire fencing.

The following are examples of barbed woven-wire strands and adaptations to make barbless woven wire barbed. Evans's 1882 design of interlocking mild steel strands with barbs Figure 172) was classified as an "Improvement in Barbed Fence-Wire," which he claimed was "exceedingly strong and easily effected." He described it as "wire-fence network."

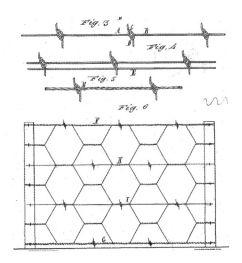

Figure 172. Evans, L. E. 1882 (#255,728) "Mesh Barbed Wire"

Clifton identified Bestor's 1877 design and Pearson's 1889 design as interlaced fence designs or as redefined here as -woven wire stands. Bestor's patent twelve months after Decker's 1877 design was for a four-point wire barb wrapped around the horizontal mild steel strands of a fence forming a four-point barb (Figure 173). This design resulted in converting a continuous-wire-strand fence design into a mesh or woven fence design.

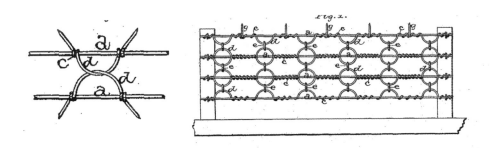

Figure 173. Bestor, F. L. 1877 (#197,757) "Tied Parallel Strands"

Bestor claimed the design made the fence ornamental and visible to keep animals from running into it. His design also attempted to address the problem of cattle getting their heads stuck between barbed wires by linking the wires in an interlaced pattern. It was classified as an "Improvement in Barbs for Wire Fences."

Pearson's design (Figure 174) was a wire fence composed of wire netting or woven mild-steel strands that formed rectangles that varied in size from the top of the fence downward; the larger mesh rectangles were at the top of the fence and the smaller meshes were at the bottom. The barbs were attached so they could pivot on the cross-wires. This design had several purposes in animal control, including controlling cattle, rabbits, and dogs. It could also be set up to trap sparrows.

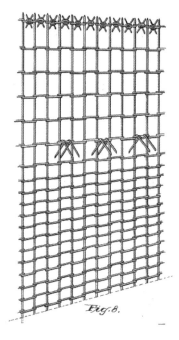

Figure 174. Pearson, A. N. 1889 (#403,774) "Two-Point Swing Barb Mesh Fence"

In 1902, Blommer (#715,541) actually used the term "woven wire" to describe his interlaced wire strand fence with barbs. It was classified as a "Woven-wire fence." Clifton (1970) did not identify it. Hagemeier (2010) listed it as barbed wire but did not provide any picture or description of the woven wire system. Bloomer's design was a combination of horizontal double-wire strands (they could be single strands) interconnected with vertical pieces of single-wire strands called "stay stands" with single-point barbs at the interconnections on the top-most strand. On the bottom, the double-wire strands were alternated with single-wire strands, each with single-point barbs at the interconnections. The weave was closer and barbed "to repel animals attempting to worry through."

Bloomer's design was similar in form to Decker's 1877 patent, but used a combination of single- and double-strand wires.

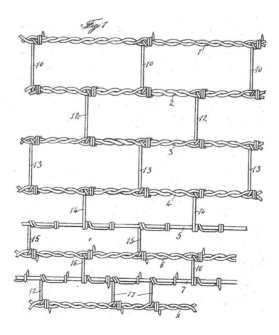

Figure 175. Bloomer, R. H. 1902 (#715,541) "Eight Strand Woven Wire with Barbs on Top Strand and Bottom Three Strands."

239

The use of barbed wire with woven fences was common. Barbed wire strands were often attached to the top of barbless woven wire (see Humphries 1916, Horton 1916). I. L. Ellwood, one of the DeKalb inventors with a sheet metal strip design (#147,756) in 1874, patented a woven-wire design with combinations of woven-wire strands and barbed wire strands in 1893 (Figure 176). He showed several alternating combinations of woven-wire mesh at the bottom of the fence and two or three barbed strands in the middle or at the top of the fence for the purpose of turning away small animals at the bottom of the fence and barb strands at the top to repel large animals.

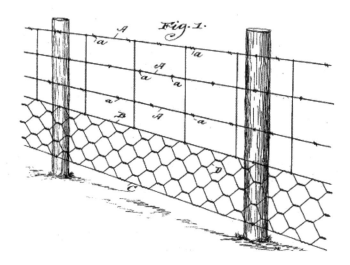

Figure 176. Ellwood, I. L. 1883 (#502,512) "Mixed Bands of Barbed Wire Mesh with Woven Barbed Wire" (One Design Shown)

Ellwood was one of the original inventors of barbed fencing and apparently took the opportunity to design a woven-wire fence, which was becoming more popular than single-strand barbed fencing at the time. It was classified as an "Improvement in Metallic Fencing." His first patent was a sheet metal barb and strip design.

In 1904, J. H. Aikin (#756,313) designed a four-point wire barb that served the purpose of converting woven fences to barbed fences and for connecting the horizontal wires with the vertical stays. In 1905, A. W. Swender patented a woven fence design (#801,417) that focused on placing barbs on the stays that had barbs facing in one direction between the horizontal strands along with barbs at the tops and bottoms of the stays. The barbs could be turned in any direction so that a smooth side fence could be erected.

In 1908, D. C. Smith was issued a patent (#905,942) for a woven fence that had longitudinal stays called "binders" that projected up from the woven fence wire and could be used to connect to higher barbed wire strands (Figure 177).

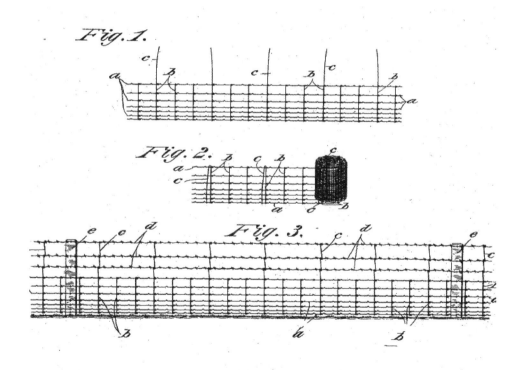

Figure 177. Smith, D. C. 1908 (#905,942) "Woven Wire with Binders"

Smith referred to the fact that barbed wires "universally" had been placed on the top of the wire "fabric" or ran above the fabric. These unsecured barbed wire strands required special fence stays to hold the barbed wire on the top of the fence. If not secured, the barbed wire would come loose. He provided recommendations on the height of the fence, including woven-wire fences that needed barbed wire or would be "ridden down by horses."

### Appearance of Strand (Shape and Form)

A closer look at wire strands themselves can reveal significant differences in their appearance. Wire strand appearance can be described two ways: (1) by the shape of the wire or its two-dimensional appearance or (2) by the form of the wire or its three-dimensional appearance. Inventors developed hundreds of wire strand shapes and forms in attempts to improve barbed wire for commercial acceptance.

*Shape of wire strands.* Clifton (1970) and Hagemeier (2010, 2012) characterized the shape of the wire(s) comprising a strand in several ways, including round, oval, polygon, flattened, ribbed, and grooved shapes and combinations of these shapes. Some of these are patented designs and others have been found as variations resulting either intentionally or unintentionally from manufacturing irregularities (see Chapter 4 on manufacturing variations). The most common shape found in antique barbed fencing is round. This shape was first seen with Kelly's 1868 patent design. It is not surprising that the round shape was first used in barbed wire fencing since barbed wire fencing evolved from the plain round fence wires (see Chapter 2). The first patented variation from the round shape design of straight single-wire strands occurred within two years of the invention of barbed wire in 1874. In February 1876, W. Collins of Ames, Iowa, was issued a patent for a ribbed wire (#173, 271) (Figure 178).

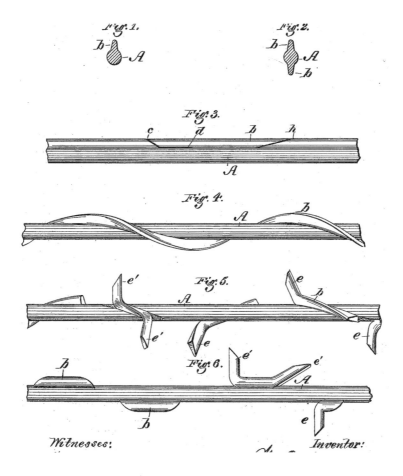

Figure 178. Collins, W. 1876 (#173,271) "Ribbed Wire Two Point"

The rib was formed into barbs (see later discussion on extruded barbs). The purpose of this design was to make a simpler and less expensive way of making barbs. He also stated that he was trying to design a wire to mimic "thorns on hedges."

A review of the single-wire stand designs showed the following patented shapes:

» Round Wire – e.g, Kelly, 1868 (#74,379); Baker, 1883 (#273,219)

» Round Wire with Flattened Sides - e.g., Upham, 1883 (#284,261)

» Round Wire Twisted with Rib - e.g., Collins, 1876 (#173,271)

» Round Wire with Small Rib - e.g., Decker, 1876 (#178,605); Husted, 1889 (#398,259)

» Round Wire with Projections – e.g., Lenox, 1884 (#300,793)

» Short Round Sections of Wire with Long Irregular Single Strand Wire – e.g., Shellaberger, 1908 (#904,496)

» Oval Wire – e.g., Glidden, 1876 (#181,453)

» Concave Round Wire - e.g., Haish, 1882 (#261,703)

» Polygon (Three or More Sides) - e.g., Rose, 1877 (#198,688 octagon); J. B. Fisher, 1878, (#203,536 triangle including roughened surface)

In reading the patent descriptions, intentional design differences to the shape of the wire were made to address one of the major limitations of single-wire strands with barbs discussed earlier. Barbs tended to slide along the round wire and bunch up. Glidden, who was issued his famous patent for the twisted two-wire strand to hold barbs in place in 1874, was also issued a patent for a non-round single-wire (oval shaped) strand design in August 1876. His design was a twisted oval wire (#181,433) invented to address the movement of barbs on single-wire strands (Figure 179).

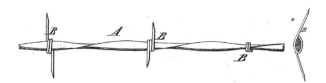

Figure 179. Glidden, J. 1876 (#181,433) "Twisted Oval"

It was classified as an "Improvement in Barbed Fence-Wire." Figure 180 provides examples of different single-wire strand shape patents:

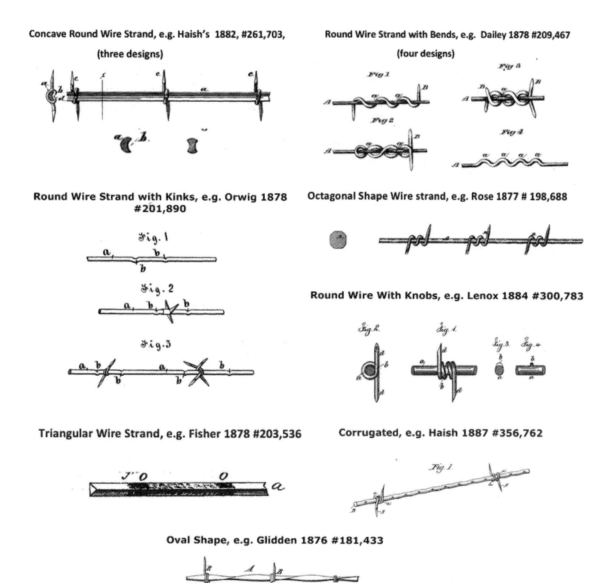

Figure 180. Examples of Different Single-Wire Strand Shape Patents

The round shape design was the dominant design shape for two-wire strands. Compared to single-wire strands, only a few patents for different wire design shapes were issued; however, a large number of variations have been found, including double grooved, oval, and polygon (e.g., square, triangular, rectangular) shapes. An example of a patented different shape for two-wire strands is Curtis (1894, #514,672), who designed two half-round strands with a two-point sheet metal barb (Figure 181).

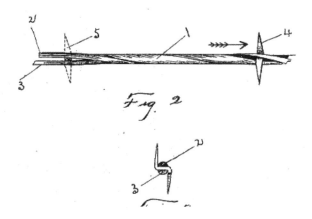

Figure 181. Curtis, J. D. 1894 (#514,672) "Flat Barb on Half-Round Strand"

Irregularities in shape also likely resulted from farm co-ops or "moonshine" manufacturers who made smooth wire of their own design, often times with crude machines lacking quality control. In addition, some manufacturers only fabricated the final product (i.e., the barbed wire) from the smooth wire. They often received wire from their wire manufacturers that was irregular in shape. This resulted in considerable variations on the shape of the wire (Hagemeier 2010). Glidden's 1874 patent (#157,124) is an example of a patent design that has a large number of wire shape variations that have been identified (Hagemeier 2010).

*Form of wire strands.* Inventors designed different forms of wire strand besides the straight design, including:

»   Undulating Round Wire - e.g., Briggs, 1884 (#301,086)

»   Undulating Round Wire with Flattened Spaces - e.g., D. Smith, 1907 (#853,938)

»   Corrugated Round Wire with Ribs - e.g., Haish, 1887 (#356,762)

»   Flattened Round Wire (or Bars) with Knobs – e.g., Huffman, 1890 (#442,525)

»   Flattened Round Wire with Barbs Cut from Flattened Section – e.g., Bagger, 1876 (#183,883)

»   Flattened Round Wire Sections with Alternating Reverse Twists - e.g., Rogers, 1888 (#376,418)

»   Kinked Wire Round Wire - e.g., Sunderland, 1884 (#303,406); Orwig, 1878 (#201,890)

»   Spiral Indentations along Round Wire - e.g., Putnam, 1877 (#187,172)

»   Oval or Eliptical and Serpentine in Form - e.g., Carpenter, 1882 (#258,888)

Figure 182 shows several examples of these variations in the form of wire used in a single-wire strands

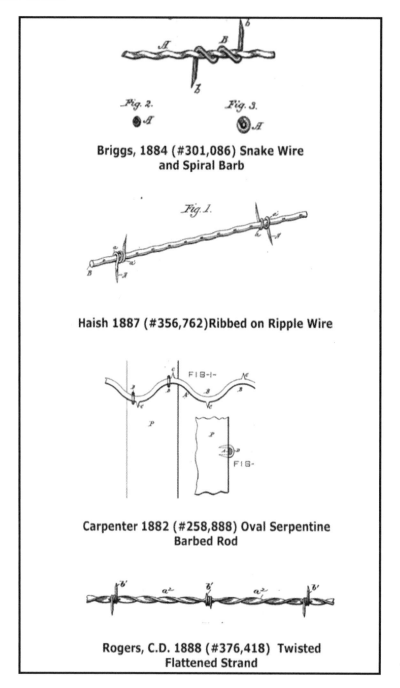

Figure 182. Examples of Different Forms of Strand Designs

## Other Wire Strand Design Variations

Other wire strand variations and patents that have been found include differences in size of the wire or gauge of the wire, whether the wires of the strand were twisted or not, and the degree of twist. In 1868, Kelly (#74,379) stated that he preferred to use No. 15 wire, although larger gauge wires could be used. Although no gauge was specified, within two years of the DeKalb inventions in 1876, L. Evans of New York City was issued a patent (#183,552) for a single strand (see Chapter 5 on linked wire) that linked two wires of different sizes and different colors to make the wires more visible.

Two-wire strand and other multiple-wire strand designs can exhibit differences in the degree of twist of the two wires with loose and tight twists in the two wires of the strands. This variation in twist is likely due to variations in manufacturing of the strands (see Chapter 4 discussion on manufacturing variations). No specific patents have been identified, but variations of right and left or reverse twists have been identified by Hagemeier (2010, 2012) and tools and machines were patented for twisting wire (see Campbell and Allison 1986).

## Summary of Mild Steel Strand Designs

Most antique barbed fencing patents were for mild steel-wire-strand designs. The major design differences in the mild steel-wire strands are differences in the configuration of the strands, whether they are continuous strands, linked strands, interlaced strands, or woven wire. The number of mild steel wires in a strand is a distinguishing design feature. Single- and double-wire continuous strands were the most commonly designed wire strands. Figure 183 provides a summary of the different mild steel-wire-strand design differences.

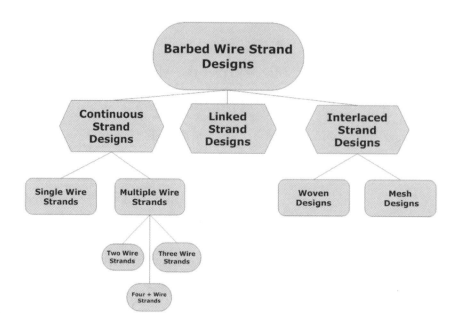

Figure 183. Mild Steel-Wire-Strand Designs

### Sheet Metal Strips (Barbed and Barbless): Attachment Mode and Appearance

Sheet metal strips, also known as ribbon wires, are another horizontal component of antique barbed wire fence. One of the designs by Brinkerhoff was referred to as a "strap" (American Agriculturist 1880). Sheet metal strips were stamped out of sheet metal rather than being steel rolled out as round mild-steel wire. Sheet metal strips were invented at the same time as mild steel barbed wire strands were invented. The Massachusetts Board of Agriculture discussed the pro and cons of "ribbon wire." Their 1882 article indicated that sheet metal strips were commonly used in Massachusetts in the early 1880s and were referred to as "Brinkerhoff wire." The article said the wire was "very easily discernable by horses or by cattle." It was preferable to mild steel barbed wire for sheep and horses because it did not cause serious injury. It cost the same as mild steel barbed wire. One of its shortcomings was that it tended to break or snap more often than the double-strand mild-steel-wire strands, especially in the snow.

According to Clifton (1970), metallic strip fences could be made cheaper and easier than round wire and were easier to maintain. Sheet metal strips with barbs could be stamped out or cut in one piece. USPTO classified these designs as "Improvements in Barbed Wire." In some cases, these sheet metal designs were described as "rods" or "bars," even though they were not as heavy and inflexible as the terms rod and bar imply (see later discussion on rods and bars).

Sheet metal strips have been found as "barbless" strip designs and "barbed" strip designs. Based on the type of barb attachments (See earlier discussion on barbs) sheet metal strips can be grouped in three ways: (1) barbed mounted strips: (2) barbed mounted double strips: and (3) integrated barbed strip. As with mild-steel strands these sheet metal strip designs can be characterized by their appearance, or shape and form.

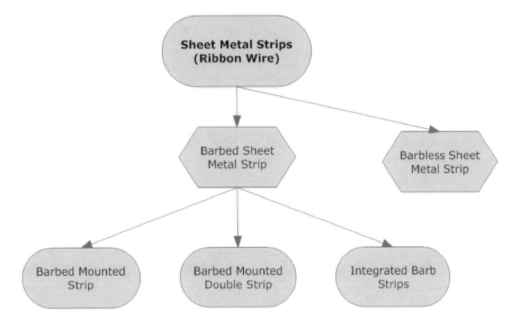

Figure 184. Major Sheet Metal Strip Designs

According to Clifton identification, there are nearly 200 sheet metal patents and patent variations and more than eighty percent were barbed sheet metal strip designs. The earliest sheet metal strip patent (#118,135) was in 1871 by L. P. Judson of Rose, New York. His design was a sheet metal strip fence design with sheet metal barbs integrated into the strip. His design involved serrated projections along the edge of the strip (Figure 185).

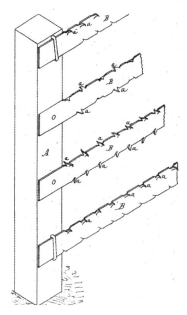

Figure 185. Judson, L. P. 1871 (#118,135) "Opposed Single-Cut Barb along Both Edges"

His sheet metal design was a "New and Useful Improvement in Fences." He stated that the use of fences "formed with loop or band-iron" were known, but the edges " … have been straight and unbroken" (i.e., barbless). His patent description stated that his motivation for his invention was to come up with a more useful wire fence and/or rail fence. He said his design would present an "armed or barbed surface" to keep animals at proper distances: "Hogs will not attempt to pass under, nor cattle and horses to jump over." He stated that his design was also better than a board or wooden fence rails since it would be visible using the bands and would have greater strength and firmness. It is important to note that he assigned his 1871 patent to J. Brinkerhoff in 1878, one year after Brinkerhoff had assigned his patents to Washburn & Moen Co. One may surmise that there was an attempt to consolidate these sheet metal designs.

The second sheet metal design patented was by I. L Ellwood in February 1874 (one of the three original DeKalb inventors). This design was a four-point sheet metal barb attached to a metal strip, a barb mounted strip design with the strip placed between two plain round-wire strands (Figure 186). It was classified as an "Improvement in Barbed Fences" and was designed to keep animals from rubbing against fences.

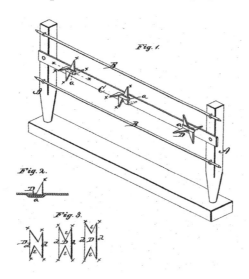

Figure 186. Ellwood, I. L. 1874 (#147,756) Centered "V" Barb

He patented one other patent (#502,521) nineteen years later in 1893 for woven wire design (see earlier discussion on woven wire). These were his only patents. He went into business with Glidden and Washburn & Moen Co. in the mid-1870s to manufacture barbed fencing.

The third sheet metal strip design was by J. Haish, also in February 1874 (#152,368). His design combined sheet metal barbed fence involving a continuous spirally twisted band of sheet metal with spikes cut from the opposite edges of the sheet metal strip that had a reinforcing core (Figure 187).

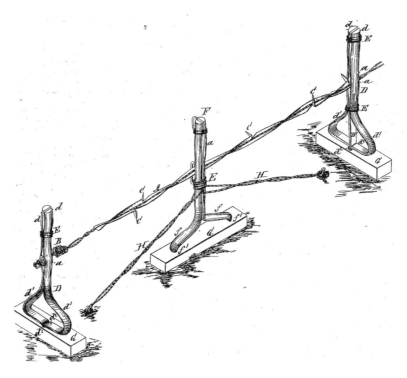

Figure 187. Haish, J. 1874 (#152,368) "Barbed Ribbon"

This design included iron posts and was classified by USPTO as an "Improvement to Barbed-Wire Fences." He apparently felt it would be easily detachable and portable and could be used in smaller areas such as yards. Haish claimed his design was durable, easily transportable, and not easily overturned by "winds, heavy snow, and storms."

**Barbed Sheet Metal Strips**

There are three different types of barbed sheet metal strips based on how the barbs are attached to the strip as applied barbs or integral barbs (Figure 189).

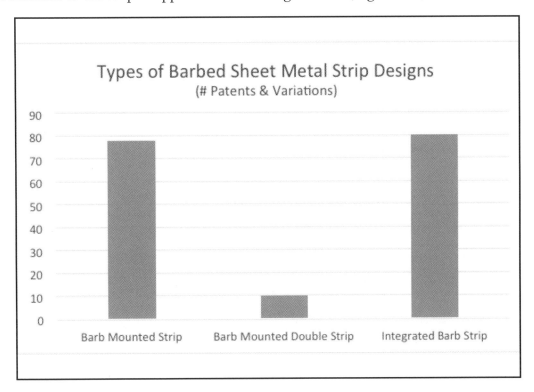

Figure 188. Percent of Patents and Variations for Sheet Metal Strip Designs (n =168) Based on Clifton 1970

Barb mounted strips and integrated strips have the most designs (approximately 160 patents and patent variations) and account for 80% of the patents and variations found in sheet metal strips.

*Barbed mounted strips.* Barbed mounted strips are single strips of sheet metal with sheet metal barbs attached (crimped) to the strip. It is the most common sheet metal strip design found in barbed sheet metal strip designs (more than seventy-five patents and patent variations). This design is exemplified by the designs of J. Brinkerhoff (Figure 189). His design was for a new "Improvement in Barbed Fences."

255

Figure 189. Brinkerhoff 1879 (#214,095) "Ribbon Wire" (Sheet Metal Strip)

For this type of design, barbs were clamped or crimped on the sheet metal strip (see Chapter 5 on attachments).

*Barb mounted double strips.* Barb mounted double strips were designs using two sheet metal strips secured together, often with the sheet metal barb sandwiched between the two strips (Figure 190).

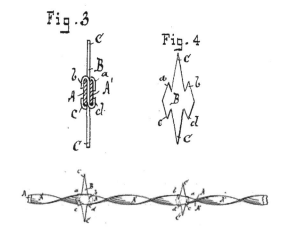

Figure 190. Childs 1883 (#285,229) "Twisted Double Strip with Four-Point Plate"

*Integrated barb strips.* Integrated barb strips are the simplest sheet metal strip design consisting of a single sheet metal strip, with the barb integrated into the strip by being stamped out of the sheet metal strip, extended, or extruded as part of the strip (Figure 191).

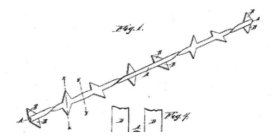

Figure 191. Allis, T. V. 1882 (#266,336) "Integrated Barbed Strip Systems with Stamped Barbs"

J. Brinkerhoff had two such early designs (#183,531 in 1876 and #186,922 in 1877), which were sheet metal strips with barbs pushed out (Figure 192).

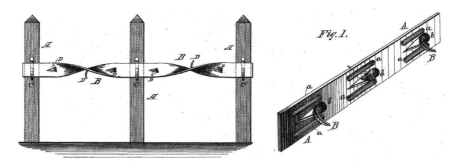

Figure 192. Brinkershoff, J. 1876 (#183,531) and 1877 (#186,922) "Integrated Sheet Metal Punched Out Barb"

His patent was classified as an improvement on his first patent, a barbed mounted strip shown above, by making the punched out barbs concave and thereby stronger. The design was also improved with barbs coming out on both sides of the flat strip.

**Barbless Sheet Metal Strips**

Both barbless and barbed sheet metal strip fences were patented at this time. Barbless strips were sheet metal strips without barbs and were often variations to the barbed sheet metal strips. Clifton (1970) identified nine barbless sheet metal strip patents. Many barbless strips are considered ornamental (Hagemeier 2010; Clifton 1970).

Other barbless sheet metal strips were designed so they could be manufactured to be barbless and later cut to make barbed sheet metal strips.

In 1885, Kilmer designed a "Barbed Fence Rail" using sheet metal that could be used barbless or barbed by cutting some of the triangular connection bars and bending them out to form a barb (Figure 193). It was classified as an "Improvement in Barbed Fence Rails." One of its stated advantages was its visibility to cattle.

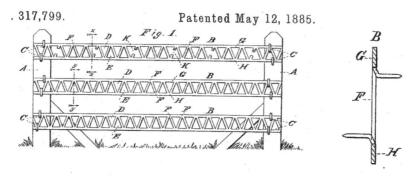

Figure 193. Kilmer, I. A. and Kilmer, M. D. 1885 (#317,799) "Barbed Window Wire With Barbs Punched Out"

Although without obvious barbs, some barbless strips (e.g., Massey 1882 [#261,619]) were designed to act as barbed strips with sharp serrated edges to scratch livestock "….instead of tearing animals' skin and flesh, as barbs do" (Figure 194).

Figure 194. Massey, W. E. 1882 (#261,619) "Swaggered Rail"

### Appearance of Sheet Metal Strips (Shape and Form)

Similar to mild steel wire strands, sheet metal strips have different appearances or designs based on the shape of the strips (2-D) and form (3-D) of the strips. Because of the wide nature compared to mild steel strands, this fencing was often referred to as "ribbon wire." Within the flat strips, several shapes were patented, including a half-round strip (Watkins-Scutt 1875 [#163,955]), ribbed strip (Scutt 1883 [#287,059]), a serrated strip (Massey 1882 [#261,619]), and concave strip (Haish 1885 [#332,393]). In 1891, A. Woodward (#452,887) patented five different types of barbless sheet metal strips, and in 1892, Allis patented three different ripple shapes (Figure 195). Woodward's designs were to provide strength without being as heavy as regular sheet metal strips.

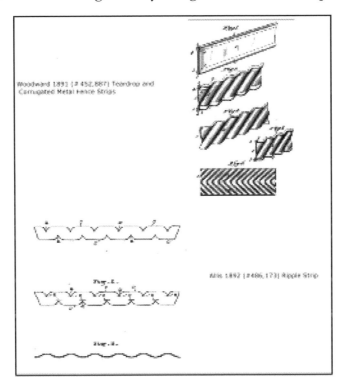

Figure 195. Examples of Sheet Metal Strip Shapes

**Summary of Sheet Metal Strip Designs**

Sheet metal strip or ribbon wire design is the second most common horizontal component found in the designs of antique barbed fencing. Although considered more visible than mild steel wire strands, it could be just as injurious. This type of design was considered by some not to be as durable as mild strand fencing in freezing conditions. Sheet metal strips can be initially grouped or classified by the type of strip, either as barbless sheet metal strips or barbed sheet metal strips. Barbed sheet metal strips are then broken down into three specific barbed strip designs: (1) barbed mounted strip, (2) barbed mounted double strip, and (3) integrated barbed strip based on how the barbs are attached and the number of strips within a strip. The two most common forms of sheet metal strips were flat and twisted rectangular strips, which were exemplified by the Brinkerhoff's designs. Figure 196 summarizes the sheet metal strip designs:

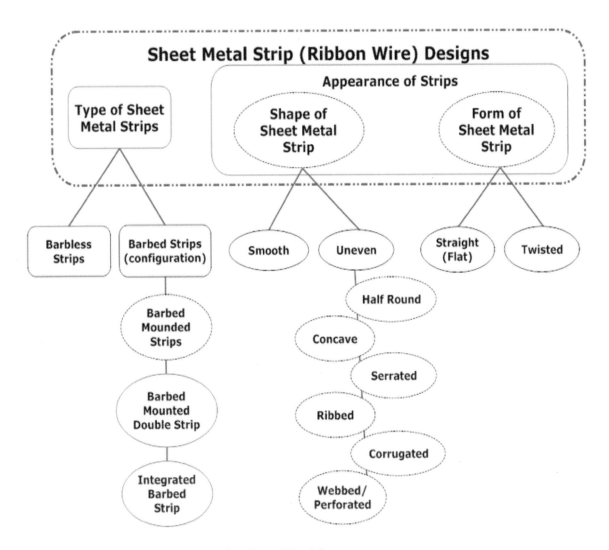

Figure 196. Design Classification for Sheet Metal Strips

## Combination Sheet Metal Strip and Wire Strand Designs

Although uncommon, there were attempts to combine mild steel wire strands and sheet metal strips. In 1885, J. J. Brinkerhoff patented a combination of a wire strand and sheet metal strip (Figure 197).

261

Figure 197. Brinkerhoff, J. J. 1885 (#324,221) "Ribbon and Single Wire Strand"

His design intended to make it easier to attach the sheet metal strip to a fence and to withstand contraction and expansion. Several variations have been found (Hagemeier 2010). In 1892, C. Mann of Buffalo, New York, was issued a patent for an "Improvement in Wire Fences" that involved a wire twisted with a flat sheet metal strip with an interior groove for the wire. A two-point barb was twisted around the wire and strip (Figure 198).

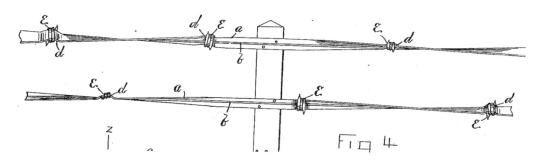

Figure 198. Mann, C. H. 1892 (#266,705) "Ribbon and Single-Strand Wire"

In his patent statement, he said he was only claiming the combination of a wire strand and sheet metal strip with a groove, not using the two together in the construction of fences or the type of barb that J. J. Brinkerhoff had patented in 1885. Mann's design differed from Brinkerhoff's in the attachment of the barb. It was twisted around both the wire and strip. He claimed that by adding the mild steel wire, the durability was increased to the sheet metal strip fence.

## Bars, Rods, and Rails: Designs and Patterns

The third major horizontal design group is rigid metal or wood horizontal components or bars, rods, and rails. These horizontal components were heavier than mild steel wire strands or sheet metal strips. They were made of metal, wood, or a combination of the two. They were sold as sections for fencing that could be assembled and disassembled. They could also be grouped by appearance (i.e., different shapes and forms). There are two major material divisions: whether they are made of (1) metal or (2) wood.

## Metal Bars, Rods, and Rails: Design Patterns

Metal bars, rods, and rails with barb wire were invented early in the barbed fencing design period; they were designed at the same time mild steel strands and sheet metal strips were invented (e.g., Sims's 1876 "Barbed Triangle Rod" [#176,195]). The terms "bars", "rods", and "rails" don't have specific definitions and the names are often times used interchangeably by different inventors (e.g., Perry 1886 [#333,887]). They represent a group of designs for rigid barbed metal units that were made for fencing. Less than a dozen patents have been identified. Bars, rods, and rails were claimed to be more durable than wire strands and sheet metal strips, considered more visible to livestock, and were not subject to stretching. They were produced in varying lengths, such as sixteen to twenty feet (Sims 1876 [#176,195]), sixteen to seventeen feet (Randall 1887 [#359,178]), and up to thirty feet (Connelly 1891 [#247,537]). They could be transported in a stack. Once the fence post was in the ground, they could be easily and quickly assembled and dismantled to allow for passage of animals or vehicles. They could be bundled for storage. Except for small enclosures, these horizontal components were not practical for large areas on the plains and prairies. They were heavy and harder to erect (Clifton 1970).

Clifton (1970) identified seven bar designs representing four patents. The four bar patent designs were classified differently by USPTO, including "Improvement in Fencing-Strips" (e.g., Allis 1878 [#209,790]), "Material for Making Wire Fences" (e.g., Beresford 1891 [#449,279]), "Metallic Fence" (e.g., Connelly 1881 [#247,537]), and "Improvement in Barbed Iron-Fences" (e.g., Sims 1876 [#178,195]). Clifton (1970) also identified five rod designs representing three patent designs, including W. H. Perry for his 1886 "Improvement in Grooved and Barbed Rods and Bars" (#333,887), Randall for his 1887 "Barbed Metallic Fencing" (#359,178), and Beresford for his 1891 "Serrated Triangle Fence Rod" (#449,279). Beresford[87] had two forms, including a saw-tooth design and smooth-edge design. Both Clifton (1970) and Hagemeier (2010) identified Beresford's designs as bars and rods. Beresford said his triangular designs would more likely keep people from sitting on the fence, keep cattle from "wanton rough usage," provide less wind resistance, and allow snow to fall off. Beresford also claimed that his triangular wire could be used as "telegraph wire." The patent was classified as "Material for Making Wire Fences." Figure 199 provides examples of these barbed metal rods and bars:

---

[87]    He was one of the few foreign antique barbed fencing inventors.

## Examples of Metal Rods and Bars

**Sims 1876 (#178,195) Barbed Triangle Rod**

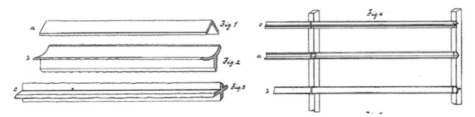

**Allis 1878  (#209,790) Fence Bar**

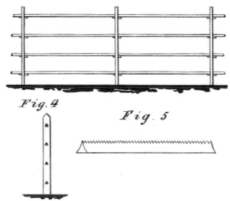

**Connelly 1881 (#247,537) Knife Edge Designs: V-Bar, T-Bar, and Crossbar**

**Beresford 1891 (#449,279) Serrated Triangle Rod**

Figure 199. Examples of Metal Rods and Bars

## Wooden Rails and Wooden Strips

Wooden rail fences long preceded barbed wire fences or plain wire fences and were common in the East, South, and Midwest where wood was available (see Chapter 2 on plain wire fences as the forerunner of barb wire); therefore, it was only natural that there was an attempt to adapt these wood fences with barbs in the beginning of the barbed wire period. This "Improvement of Fences" was manifested in two ways: (1) by attaching barbs to existing wooden rails and (2) by using wooden boards with barbs as a new barbed fence design. At the beginning of the barbed wire era, a few inventors received patents that used wooden rails or strips with barb-like attachments. Clifton (1970) and Hagemeier (2010, 2012) identified less than ten patents and variations. A few inventors recognized that many farmers and cattlemen had wooden fences. This provided an opportunity to adapt and utilize these wooden fences as barbed fences by designing barbs to attach to the wooden fences. One patent issued to Housum in 1878 (#204,735) was for a hand tool for attaching wires with points to wooden rails. In 1874, Haish was issued a patent (#147,634) for a sheet metal barb that could be attached to a wooden panel.

The inventors with patent designs involving wooden rails using mild steel barbs (e.g., staples and sheet metal strip barbs) included Richards, Topliff, Chapman, Haish, Housum, Orwig, Stout, Walsh and Dutot, and Rose. Rose's seminal barbed fence invention in 1873 (#138,763) was referenced by McCallum and McCallum (1985) as triggering the idea of barbed fencing with his use of it at the DeKalb County Fair in 1873. His design was a wooden rail supported by an iron rod with sharp wire barbs driven into the four sides of the rail (Figure 200). The USPTO considered his design as an "Improvement in Wire Fences."

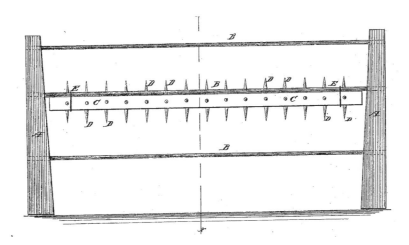

Figure 200. Rose, H. M. 1873 (#138,763) "Wooden Rail and Iron Rod"

These combination wooden rail and metal barb designs were short lived starting with Rose's patent of 1873 to the last patent in 1881, which was issued to Chapman for his "Barb Rail" (#246,866). In 1875, Stout was issued a patent for three-point metal barbs inserted into boards suspended between mild steel wire strands. His design was classified as an "Improvement in Farm Fences," more specifically as a "Combined Wire and Board Fence." There was a combination wire and wood fence design by King in 1876 (#178,645) called the "Diagonal Barbed Picket Fence." It was patented as an "Improvement in Wire Fences" by adding wooden slats "armed" with steel barbs three-quarters-of-an-inch in length. In 1877, Richard (#191,468) specifically stated that his barb design was to be used for existing wooden fences and included a device to insert these barbs. In 1881, Chapman (#246,866) was issued the last combination wood rail metal barb design patent. It was classified as an "Improvement in Barbed Fences" with the purpose of making the barbed fence more visible to stock and preventing stock "from running blindly against it and causing injury to themselves from the barbs."

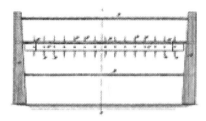

Rose 1873 (#138,763) Barbed
Wood Rail

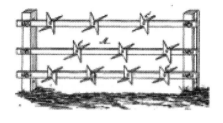

Haish 1874 (#147,634) Square Rail
with Four Point Sheet Metal Barbs

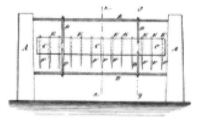

Stout 1875 (#163,116) Combined
Wire and Board Fence

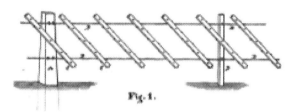

King 1875 (#178,645) Barbed Pickets

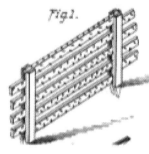

Richards 1877 (#191,466) Square Rail
with Spike Sheet Metal Barbs

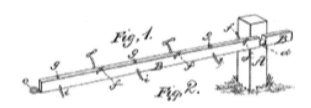

Walsh and Dutol 1880 (#223,780) Wood Rail
and Rod

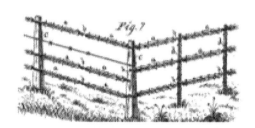

Orwig 1880 (#225,717) Square Rail with
Two Point Barbed Insert

Chapman 1881 (#246,866) Barbed Rail
with Three Point Brads

Figure 201. Examples of Wooden Rail Barbed Fences

**Summary of Bars, Rods, and Rails**

The following is a summary (Figure 202) of the characteristic designs of metal bars, rods, and rails. These designs arose from Rose's 1871 design. Although wooden rail fences were common in the East and Midwest, they were not practical as far as cost and maintenance. This encouraged inventors to design metal rods and bars as substitutes for wood and adding mild steel and sheet metal barbs to existing wooden fences, but in the long run, bars, rods, and rails could not compete with the metal strands and strips.

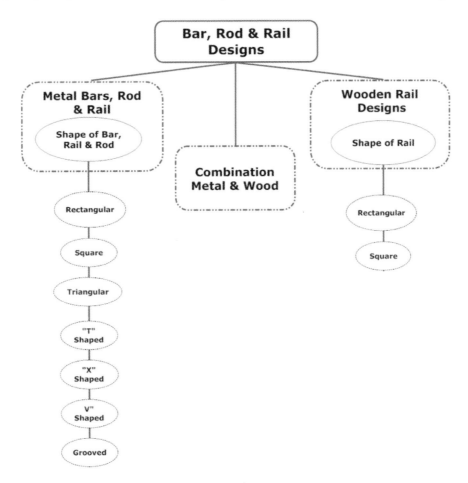

Figure 202. Summary of Bars, Rods and Rail Designs

## UNIQUE HORIZONTAL COMPONENT DESIGNS

The preceding discussion describes in detail the unique differences in designs of the horizontal components. Some designs are considered "more unique" because of other characteristics. For example Kelly's "Thorny Barb" the first commercially successful single-strand wire with sheet metal barb design (Figure 202) and the sheet metal strip or ribbon wire designs especially the barbed mounted and double barbed mounted designs of J. Brinkerhoff (Figure 203) and the integrated barbed strip designs of Allis (Figure 204) compared to the more common mild steel strand designs.

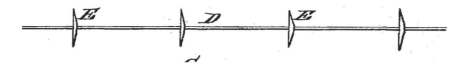

Figure 203. Kelly, M. 1868 (#74,379) "Thorny Single Strand"

Figure 204. Brinkerhoff, J. 1879 (#214,095) "Harrow Point"

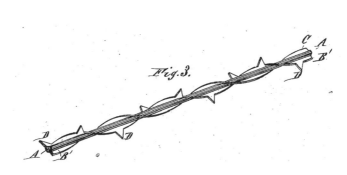

Figure 205. Allis, T. V. 1881 (#244,726) "Buckthorn"

270

In addition, the single strand with a sheet metal wrap design by Hallner in 1878 (#199,538) called "Greenbrier" was considered unique (Figure 206).

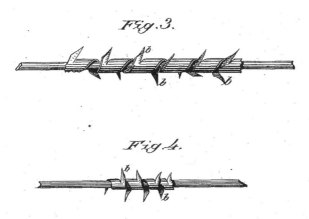

Figure 206. Hallner, J. 1878 (#181,433) Single-Cut "Greenbrier"

## THE NUMBER OF STRANDS, STRIPS, BARS, RODS, AND RAILS IN ANTIQUE BARBED FENCING

What is the standard number of stands, strips, bars, rods, and rails found in antique barbed fencing? In this review, the number of strands or strips on a fence varied in patent descriptions from two or more strands or strips depending upon if the barbed fencing was put on top of an existing stone fence, used in conjunction with woven wire, or used as a complete stand alone barbed wire strand or sheet metal fence system. The purpose of the fence was for controlling different species of livestock. One to five levels of wire strands were found in patent descriptions, with three to four horizontal components common. A review of agricultural literature (e.g., Massachusetts Agricultural Department 1882) revealed that there were many reasons for the number of stands, strips, bars, rods, and rails used in a fence.

The specific number seems to be determined by a combination of factors: the cost of the wire (i.e., for inexpensive fencing [one to two wire strands]); the purpose of fencing (e.g., for sheep to keep out dogs in a sheep pasture [four wire strands], for cattle [three wire strands], for horses [two wire strands with spruce board on the top]); for boundary delineation (one to two wire strands); adding barbed wire to existing stonewalls and wooden fences (one to two wire strands); and mixing mild steel wires with sheet metal wire (some mixed number).

The *American Agriculturist* of 1890[88] provided a list of barbed wire laws in the states that defined the number of barbed wire strands in a barbed fence. Of the forty-three states described in the article, nine states, including Wyoming (two to three strands), Washington (three strands), Idaho (two strands), Iowa (three strands), Wisconsin (two plus strands), Georgia (six strands), Texas (two to three strands), Mississippi (three strands), and West Virginia (no less than five strands) defined or stipulated the number of strands in barbed fencing as of 1890. This same article identified three states which defined the height of barbed fencing: New Jersey (four to six feet), Florida (greater than five feet), and Mississippi (four feet).

The Natural Resource Conservation Service (2008) published construction specifications for barbed fencing in Missouri. Although these were present day recommendations, Table 14 and Table 15 provide a good summary of the considerations in the number of strands, strips, height of the fence, spacing of the strands and strips, and how they might differ for different species of livestock that early farmers and ranchers considered in the construction of barbed fencing using barbed wire and woven wire with barbed wire. Slight differences were seen in the specifications if the purpose of the fencing was for containment or deterrent. Greater differences in design were seen between barbed wire fences and woven-wire fences.

---

88    Vol 49: page 87

Table 14. Wire Height and Spacing For Barbed Wire Fences (Adapted from Natural Resources Conservation Service 2008)

| Fence Type | Livestock Type | Purpose | Min. Number of Strands | Height of Top Strands | Suggested Strands Spacing* |
|---|---|---|---|---|---|
| Barbed Wire (12.5 gauge standard; 12.5 gauge, 2 strand, twisted, barbless; or 15.5 gauge high tensile) | Cattle | Containment | 4 | 48" | 12, 12, 12, 12 |
| | | Deterrent | 4 | 48" | 12, 12, 12, 12 |
| | Sheep/ Goats | Containment | 6 | 48" | 6, 6, 6, 8, 10, 12 |
| | | Deterrent | 5 | 36" | 6, 6, 6, 8, 10 |
| | Horses | Containment | 4 | 48" | 12, 12, 12, 12 |
| | | Deterrent | 4 | 48" | 12, 12, 12, 12 |
| | Hogs | Containment | 7 | 48" | 0, 6, 6, 6, 8, 10, 12 |
| | | Deterrent | 6 | 36" | 0, 6, 6, 6, 8, 10 |
| | Deer/ Predators | Deterrent | 8 | 60" | 0, 6, 6, 6, 8, 10, 12, 12 |

* Indicates inches between strands of wire, the first number represents distance from the ground to the first or bottom of woven wire

273

Table 15. Wire Height and Spacing for Woven-Wire Fences (Adapted from Natural Resources Conservation Service 2008)

| Fence Type | Livestock Type | Purpose | Min. Number of Wires | Height of Top Wire | Suggested Wire Spacing* |
|---|---|---|---|---|---|
| Woven wire (Conventional – top & bottom strands 12.5 gauge with 14.5 wire for intermediate strands with verticals every 4 – 12") (High tensile – all 12.5 gauge high tensile wire with verticals every 6 – 24") | Cattle | Containment | 39" woven + 1 barb | 48" | 4 (woven), 5 |
| | | | 32" woven + 2 barbs | 48" | 4 (woven), 6, 6 |
| | Sheep/ Goats | Containment | 39" woven + 1 barb | 48" | 2 (woven), 7 |
| | | | 36" woven + 2 barbs | 48" | 2 (woven), 2, 8 |
| | | | 32" woven + 2 barbs | 48" | 2 (woven), 6, 8 |
| | | Deterrent | 36" woven | 36" | 0-2" |
| | | | 32" woven + 1 barb | 36" | 0-2" (woven), 4 |
| | Horses | Containment | 39" woven + 1 barb | 48" | 4 (woven), 5 |
| | | Deterrent | 32" woven + 1 barb | 42" | 4 (woven), 6 |
| | Hogs | Containment | 39" woven + 2 barbs | 48" | 0, 2 (woven), 7 |
| | | Deterrent | 36" woven + 1 barb | 36" | 1 barb on ground + (woven) |
| | | | 32" woven + 2 barbs | 36" | 0 (woven), 4 |
| | Deer/ Predators | Deterrent | Woven + 4 barbs | 60" | 0, 4 (39" woven), 2, 7, 8 |

* Indicates inches between stands of wire, the first number represents distance from the ground to the first or bottom of woven wire

# 6) CLASSIFICATION OF ANTIQUE BARBED FENCING

» Identification versus Classification

» Classification System for Antique Barbed Fencing Designs

» Classification Naming Protocol

» Uses of Antique Barbed Fencing Classification System

## IDENTIFICATION VERSUS CLASSIFICATION

For collectors and historians, it is important not only to identify who patented a particular piece of barbed fencing, but also to know how similar or different the piece of antique barbed fencing is compared to other pieces of antique barbed fencing. Classification answers the question of how this piece of antique barbed fencing relates to other pieces of antique barbed fencing. Most of the efforts to date have focused on the identification of antique barbed fencing by the inventor rather than by the design. Classification differs from identification by grouping different barbed fencing patents and variations based on their common design characteristics and functions rather than inventor and the particular patent number. Classification is a morphological analysis[89] of shape and form and other structural characteristics of a piece of barbed fencing.

Classification differs from identification by grouping different barbed fencing patents and variations based on their common design characteristics and functions rather than inventor and the particular patent number. Classification is a morphological analysis of shape and form and other structural characteristics of a piece of barbed fencing.

---

89    Morphology is the study of the structure and form of things.

Classification allows an antique barbed fencing collector, historian, and antique barbed fencing enthusiast to know which patents and variations of barbed fencing are similar or different in structure, form, shape, and function to other pieces of barbed fencing. Several authors, including McCallum and McCallum (1985), Grover (1969), Clifton (1970), and Hagemeier (2010, 2012), have published books identifying different antique barbed fence patent inventors and their patent numbers. These identification guides suggest the beginnings of a classification system for antique barbed fencing.

The first comprehensive discussion of the history of barbed wire was by McCallum and McCallum (1985) in *The Wire that Fenced the West*. Their book provided a detailed description of the history of barbed wire, the inventors, manufacturing, and litigation associated with barbed fencing patents. In it, the authors presented examples of thirty-seven types of barbed fencing. They grouped wires or strips by when they were patented and how they affected livestock (e.g., "early varied", "modified", "vicious", "obvious", and "modern." For the thirty-seven representative patents, they provided a short description of each design, often with information on the history of the wire and sometimes with manufacturing information. They had a "classification" chapter that was a temporal grouping based on the different periods that barbed wire designs were invented in and what effects some of these designs had on livestock rather than a structural grouping. McCallum and McCallum (1985) also distinguished between classification and identification. They focused on categorizing or classifying by combining chronology of patent issuance with general design features but did not relate the grouping of designs and subdesigns to one another. For identification, they developed a list of "bynames" based on their review of the literature and how the strands and stands were described. The purpose of this naming was done with the intention of "giving a clue to the history of a particular pattern or its relation to the barbed-wire story as a whole" (e.g., "Scutts' Clip" for H. B. Scutt's 1878 (#205,000) four-point sheet metal barb with a central clip for attaching to a wire strand).

Glover's (1969) *The Bobbed Wire Bible,* an identification guide, provided numbered drawings of 387 types and variations of barbed fencing and 102 barbed fencing tools and accessories. Common names characterizing the barbs (e.g., "Forked Tongue Brotherton Barb") or sometimes characterizing the strand or strip (e.g., "Frye's Parallel") were provided, often without patent numbers. There was no attempt to group the designs of a particular inventor by design.

Clifton's (1970) *Barbs, Prongs, Points, Prickers, and Stickers, A Complete and Illustrated Catalogue of Antique Barbed Wire* was an identification and initial classification guide of more than 800 wires and fencing types. Barbed fencing types were grouped by general design in his table of contents (i.e., wire versus metal strip fencing), then by whether the strand or strip was barbless or barbed, then by the number of wires or strips in a strand, then by the number of points on the barb, and finally, by the shape or the type of attachment of the barb to the strand or strip. Clifton also used common names, or what he characterized as popular names, and added new names when conflicts in old names occurred. His names were not always the same as Glover's common names.

Hagemeier's (2010, 2012) *Barbed Wire Identification Encyclopedia* provided the most recent and comprehensive identification of barbed fencing and accessories with drawings. He identified over 1,500 patents and patent variations. His identification system included cross references for the identification systems of Clifton and Glover and the patent numbers of Campbell and Allison. Patent information on each wire was provided, including whether the described design was considered a variation of an earlier patent. As a basis for his table of contents, Hagemeier identified and grouped some of the patents based on general similarities of design (e.g., wire strands versus strips), somewhat similar to Clifton. More specifically, he grouped patents and patent variations by whether they were barbless or barbed wire, the number of wires in a strand, the type of sheet metal strip designs, and finally, by the number of points and type of barb (i.e., wire barb, sheet metal barb, or cast iron or malleable barb). He does not go into categorizing the different types of attachments associated with barbs. His common names were not always the same as McCallum and McCallum (1985), Glover (1969), or Clifton (1970).

The use of common names, "by-names" as McCallum and McCallum (1985) called them and "popular names" as Glover (1969) called them, would be useful if there was a consistent set of common names and principles used for naming barbed fencing that collectors, historians, and others could use. An example of the inconsistency in the use of common names is seen in Table 10 of Chapter 4, where the Jacob Haish organization (www.jacobhaishmfg.org) provided common names for his eleven patent designs that were different from Hagemeier's common names for some of his designs.

Hagemeier's cross reference index (2010) provided a very good cross reference for his numbering system with common names for patents identified by other authors. He did not compare the different designs. As stated, the use of the common name system is not consistent between authors. A review of the major barbed fencing authors, and in particular, Hagemeier's "common" names, shows that they identified the name of the patentee but not necessarily other information on the design of patent or patent date. Hagemeier varied in his descriptive information. The common names used in this analysis primarily relied on Hagemeier's common names. He provided the inventor's name along with a common name. In some cases, the common name focused on some characteristics of the barb; in other cases, it described the characteristics of the barb, strand, or sheet metal strip. As discussed earlier, most barbed fencing inventors had more than one patent and some had more than a dozen patents (see Chapter 4). This distinction was not always provided. Manufacturers of the time used their own common names to describe a particular design. These names varied often for the same patent design. Cross comparison of similar designs is not possible using only common names.

## CLASSIFICATION SYSTEM FOR ANTIQUE BARBED FENCING DESIGNS

There is no standard classification system for antique barbed fencing. USPTO uses a classification system for patent examiners and others to code documents such as patent applications according to technical features of their content. The USPTO classifications for antique barbed fencing are presented in this book when first discussing a particular patent (See Chapter 4 discussion of early patents). These are very broad groupings such as "improvements in fencing" or "improvements in metal fencing" and are not useful in identification a particular design or its relationship to another patent design. The beginnings of a classification were found in the identification books discussed above. The goal of a classification scheme is to group similar antique barbed fencing patent designs and variations based on their common structure, form, and shape with other similar antique barbed fencing designs. The proposed classification system does not depend upon knowing the names of the hundreds of individual inventors or patentees, but depends only on a few dozen design characteristics reflecting materials and the horizontal components and attachments associated with antique barbed fencing for classifying antique barbed fencing.

The following are schematic diagrams of antique barbed fencing design considerations discussed in the book. They depict the multitude of design considerations found in antique barbed fencing and the relationships of these different designs to one another.

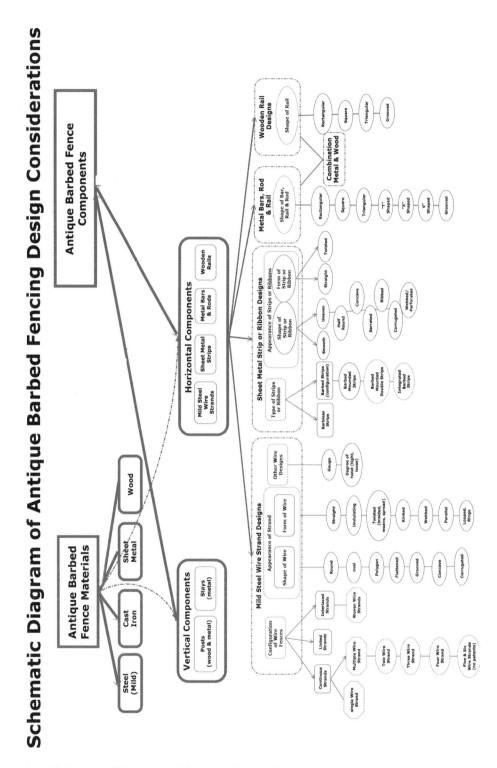

Figure 207-1. Schematic Diagram of Antique Barbed Fencing Design for
Horizontal Components

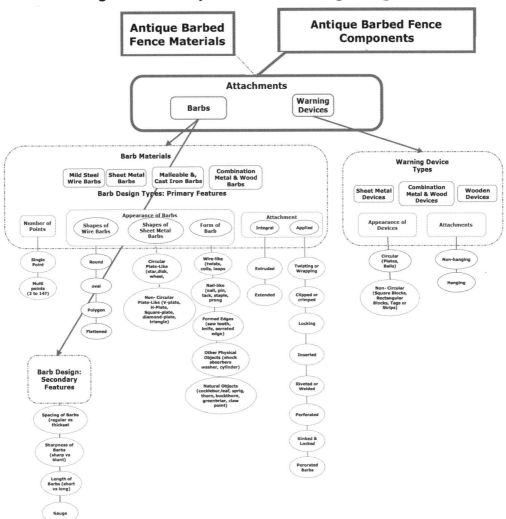

Figure 207-2. Schematic Diagram of Antique Barbed Fencing Design for Attachments

Although complex, these diagrams can be used to develop a classification system for barbed fencing designs to simplify the understanding of the complexity in the patent designs and design variations found in antique barbed fencing.

Each patentee of barbed fencing invented a barbed fencing design that was different in its material properties and/or structural components from the design of other inventors (see Chapter 4 on USPTO patent criteria). The very basic barbed fencing designs (i.e., horizontal components) with barbs arose from the plain wire fences along with the wooden fence, and hedge fences that were in use in the Midwest and East in the 1850s, 1860s, and 1870s. The idea of attaching barbs to plain wire and wooden fences was in the minds of a number of individuals in the 1850s and 1860s. Over time, inventors developed scores of different designs for the horizontal and attachment components and used different materials, sometimes in combination with one another.

Antique barbed fencing can be grouped or classified by its two major design characteristics: its material properties and then by its structural components. This allows a more understandable way for comparing the similarities and differences in different antique barbed fencing designs. As discussed earlier, there are two classes of material properties: metallic materials and non-metallic materials and three structural components: (1) horizontal components, (2) vertical components, and (3) attachments.

There are three primary metals found in antique barbed fencing (1) mild steel, (2) sheet metal, and (3) cast iron (See Chapter 3. Materials Used In Antique Barbed Fencing). The non-metallic materials found in antique barbed fencing is vegetative material either as wood used in barbs or in one instance Osage Orange branches or as wooden rails (See earlier discussion on non-metallic materials). By combining the horizontal components with their material properties, four general classes of horizontal components and material properties result: (1) mild steel strands, (2) sheet metal strips, (3) iron bars and rods, and (4) wooden rails. For barb attachments with their material properties, there are four classes of barbs: (1) mild steel barbs, (2) sheet metal barbs, (3) cast iron barbs, or (4) combination mild steel and wooden barbs (Table 16).

Table 16. General Categories and Subcategories of Antique Barbed Fencing

| General Categories of Antique Barbed Fencing | Subcategories of Antique Barbed Fencing |
|---|---|
| Mild Steel Strands and Barbs | Mild Steel Strand with Mild Steel Barbs |
|  | Mild Steel Strand with Sheet Metal Barbs |
|  | Mild Steel Strands with Cast Iron Barbs |
|  | Mild Steel Strands with Combination Mild Steel and Wooden Barbs |
| Sheet Metal Strips and Barbs | Sheet Metal Strips with Sheet Metal Barbs |
|  | Sheet Metal Strips with Mild Steel Barbs (No Patents Identified) |
|  | Sheet Metal Strips with Cast Iron Barbs |
| Iron Bars or Rods[2] and Barbs | Metal Bars or Rods with Integral Metal Barbs |
|  | Metal Bars or Rods with Iron Pegs |
| Wooden Rails and Barbs | Wooden Rails with Mild Steel Barbs |
|  | Wooden Rails with Sheet Metal Barbs |

This classification allows for the grouping of different patents and patent variations into recognizable general categories reflecting their different structural components and their material properties. Information on the inventors or patentees can be assigned to these categories and subcategories of antique barbed fencing to see the relationship of the different designs to different inventors. Table 17 shows an example of the classification scheme applied to a number of early barbed fencing inventors and their patents.

Table 17. Example of Classification of Patents of Representative Early Inventors Based on the Structure and Materials in Their Patents

| Categories and Subcategories of Antique Barbed Fencing | | |
|---|---|---|
| Categories | Subcategories | Inventor – Patent Date (Patent #) |
| Mild Steel Wire Strands | Mild Steel Barbs | Haish - 1874 (#146,671) |
| | | Merrills - 1874 (#155,538) |
| | | Glidden - 1874 (#157,124) |
| | | Wilson - 1875 (#158,451) |
| | | Haish - 1875 (#162,240) |
| | | Mack - 1875 (#162,835) |
| | | Ellwood, R. - 1875 (#163,169) |
| | | Devore - 1875 (#168,886) |
| | | Page - 1875 (#170,891) |
| | | Dobbs & Booth - 1875 (#171,104) |
| | | Dobbs & Booth - 1875 (#171,105) |
| | | Glidden - 1876 (#181,433) |
| | Sheet Metal Barbs | Hunt - 1867 (#67,117) |
| | | Kelly - 1868 (#74,379) |
| | | Kennedy - 1874 (#153,965) |
| | | Kennedy - 1875 (#164,181) |
| | | Haish - 1875 (#164,552) |
| | | Stover - 1875 (#164,947) |
| | | Duffy & Schroeder - 1875 (#165,220) |
| | | Armstrong & Doolittle - 1875 (#168,550) |
| | | Wormley - 1875 (#169,393) |
| | | Brown & Tubbs - 1875 (#192,736) |
| | | Frentress - 1875 (#171,008) |
| | | Armstrong - 1875 (#171,208) |

| | | |
|---|---|---|
| Mild Steel Wire Strands | Cast Iron Barbs | Reynolds - 1877 (#180,049) |
| | | Burrows - 1877 (#194,647) |
| | | Pederson - 1878 (#205,501) |
| | | Phillips - 1883 (#280,857) |
| | | Wheeler - 1885 (#321,264) |
| Steel Wire Strands | Cast Iron Barbs | Utter - 1887 (#369,825) |
| | | Gearty - 1892 (#472,044) |
| | Combination Wood and Mild Steel Barbs | Smith - 1867 (#66,182) |
| | | Stout - 1875 (#163,116) |
| Sheet Metal Strips | Sheet Metal Barbs | Judson - 1871 (#118,135) |
| | | Haish - 1874 (#147,634) |
| | | Ellwood - 1874 (#147,756) |
| | | Haish - 1874 (#152,368) |
| | | Brinkerhoff, J. - 1876 (#183,531) |
| | | Allis - 1881 (#244,726) |
| | Mild Steel Barbs | Kelly - 1868 (#84,062) |
| | | Wakins-Scutt - 1875 (#163,955) |
| | Cast Iron Barbs | No Patents Identified |
| Iron Bars or Rods | Integral Metal Barbs | Sims - 1876 (#178,195) |
| | | Allis - 1878 (#209,790) |
| | | Perry - 1886 (#333,887) |
| | Iron Pegs | Randall - 1887 (#359,178) |
| Wooden Rails | Mild Steel Barbs | Rose - 1873 (#138,763) |
| | | Stout - 1875 (#163,116) |
| | Sheet Metal Barbs | Haish - 1874 (#147,634) |
| Warning Devices | Sheet Metal Warning Devices for Mild Steel Strands | Crandal - 1879 (#220,912) |
| | | Briggs - 1882 (#252,071) |
| | | Sergeant - 1884 (#353,129) |
| | Sheet Metal Warning Devices for Sheet Metal Strips | No Patents Identified |
| | Wooden Warning Devices for Mild Steel Strands | Boone - 1884 (#294,572) |
| | | Bacon - 1884 (#297,487) |
| | | Boone - 1885 (#321,787) |
| | Wooden Warning Devices for Sheet Metal Strips | Boone - 1884 (#294,572) |

This level of classification can be used to group pieces of barbed fencing for collecting purposes and for displaying barbed fencing based on their structural and material property relationships.

More differentiation in the classification scheme is also possible by including additional sub design characteristics for the horizontal components and attachments. For example although the first ten inventors (See Table 17) are grouped as inventing mild steel strands with mild steel barbs designs they had different designs within this design class. Their designs differ in the number of wires in the strand and the number of point in the barbs. Haish had the first issued patent (#46,671) in the group, but it was for a two wire mild steel strand with a two-point mild steel barb. The Merrills were the next issued patent in this general category but it was a single mild steel wire strand with four-point mild steel barbs. This is a second level of classification requires characterizing the number of wires comprising a strand and the number of point on the barb. Even more detailed classification can be developed by classifying the way barbs are attached to the wire of a strand i.e. applied barbs and the specific ways the barbs were attached by including:

(1) twisted, wrapped, and coiled
(2) clipped or crimped
(3) locked
(4) inserted
(5) welded or riveted
(6) perforated
(7) extended or extruded.

With this differentiation, a more detailed level of specificity is added to the classification of antique barbed fencing. The following is an organizational breakdown of this more detailed level of classification (Tables 18, 19, 20, 21).

Table 18. Mild Steel Classification Subcategories

| MILD STEEL BARB CLASSIFICATION SUBCATEGORIES |
| --- |
| • **NUMBER OF MILD STEEL BARB POINTS** |
| o Single Point |
| o Two Point |
| o Three Point |
| o Four Point |
| o Other Multiple Points |
| • **APPEARANCE OF MILD STEEL BARB** |
| o Wire-like |
| o Nail-like |
| o Looped |
| o Circular |
| o Non-Circular |
| o Integral |
| • **TYPE OF ATTACHMENT** |
| o Applied |
| o Integral |
| **MILD STEEL WIRE STRAND CLASSIFICATION SUBCATEGORIES** |
| • **CONFIGURATION OF MILD STEEL STRAND** |
| o Continuous Barbed Wire Strand |
| a. Single Wire Strands |
| b. Multiple Wire Strands |
| o Linked Barbed Strands |
| o Interlaced Strands (Woven) |

Table 19. Sheet Metal Classification Subcategories

| SHEET METAL BARB CLASSIFICATION SUBCATEGORIES |
| --- |
| • **SHEET METAL BARB ATTACHMENT** |
| o Applied |
| o Integral |
| • **SHAPE OF SHEET METAL BARBS** |
| o Circular or Plate-Like |
| o Non-Circular (angular) |
| **SHEET METAL STRIP CLASSIFICATION SUBCATEGORIES** |
| • **TYPE OF SHEET METAL STRIP** |
| o Barbless |
| o Barbed |
| a. Barbed Mounted |
| b. Barbed Mounted Double Strip |
| c. Integrated Barbed Strip |
| • **SHAPE OF SHEET METAL STRIP** |
| o Smooth |
| o Uneven |
| a. Half Round |
| b. Concave |
| c. Serrated |
| d. Ribbed |
| e. Corrugated |
| f. Webbed/Perforated |
| • **FORM OF SHEET METAL STRIP** |
| o Straight (Flat) |
| o Twisted |
| |

Table 20. Metal Bar, Rod and Rail Classification Subcategories

| METAL BAR, ROD AND RAIL CLASSIFICATION SUBCATEGORIES |
| --- |
| • SHAPE OF METAL BARS, RODS, AND RAILS |
| o Rectangular |
| o Square |
| o Triangular |
| o "T" Shaped |
| o "X" Shaped |
| o "V" Shaped |
| o Grooved |

Table 21. Wooden Rail Classification Subcategories

| WOODEN RAIL CLASSIFICATION SUBCATEGORIES |
| --- |
| • SHAPE OF RAIL |
| o Rectangle |
| o Square |
| o Triangular |
| o Grooved |

The following is a summary for using this recommended antique barbed fencing classification process:

- First: identify the structural components and material properties.

- Second: group the structural components and material properties.

- Third: classify these grouped components and associated material properties into categories.

- Fourth: if a more detailed classification is desired classify the categories by subcategories (Appendix A) provides a summary of steps in this process.

Figure 208 depicts this classification process leading to these general classification categories for antique barbed fencing.

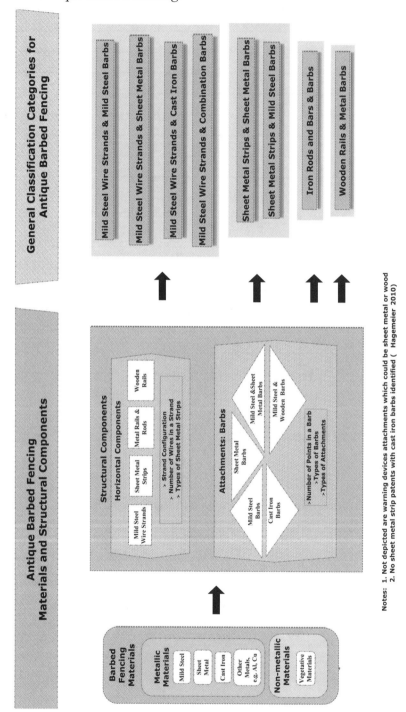

Figure 208. Antique Barbed Fencing System Classification Process

A similar classification system can be developed for Warning Devices starting with their material properties and then their structure and form (Table 22).

Table 22. Classifications of Warning Devices.

| WARNING DEVICE CLASSIFICATION CATEGORIES AND SUBCATEGORIES |
| --- |
| • SHAPES OF WARNING DEVICES |
| o Plates, strips, blocks, balls, and tags |
| • ATTACHMENT |
| o Hanging |
| o Non-Hanging (Fixed) |

The following is a list of representative warning device inventors and patents classified accordingly (Table 23).

Table 23. Examples of Classification of Patents of Representative Inventors of Warning Device

| Attachments: Warning Devices | Classes Found Within Warning Devices | Early Inventors – Date (Patent #) |
| --- | --- | --- |
| Warning Devices | Sheet Metal Warning Devices for Mild Steel Strands | Crandal – 1879 (#220,912) |
| | | Briggs – 1882 (#252.071) |
| | | Sergeant 1884 (#353,129) |
| | Sheet Metal Warning Devices for Sheet Metal Strips | No Patents identified |
| | Wooden Warning Devices for Mild Steel Strands | Boone – 1884 (#294,572) |
| | | Bacon – 1884 (#297,487) |
| | | Boone – 1885 (#321,787) |
| | Wooden Warning Devices for Sheet Metal Strips | Boone – 1884 (#294,572) |

## USES OF ANTIQUE BARBED FENCING CLASSIFICATION SYSTEM

This classification system is based on similar or different categories of designs that can be used by collectors to inventory what designs they have and do not have. It can be used to organize price guides. Exhibitors at antique barbed wire shows and other antique shows can display their collections in a more organized and understandable way.

# 7) CONCLUSIONS AND RECOMMENDATIONS

The point of this book is to describe what appears as a simple design invention that evolved into a large number and complex series of patented designs by more than four hundred inventors over a twenty-five year period attempting to change the behavior of livestock to fencing. Including mild steel barbed strands and sheet metal strip designs, their barbs, and associated barbed fencing patents (i.e., tools, machines, dies, and cattle guard designs), there are over 1,000 patents. The invention was instrumental in the expansion of livestock ranching in the West and strengthened livestock farming in the East. It affected US patent law and contributed to the wealth of the country. Barbed fencing patenting exemplifies the creativity of individuals, farmers, hardware owners, and industrialists who understood the limitations to existing fencing and saw an economic opportunity to improve livestock fencing. Inventors attempted to improve on the designs of previous inventors and "to build a better mouse trap" or to improve barbed fencing as USPTO classified these antique barbed fencing designs. More than 2,000 patents and patent design variations for antique barbed fencing exist. Many designs and variations of existing designs were authorized while many were unauthorized and were illegal. Many variations were due to intentional and unintentional manufacturing errors of existing patent designs.

Antique barbed fencing has three fundamental components: (1) horizontal components (i.e., strand, strip, rods, bars, and rails), (2) attachments to the horizontal components (i.e., barbs and warning plates), and (3) vertical components (i.e., posts and fence stays).

As a general term "barbed wire" is somewhat of a misnomer since it is used to cover barbed sheet metal strips, rods, bars, and rails as well as barbed wire. More correctly, the invention of fencing with barbs to control livestock should be referred to as "barbed fencing," which covers all the different patents and variations of the antique barbed fencing design periods.

The period of antique barbed fencing design was a relatively short lived period which started in the late 1860s and mid-1870s and lasted approximately forty years; it was finally affected by lawsuits and the consolidation or monopolization of barbed fencing manufacture by a few manufacturing companies (McCallum and McCallum 1985). A few barbed fencing patents continued to be applied for after the beginning of the 20th century, but the early designs, e.g., Glidden's # 157,124 design, turned out to be the most effective and are still manufactured today.

Antique barbed fencing design can be broken down into three periods:

1. Initial Antique Barbed Fence Patent Designs (1867 to 1874)
2. Major Antique Barbed Fence Patent Designs (1875 to 1893)
3. Decline of Antique Barbed Fence Patent Designs (Mid-1894 to 1914)

Based on the frequency of new patents issued over time and the change in the use of barbed fencing from agricultural purposes, the antique barbed wire design era came to an end around 1914 when the number of barbed fencing patents for agricultural purposes declined. WWII started and those patents that were applied for tended to focus on non-agricultural uses, such as security and war uses.

According to estimates of the several hundred patents and some two-thousand patent variations, only about 50% of the patent designs of antique barbed fencing were manufactured and less than ten percent were considered successful (Hagemeier 2010, 2012). The most successful designs were Glidden's two- and four-point double-wire strand in 1874 (#157,124) and Baker's two-point double-wire strand in 1883 (#273,219).

As stated earlier, no one person invented barbed fencing. It was an idea that found its fruition in the late 1860s and early 1870s in response to farmers and ranchers who were dealing with the limitations of existing metal, wood, hedge, and stone fencing. In some ways, the invention of barbed fencing was a simultaneous invention that originated from Rose's patented fence design at the DeKalb County Fair in 1873. His design is considered as triggering early barbed fencing designs. The invention of barbed fencing as we know it today should be attributed to three and possibly two other individuals, who happened to attend a county fair in DeKalb County, Illinois, in 1874 and saw or heard about Rose's wooden rail fence. In actuality, there were earlier attempts in the late 1860s at improving barbless plain wire fences in common use at the time (e.g., L. B. Smith from Kent, Ohio, in 1867 [#66,182] with two-point wire spurs or nails attached to wood or cast iron spools on a single-wire strand and M. Kelly from New York City in 1868 [#74,379] with a two-point "hard iron-tinned" sheet metal barb on single- mild steel wire strand). In 1871, Judson from Rose, New York, was issued the first patent for a sheet metal strip fence with integral barbs (projecting spurs). From Supreme Court records, it appears that there may have been unpatented barbed fencing attempts in the 1850s.

Since the 1840s, plain or barbless wire fences, stonewalls, thorny hedges, and wooden fences were used to control livestock. Plain wire fences are the forerunner of barbed fencing. It was the fence of choice because it was easy to construct and took up less space in a field than stone and wooden fences and thorny hedges. However, plain wire fences had major limitations for livestock fencing, especially for cattle who were able to push through and break the fence. The first patents using barbs were classified by the USPTO as "Improvements to Wire Fences."

A problem with many of the early barbed single-strand wire fence designs was that the barbs often bunched together along the wire strand. There was a need for a better design to hold the barbs in place. This need resulted in scores of different designs in the shape of barbs for use on single wire strands, the shape of the single-wire strand, and the development of multiple-wire-strand fences. The issue of securing barb in place along a wire was solved with J. Glidden's 1874 two-point double-wire strand design (#157,124), where he claimed the second twisted wire had the purpose of holding the barb in place. The myriad of barbed fence designs resulted in numerous lawsuits as to who had the patent right for barbed fencing. The United States Supreme Court, in defining primary barbed wire design, recognized Giddens's simple design in 1892.

The material properties of antique barbed fence are metallic, non-metallic, or a combination of the metal and non-metallic materials. The predominant metal used in antique barbed wire fencing is mild steel used in the horizontal structures (i.e. wire strands) and the attachments or barbs. The second most common metal found in barbed fencing is sheet metal made from rolled and flattened mild steel; this is called sheet metal strip fencing or ribbon wire. Cast iron is a minor metal found primarily in barbs. Non-metals such as wood and woody materials are found in rails and in combination with metals in barbs and warning devices.

Wire strands have been designed in the three ways (1) as continuous-wire strands comprised of different numbers of wires, (2) linked wire strands to form linked barbed strands, and (3) interlaced wire strands to form woven fences. Additional design differences in wire strands include shape of the wire(s) in the strand (e.g., round, square, triangular, flat, twisted, etc.), sharpness of the barbs, and spacing of the barbs. Most of the barbed fencing designs are based on the two-twisted mild steel wire design of J. Glidden. Barbed sheet metal strips were designed in three ways: (1) barbed mounted strips, (2) barb mounted double strips, and (3) integrated barb strips. Barbed sheet metal strips were invented at the same time barbed mild steel wire strands were invented. These sheet metal strips could be flat or twisted. Barbless strips were also patented. Barbs for sheet metal strips were often different from wire strands in that inventors more often integrated the barb designs into the strip. Sheet metal strips were considered a more visible alternative to mild steel wire strands.

The greatest patented design variations in antique barbed fencing are found in the attachments or barbs to the horizontal components (i.e., strands and strips). Barbs were designed using mild steel, sheet metal, and sometimes in combination with the two metals. Cast iron barbs were patented, but in fewer numbers. A few metal/wood combination designs were patented. Besides the differences in materials, barb designs can be classified into the number of points on a barb (i.e., single to multiple points). Two-point barbs are the most common. Some barb designs have complicated shapes and forms (e.g., plates, rowels, discs, and cylinders).

Barbs can be classified by their different shapes and forms, including:
» Wire-like barbs

» Nail- or staple-like barbs

» Circular-plate-like sheet metal barbs

» Non-circular plate-like barbs

» Looped barbs

» Integral barbs

One major design factor that accounts for many of the different designs is how the barbs are attached. There are two basic groups of barb attachments: (1) applied barbs and (2) integral barbs. There are seven groups of attachment designs found:

1. Twisted, wrapped, and coiled around a wire strand or sheet metal strip
2. Clipped or crimped on the strand or strip
3. Locked in some fashion to the strand or strip
4. Inserted into a strand or strip
5. Perforated for attachment
6. Welded and riveted to a strand or strip
7. Extended or extruded from the sheet metal strip

After the hundreds of antique barbed fencing designs were patented, modern barbed fencing is essentially a twisted two-steel wire strand with two-point or four-point steel barbs based on Glidden's earliest design of 1874. This design is now made of high tensile (H-T or HT) steel, which is a special hard, springy steel wire introduced in the 1980s. It is capable of much higher tension than the mild or soft steel found in antique barbed fencing.

The most successful barbed designs can be measured in several ways, including the most effective design, most manufactured design, most copied design in the antique barbed fencing period, and finally, the most used design today. Based on the stated purpose of barbed fencing, one might argue all the designs were effective. Some were too effective in that they caused unnecessary injury to livestock. Some designs were complicated and too expensive to manufacture. At this time, manufacturing records are not available to provide a comparative analysis of the manufactured volume for antique barbed fencing designs. According to McCallum and McCallum (1985), J. Glidden's two- or four-point round barb attached to a two-wire strand, "The Winner" (#157,124), as it is called was the most manufactured (Figure 209).

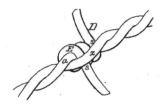

Figure 209. Glidden, J. 1874 (#157,142) "The Winner"

G. Baker's 1883 two-point double-wire strand, "Baker Perfect" (#273,219), was the second most commonly manufactured wire (Figure 210).

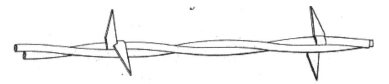

Figure 210. Baker, G. 1883 (#273,219) "Baker Perfect"

Baker's design was a two-point flat-wire barb that was notched and attached to one of the wires on a two-wire strand. The major difference in these two barb designs is the barb: Glidden's barb was round and Baker's was flat and notched. The Glidden barb was wrapped twice around one of the two wires in the double strand being held in place by the second wire. Baker's barb was wrapped only once around one of the two wires of the strand and held in place by the notch. The most copied design is the Glidden design. Hagemeier (2010) identified nearly 300 variations and said more have been reported. He considered the Glidden design the most practical and successful. According to McCallum and McCallum (1985), the most acceptable barb designs were the two-point barb design exemplified by Glidden and Baker. The next most important barb antique design group was the four-point wire barb design, followed by the sheet-metal barb design.

McCallum and McCallum (1985) concluded that two years before Rose's fence was used at the DeKalb County Fair in 1873, three US patents had incorporated most of the design features that were used in future barbed fencing.

» Single-wire strands, first patented by L. B. Smith in 1867 (#66,182)

» Double-wire strands, first patented by Kelly in 1868 (#74,479)

» Sheet metal strips or ribbon wire, first patented by Judson in 1871 (#118,135)

For attachments, the following barb patents of the early inventors cover most of the future barb designs, including:

» Steel wire points or barbs (block and nail), patented by L. B. Smith in 1867 (#66,182)

» Sheet metal barbs (spur-rowel), patented by W. D. Hunt in 1867 (#67,117)

» Sheet metal points (thorns), patented by M. Kelly in 1868 (#74,479)

» Sheet metal integrated or extended points (serrated), patented by L. P. Judson in 1871 (#118,135)

Although the emphasis of antique barbed fencing literature focused on occurrence and use in the West, barbed fencing was invented, manufactured, and used just as much in the East and Midwest. There is regional bias in viewing the development and use of barbed fencing as primarily a western invention. What can be said is that barbed fencing replaced much of the existing plain wire fencing and other fence types (e.g., wood, hedges, and stone walls) in the East and became the preferred fencing in the West where natural fencing resources (e.g., wood and stone) were scarce. Systematic or formal inventories and surveys of antique barbed fencing in different regions of the country have not been conducted to date. Old styles of barbed wire fencing such as Allis' 1881 "Buckthorn" design (# 244,746) is found in the East as well as the West and is associated with sheep farming and ranching. Early agricultural journals and fencing descriptions (e.g., Washburn and Moen 1882), provided an indication of the importance of barbed fencing in the East, Midwest, and West. At the same time barbed fencing was developing in the United States, it was being sold and manufactured across the border in Canada and imported into Australia and England.

Most of the modern barbed fencing came from design variations of one of the earliest designs, Joseph Glidden's 1874 patent (#157,142) for two- or four-point barbs on double-wire strand. Most modern changes in design of barbed fencing that have occurred are not in the structure, form, and shape of the horizontal component or its attachments, but are changes in the type of materials used in making barbed fencing (e.g., high tensile steel to provide improved strength and flexibility). Some variations have resulted in variations of twist (e.g., reverse twist between barbs).

At first glance, understanding the more than two-thousand designs and design variations is overwhelming and seemingly impossible to characterize. Are there any common patterns or similarities in designs that can be used to classify these designs and variations into simpler groups? Yes, there are. The myriad of designs and variations can be better understood by classifying barbed fencing by their material properties, structural components, and specific design characteristics. Classifying antique barbed wire leads to a more logical and understandable way to compare the categories of the hundreds of designs rather than focusing on or remembering the names and designs of individual inventors. Collectors should consider organizing their collections first by their material properties, and then by barbed fencing components, and finally by the specific shapes and forms of the components.

Compared to the past, much of the present barbed fencing is manufactured overseas (e.g., in India and China) and is primarily the two-point or four-point double-wire strand design. As with the change in farm and ranch fencing that occurred in the 1860s and

1870s that led to barbed fencing, a change in barbed fencing is occurring today with the invention of electric fencing in the 1950s and 1960s. Electric fencing is replacing barbed wire. As barbed fencing is replaced, the original barbed fencing designs are becoming rarer, and lost in overgrown farm fields, ranches, and woods. Antique barbed fencing can last a long time and can be found today attached to old fence posts and trees in the fields and pastures (Newman 2014). It is a reminder of the agricultural conditions of the 19th and 20th centuries and how this invention helped change how livestock were raised. It will continue to be an interest to collectors, historians, and those of us who have ripped our pants crossing an old barbed fence.

# REFERENCES

Aldrich, M. *Death Rode the Rails: American Railroad Accidents and Safety, 1828–1965*. JHU. Press, 2008.

Bennett, L., and S. Abbott. "Barbed and Dangerous: Constructing the Meaning of Barbed Wire in the Late Nineteenth-Century." *Agricultural History* 8 (2014): 566-590.

Birkett. S., and P. Poletti. "Reproduction of Authentic Historical Soft Iron Wire for Musical Instruments." Proceedings of the 2002 Harmoniques Conference, Lausanne, Peter Lang Publisher.

Bureau of Land Management. "Fences." USDA Forest Service Technology and Development Program, Denver, July 1988, 2400-Range 8824 2803.

Campbell, R. O., and V. L. Allison. *Barriers - An Encyclopedia of United States Barbed Fence Patents*. Denver: Western Profiles Publishing Company, 1986.

Clifton, Robert T. *Barbs, Prongs, Points, Prickers & Stickers: A Complete and Illustrated Catalogue of Antique Barbed Wire*. Norman, OK: University of Oklahoma Press, 1970.

Cushman, A. S. "The Corrosion of Fence Wire." U.S. Department of Agriculture, Bulletin 239, Washington, D.C., Government Printing Office, 1905.

Engle, D. M., and J. R. Weir. "Grassland Fire Effects on Corroded Barbed Wire." *Journal of Range Management* 53 (2000): 611–613.

Flint, C. L. "Farm Fences." In *The American Farmer: A Complete Agricultural Library, With. Useful Facts for the Household, Devoted to Farming In All Its Departments And Details. Illustrated With Over Seven Hundred Engravings*. Vol. 1, 560-570. Hartford: R. H. Park and Company, 1884.

Glover, Jack. *The "Bobbed" Wire Bible*. Sunset, TX: Jack Glover, 1969.

Greer, H. "The Lord's Caltrop." *The Barbed Wire Collector*. Kearney, NE: Antique Barbed Wire Society, 2014.

Hagemeier, H. L. *Barbed Wire Identification Encyclopedia*. 5th ed. 2010.

Hagemeier, H. L. *Supplement to Edition Five of Barbed Wire Identification Encyclopedia*. 4th printing, 2012.

Hayter, Earl W. "Barbed Wire Fencing—A Prairie Invention." *Agricultural History* 13 (1939): 189–207.

Hornbeck, R. "Barbed Wire: Property Rights and Agricultural Development." *Quarterly Journal of Economics* 125, no. 2 (2009): 767-810 [journal online] [cited 16 December 2013]. Available from http://www.fs.fed.us/outernet/r2/psicc/projects/forest_revision/prv2/5e42d31_fences/06_options_wire.pdf

Horton, H. R. "Fencing the Farm." *Meeting of the American Society of Agricultural Engineers.* Vol. 4: 116-135. Ames, IA: 1910.

Horton, H. R. "Fences: Materials, Manufacturing, and Building." *Transactions of American Society of Agricultural Engineers.* Vol. 9: 134-180. Ames, IA: 1916.

Humphrey, H. N. "Cost of Fencing Farms in the North Central States." *United States Department of Agriculture Bulletin,* No. 321 (1916): 1-31.

Kerr, J. S. "A Brief Account on the Development of Fencing in Australia in the Nineteenth Century." In *Papers in Australian Historical Archeology*, edited by Birmingham, J. and E. Bairstow, 129-136. Sydney: Australian Society for Historical Archaeology, 1987.

Massachusetts Board of Agriculture. *Thirtieth Annual Report of the Secretary of the Massachusetts Board of Agriculture, with the Returns of the Finances of the Agricultural Societies, for 1882.* MA: State Board of Agriculture, 1882.

McCallum, H. D., and F. T. McCallum. *The Wire That Fenced the West.* Normal, OK: University of Oklahoma Press, 1985.

Mc Fadden, J. M. "Monopoly in Barbed Wire: The Formation of the American Steel and Wire Company." *The Business History Review* 52, no. 4 (Winter 1978): 465-489 [journal online] Availabe from http://books.google.com/books?hl=en&lr=&id=Q_sehltsi1AC&oi=fnd&pg=PP13&ots=KXKR_c347q&sig=nGfiX20bMa7yS2Gb3ER7YNgTvis#v=onepage&q&f=false

Natural Resources Conservation Service (NRCS). "Missouri Construction Specifications." Fence (Barbed Wire, Woven Wire or Suspension Fence). Missouri, 2008, Transmittal No. 448: 328-1 to 328-7.

Naylor, R. T. *History of Canadian Businesses (1867-1914).* Montreal: McGill-Queen's Press, 2006.

Netz, R. *Barbed Wire: An Ecology of Modernity.* Middleton, CT: Wesleyan University Press, 2004.

Newman, J. "Aging Antique Barbed Wire." *The Barbed Wire Collector*. Vol. 31, no. 3: 10-11; Vol. 31, no. 4: 12-12. Kearney, NE: Antique Barbed Wire Society, 2014.

Nix, S. "Estimating a Tree's Age. Noninvasive Measurements that Roughly Estimate the Age of a Tree." *About.com*. Accessed 16 December 2013. Available from http://forestry.about.com/od/silviculture/a/Estimating-A-Trees-Age.htm?p=1.

Prairie Farmer. *A Weekly Journal for the Farm, Orchard and Fireside* 56, no. 1 (January 5, 1884) [ebook]. Chicago.

Pryor, A. *Cowboys: The End of the Trail*. Roseville, CA: Stagecoach Publishing, 2005.

Reinhart, F. M. *Twenty-Year Atmospheric Corrosion Investigation of Zinc-Coated and Uncoated Wire and Wire Products*. American Society for Testing Materials, 1961.

Smith, H. M. "Barb Wire and The Fence Questions." *Massachusetts Board of Agriculture. Thirtieth Annual Report*. Wright and Potter Printing, 1882, 196-231.

Stoddard, C. L. "The Family Cow and Her Owner – Their Prospective Rights." *The Annual Report; Illinois Framers' Institute* 5 (1890): 345-346.

Storey, O. W. "The Corrosion of Fence Wire." Proceedings of the American Electrochemical Society, October 3–6, 1917. *Journal of the Franklin Institute* 186, no. 1 (July 1918): 75- 76.

Storey, O. W. "Fence Wire Corrosion and Its Causes." *The Iron Age* 100 (December 13, 1917): 1449 -1451.

Tanner, A. M. "The Barb Wire Patent." *Scientific American* 60 (1889): 21.

Washburn and Moen Manufacturing Co. and I. L. Ellwood & Co. *The Utility, Efficiency and Economy of Barb Fence, A Book For The Farmer, The Gardener, and Country Gentleman*. Worcester, MA: Lucius P. Goddard, 1876.

Washburn and Moen Manufacturing Co. *The Fence Problem in the United States as Related to General Husbandry and Sheep Raising, Facts and Statistics from Authoritative Sources with a View of Fence Laws and Customs*. Worcester, MA: Washburn and Moen Manufacturing Company, 1882.

Western Historical Co. *The History of Marshall County, Iowa: Containing a History of the County, Its Cities, Towns, & Etc*. Chicago: Novel Co., 1878.

# APPENDIX A: ANTIQUE BARBED FENCING CLASSIFICATION SYSTEM

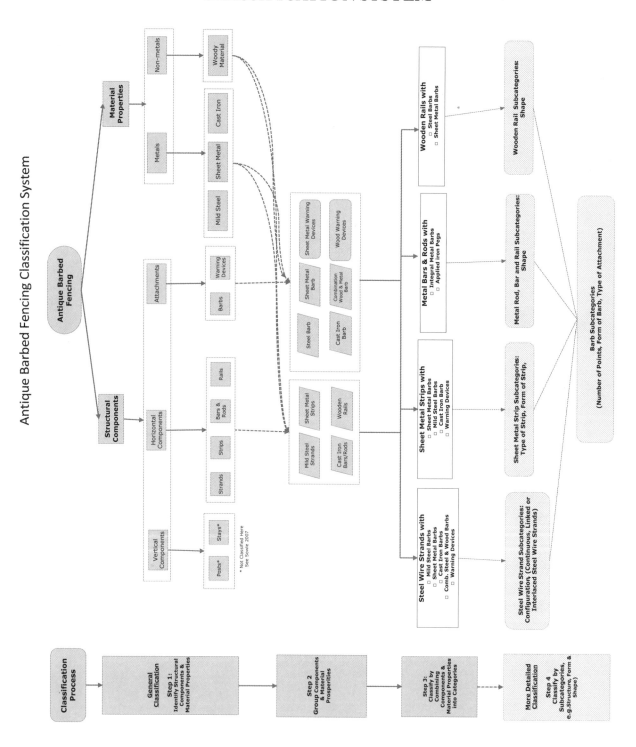

Antique Barbed Fencing Classification System

306

# APPENDIX B: SUPPORTING INFORMATION

Table 1. List of 1883 Companies with Licenses to Manufacture Glidden's Barbed Wire (Prairie Farmer 56, no. 1 [January 5, 1884])

Aaron K. Stiles and John W. Calkins, Chicago, Ill.

Alfred Van Fleet & A.H. Shreffler, Joliet, Ill.

Arthur H. Dale, Leland, Ill.

Baker Manufacturing Co., Des Moines, Iowa.

Cedar Rapids Barb Wire Co., Cedar Rapids, Iowa.

Chicago Galvanized Wire Fence Co., Chicago, Ill.

Cincinnati Barbed Wire Fence Co., Cincinnati, Ohio.

Cleveland Barb Fence Co., Cleveland, Ohio.

Crandal Manufacturing Co., Chicago, Ill.

Daniel S. Marsh, Chicago, Ill.

David G. Wells, Joliet, Ill.

Edwin A. Beers & Co., Chicago, Ill.

Frentress Barbed Wire Fence Co., East Dubuque, Ill.

Grinnell Manufacturing Co., Grinnell, Iowa.

H.B. Scutt & Co., Buffalo, N.Y.

H.B. Scutt & Co.--Limited, Pittsburg, Pa.

Hawkeye Steel Barb Fence Co., Burlington, Iowa.

Herman E. Schnabel, Chicago, Ill.

Indiana Wire Fence Co., Crawfordsville, Ind.

Iowa Barb Steel Wire Fence Co., Marshaltown, Iowa.

Iowa Barb Wire Co., Johnstown, Pa.

J.H. Lawrence & Co., Sterling, Ill.

Jacob Haish, DeKalb, Ill.

James Ayers and Alexander C. Decker, Bushnell, Ill.

Janesville Barb Wire Co., Janesville, Wis.

Lambert & Bishop Wire Fence Co., Joliet, Ill.

Lock Stitch Fence Co., Joliet, Ill.

Lockport Wire Fence Co., Lockport, Ill.

Lyman Manufacturing Co., Chicago, Ill.

Missouri Wire Fence Co., St. Louis, Mo.

National Wire Co., Chicago, Ill.

North Western Barb Wire Co., Sterling, Ill.

Norton & DeWitt, Lockport, Ill.

Novelty Manufacturing Co., Sterling, Ill.

Ohio Steel Barb Fence Co., Cleveland, Ohio.

Omaha Barb Wire Co., Omaha, Neb.

Oscar F. Moore, Chicago, Ill.

Robinson & Hallidie, San Francisco, Cal.

Sandwich Enterprise Co., Sandwich, Ill.

Southwestern Barb Wire Co., Lawrence, Kan.

St. Louis Wire Fence Co., St. Louis, Mo.

Superior Barbed Wire Co., DeKalb, Ill.

The Hazard Manufacturing Co., Wilkes Barre, Pa.

Thorn Wire Hedge Co., Chicago, Ill.

Union Barb Wire Co., Lee, Ill.

William J. Adam, Joliet, Ill.

Worcester Barb Fence Co., Worcester, Mass.

Pittsburg Hinge Co.--Limited, Beaver Falls, Pa.

# FIGURES

# TABLES

# INDEX

# E

# F

# G

## N

## S

## About the Author:

James R. Newman has been a collector of barbed fencing since the 1960s and is a member of the Antique Barbed Wire Society. As a doctoral student at the University of California at Davis his interests in zoology involved wildlife field studies that often resulted in climbing over barbed wire fences. These "scientific" observations of barbed fencing led to an interest in their history and design. Following graduate school he continued to encounter barbed fencing as wildlife and environmental scientist in the US and Overseas. Writing this book has been a goal of his from his early collecting days.

# NOTES

# NOTES